MARK WAID · MARCIO TAKARA

INCORRUPTIBLE

VOLUME 3

D1408786

BOOM! STUDIOS

Ross Richie - Chief Executive Officer
Mark Waid - Chief Creative Officer
Matt Gagnon - Editor-in-Chief
Adam Fortier - VP-New Business
Wes Harris - VP-Publishing
Lance Kreiter - VP-Licensing & Merchandising
Chip Mosher - Marketing Director
Bryce Carlson - Managing Editor

Ian Brill - Editor
Dafna Pleban - Editor
Christopher Burns - Editor
Christopher Meyer - Editor
Shannon Watters - Assistant Editor
Eric Harburn - Assistant Editor
Adam Staffaroni - Assistant Editor

Neil Loughrie - Publishing Coordinator
Brian Latimer - Lead Graphic Designer
Erika Terriquez - Graphic Designer
Travis Beaty - Traffic Coordinator
Ivan Salazar - Marketing Assistant
Kate Hayden - Executive Assistant

First Edition: December 2010
10 9 8 7 6 5 4 3 2 1
Printed in CANADA

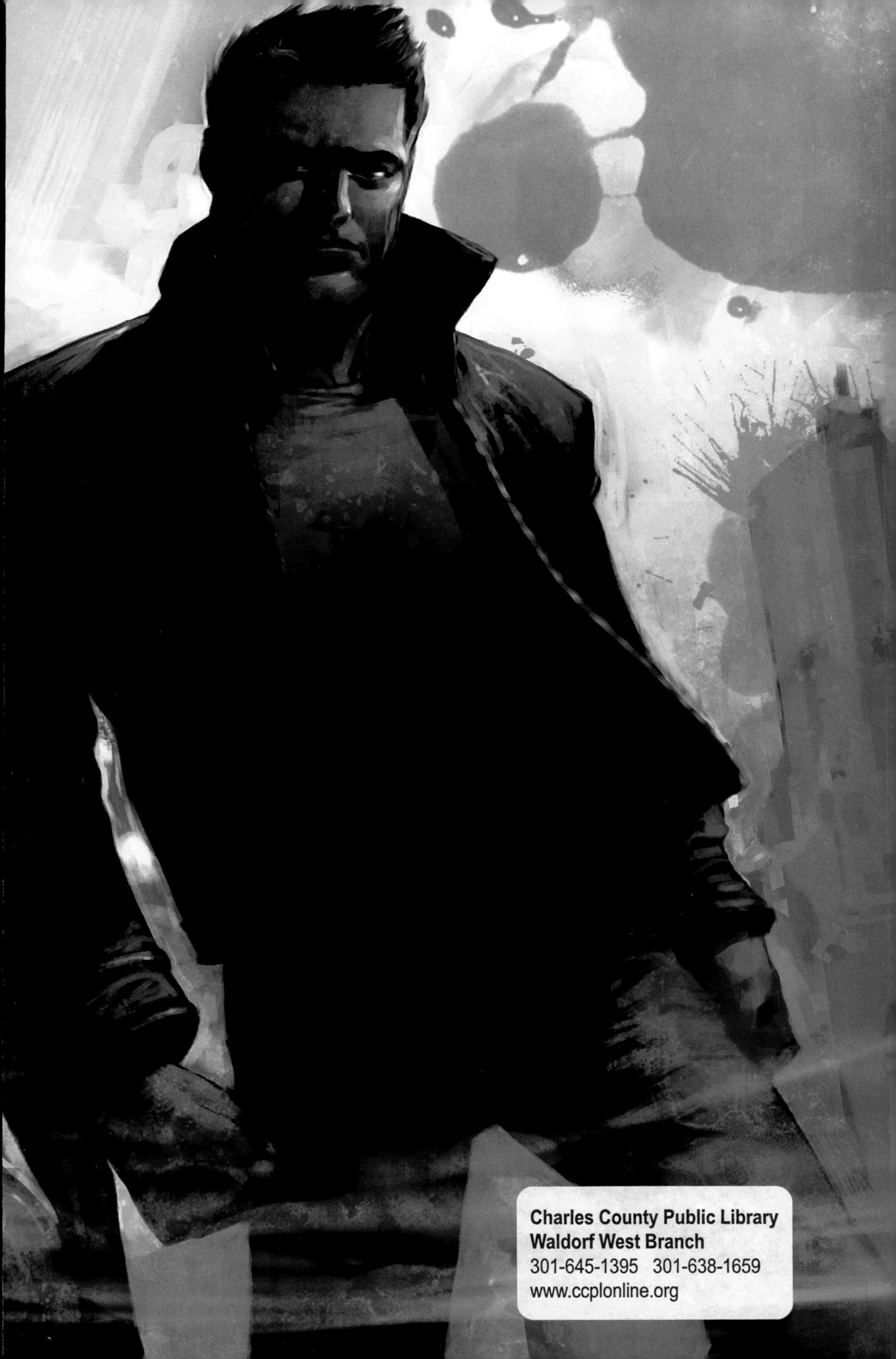

CREATED AND WRITTEN BY:

MARK WAID

ARTISTS:

HORACIO DOMINGUES
(ISSUES 9-10)

MARCIO TAKARA
(ISSUES 11-12)

INKS: **JUAN CASTRO** (ISSUE 9, ISSUE 10 PAGES 1-22, 15-19, 21, 22)
MICHAEL BABINSKI (ISSUE 10 PAGES 12-14, 20)

COLORISTS: **ANDREW DALHOUSE** (ISSUE 9)
NOLAN WOODARD (ISSUES 10-12)

LETTERER: **ED DUKESHIRE**

EDITOR: **MATT GAGNON**
ASST. EDITOR: **SHANNON WATTERS**

COVER: **CHRISTIAN NAUCK**

DESIGN: **STEPHANIE GONZAGA**

INCORR

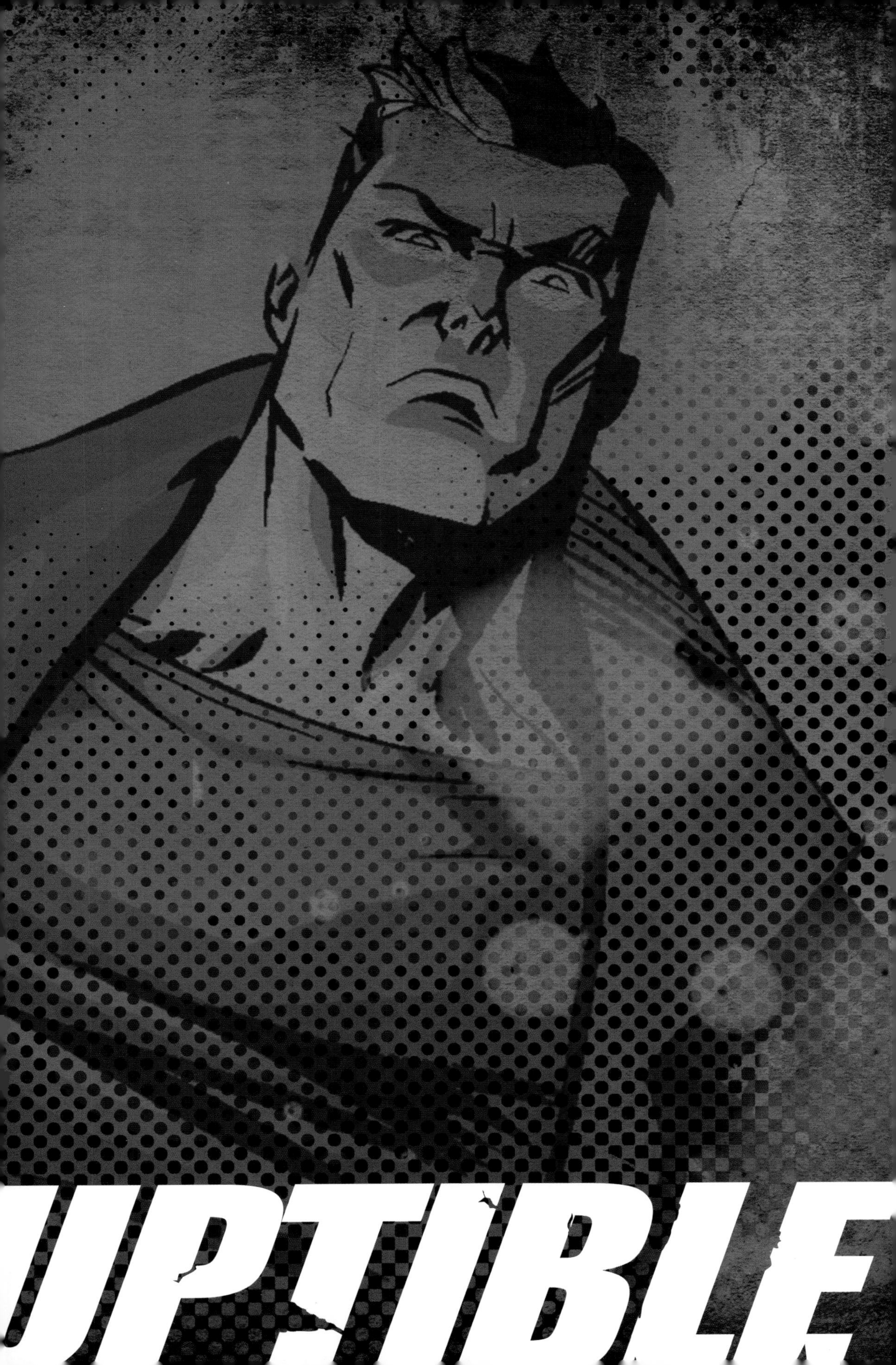
UPTIBLE

CHAPTER 9

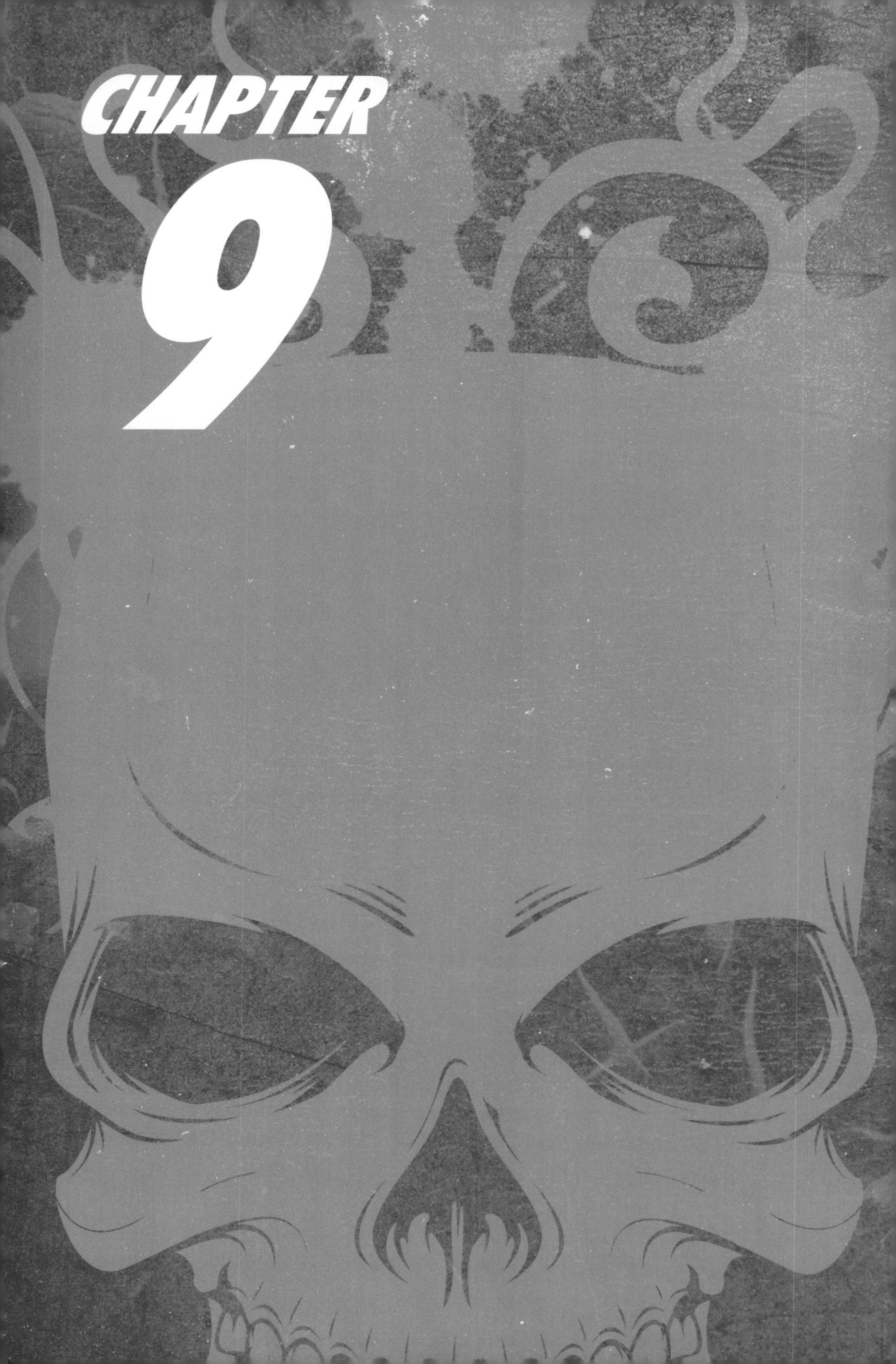

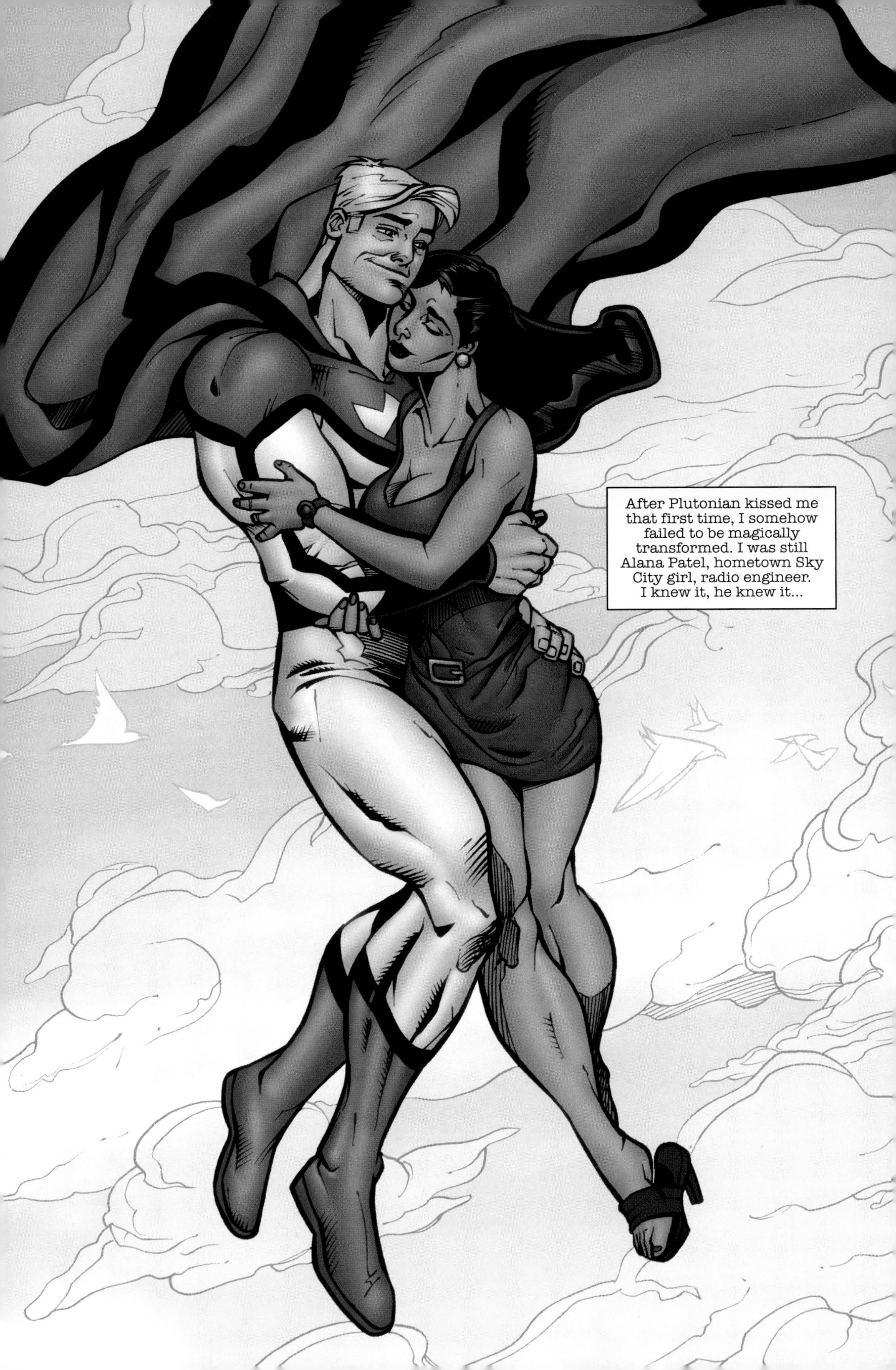
After Plutonian kissed me that first time, I somehow failed to be magically transformed. I was still Alana Patel, hometown Sky City girl, radio engineer. I knew it, he knew it...

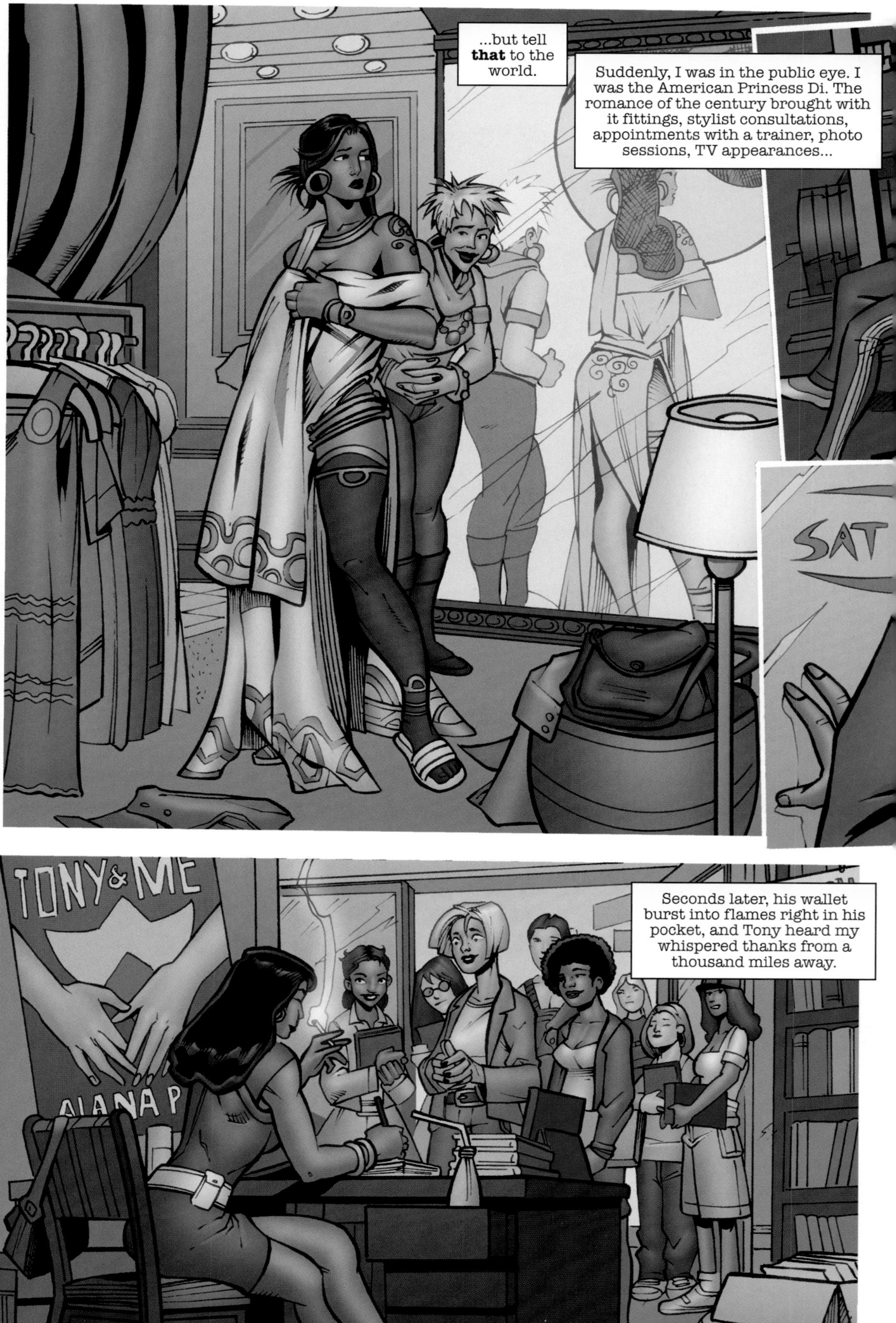
...but tell **that** to the world.
Suddenly, I was in the public eye. I was the American Princess Di. The romance of the century brought with it fittings, stylist consultations, appointments with a trainer, photo sessions, TV appearances...
TONY & ME
Seconds later, his wallet burst into flames right in his pocket, and Tony heard my whispered thanks from a thousand miles away.

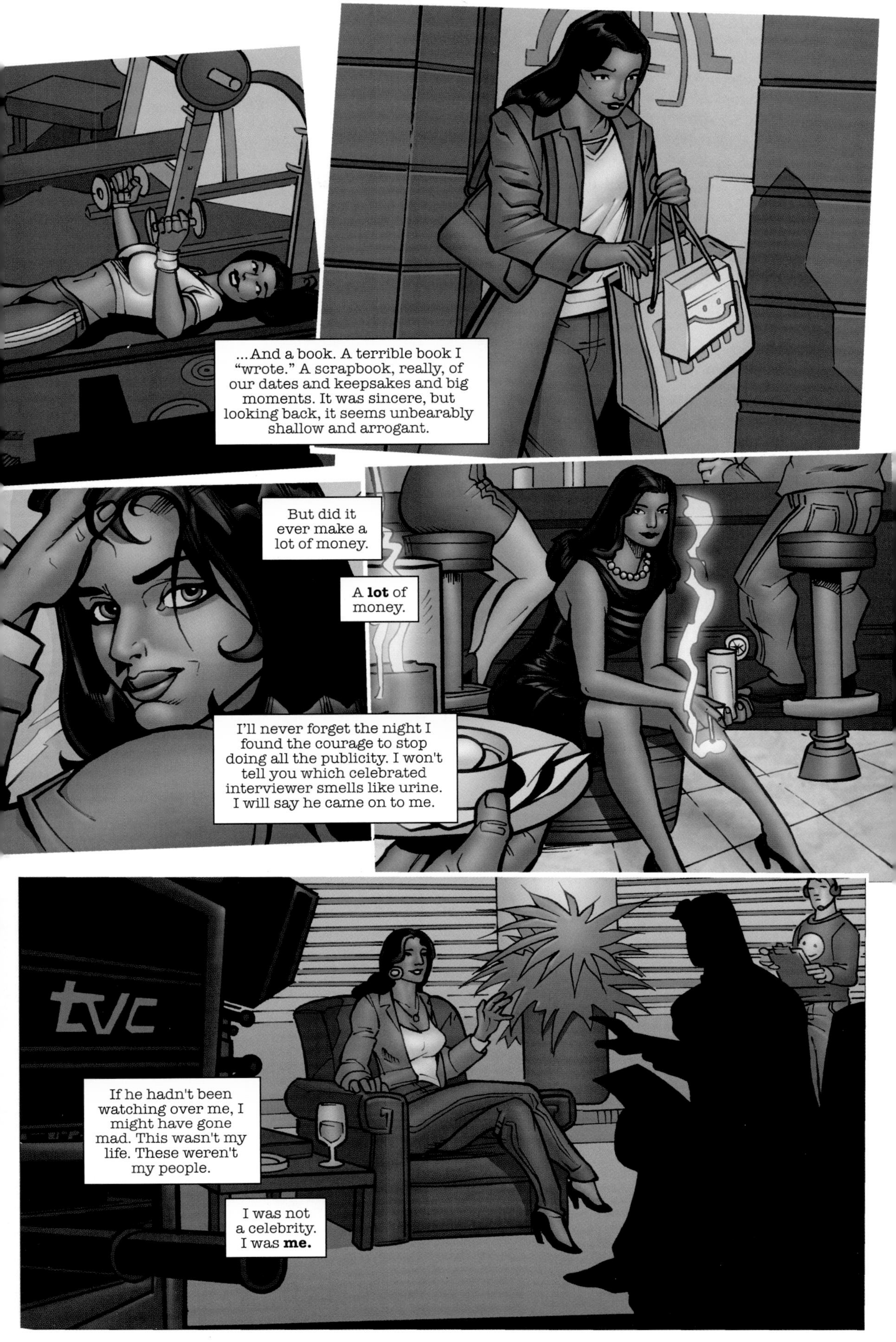
...And a book. A terrible book I "wrote." A scrapbook, really, of our dates and keepsakes and big moments. It was sincere, but looking back, it seems unbearably shallow and arrogant.
But did it ever make a lot of money.
A **lot** of money.
I'll never forget the night I found the courage to stop doing all the publicity. I won't tell you which celebrated interviewer smells like urine. I will say he came on to me.
tvc
If he hadn't been watching over me, I might have gone mad. This wasn't my life. These weren't my people.
I was not a celebrity. I was **me.**

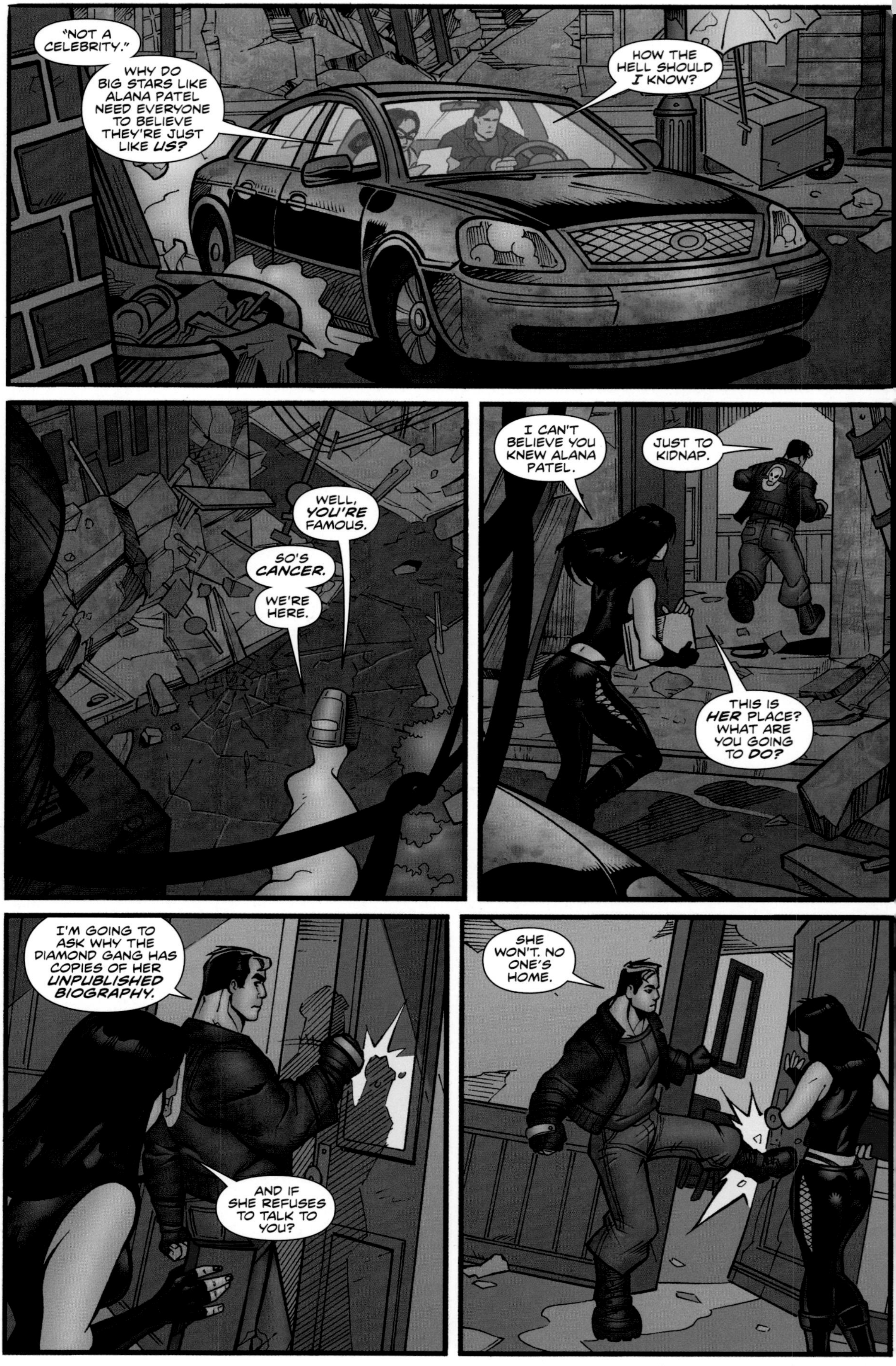
"NOT A CELEBRITY."
WHY DO BIG STARS LIKE ALANA PATEL NEED EVERYONE TO BELIEVE THEY'RE JUST LIKE *US?*
HOW THE HELL SHOULD *I* KNOW?
WELL, *YOU'RE* FAMOUS.
SO'S *CANCER.*
WE'RE HERE.
I CAN'T BELIEVE YOU KNEW ALANA PATEL.
JUST TO KIDNAP.
THIS IS *HER* PLACE? WHAT ARE YOU GOING TO *DO?*
I'M GOING TO ASK WHY THE DIAMOND GANG HAS COPIES OF HER *UNPUBLISHED BIOGRAPHY.*
AND IF SHE REFUSES TO TALK TO YOU?
SHE WON'T. NO ONE'S HOME.

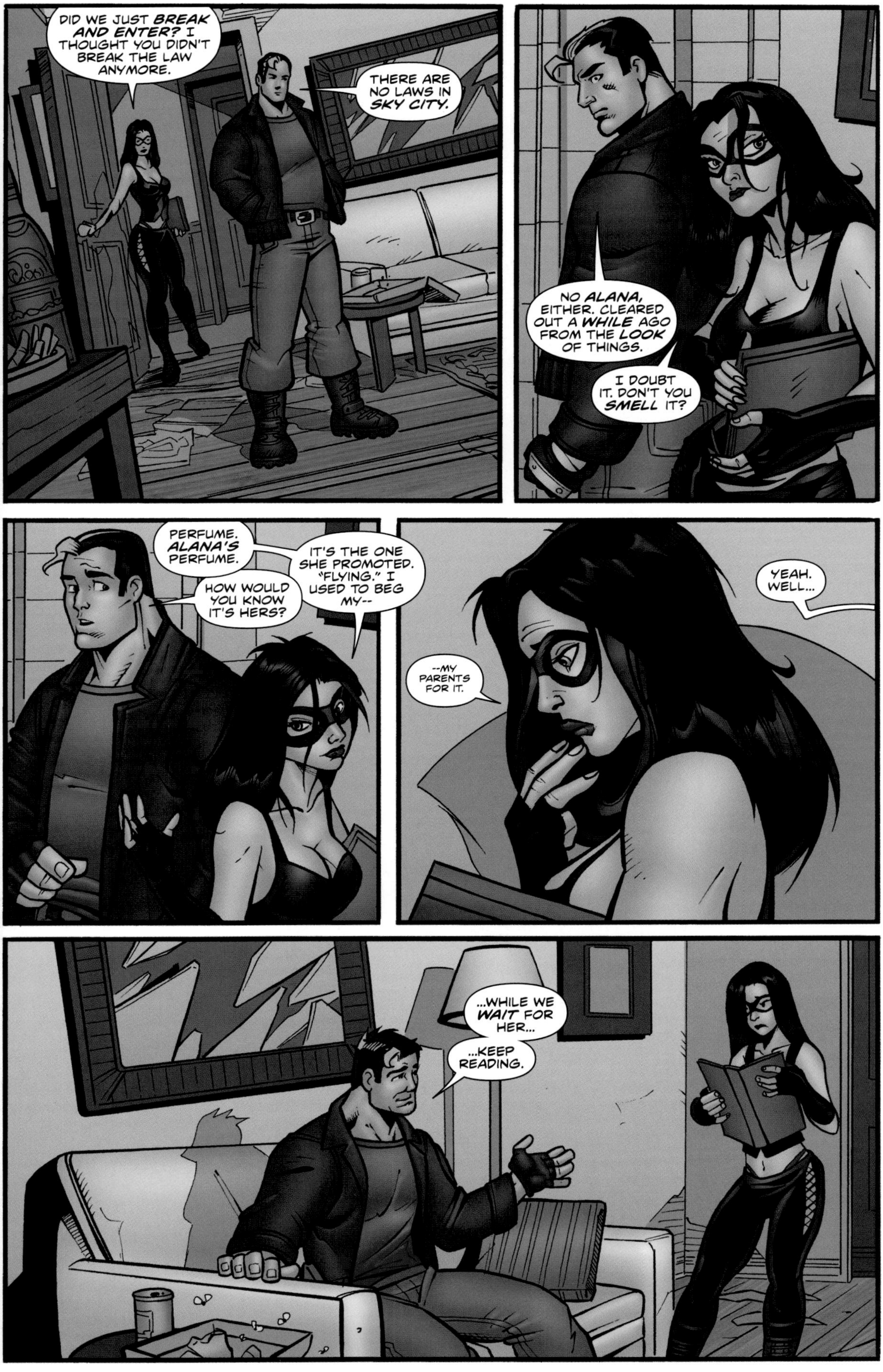
DID WE JUST BREAK AND ENTER? I THOUGHT YOU DIDN'T BREAK THE LAW ANYMORE.
THERE ARE NO LAWS IN SKY CITY.
NO ALANA, EITHER. CLEARED OUT A WHILE AGO FROM THE LOOK OF THINGS.
I DOUBT IT. DON'T YOU SMELL IT?
PERFUME. ALANA'S PERFUME.
HOW WOULD YOU KNOW IT'S HERS?
IT'S THE ONE SHE PROMOTED. "FLYING." I USED TO BEG MY--
--MY PARENTS FOR IT.
YEAH. WELL...
...WHILE WE WAIT FOR HER...
...KEEP READING.

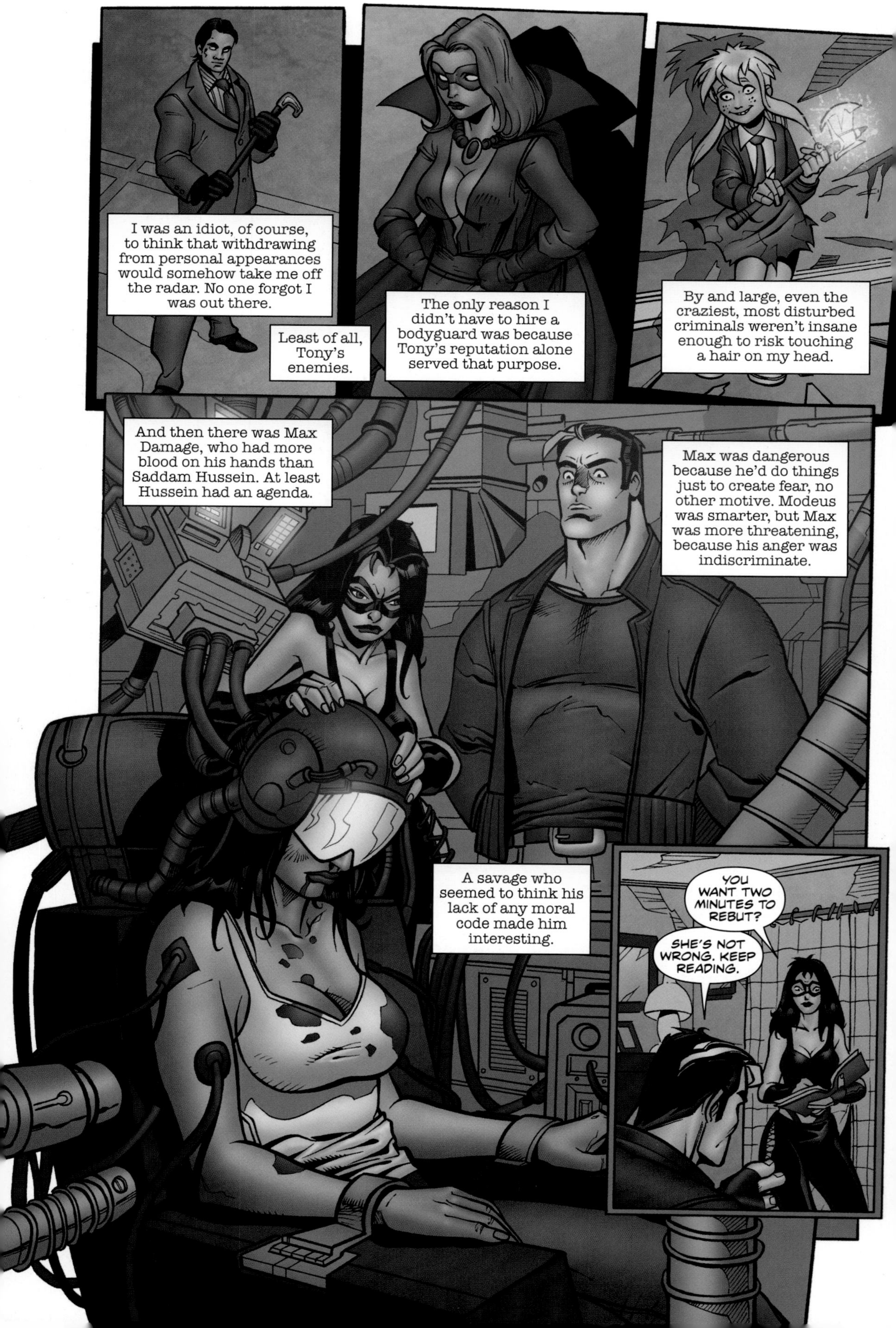

I was an idiot, of course, to think that withdrawing from personal appearances would somehow take me off the radar. No one forgot I was out there.
Least of all, Tony's enemies.
The only reason I didn't have to hire a bodyguard was because Tony's reputation alone served that purpose.
By and large, even the craziest, most disturbed criminals weren't insane enough to risk touching a hair on my head.
And then there was Max Damage, who had more blood on his hands than Saddam Hussein. At least Hussein had an agenda.
Max was dangerous because he'd do things just to create fear, no other motive. Modeus was smarter, but Max was more threatening, because his anger was indiscriminate.
A savage who seemed to think his lack of any moral code made him interesting.
YOU WANT TWO MINUTES TO REBUT?
SHE'S NOT WRONG. KEEP READING.

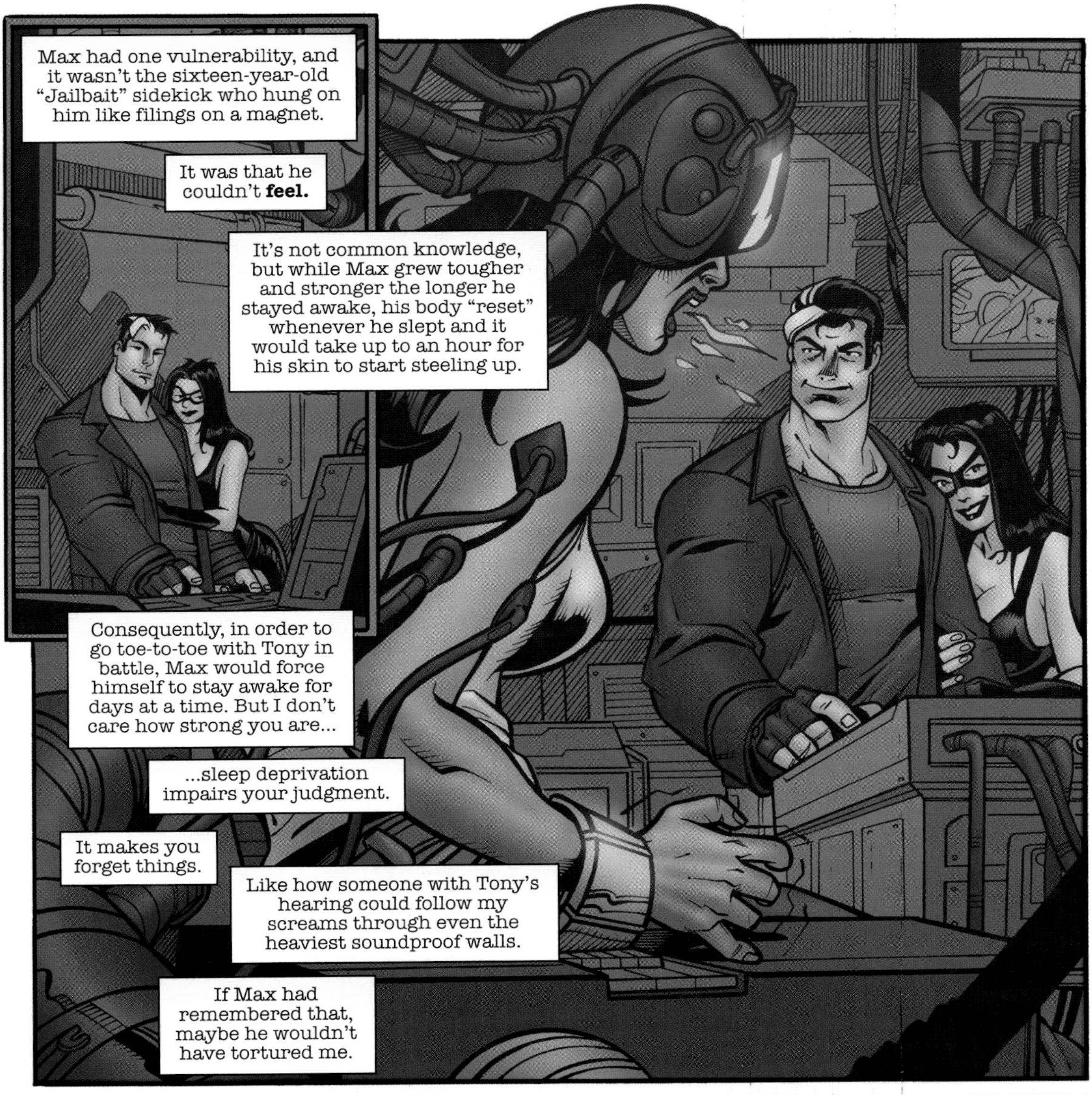
Max had one vulnerability, and it wasn't the sixteen-year-old "Jailbait" sidekick who hung on him like filings on a magnet.
It was that he couldn't **feel.**
It's not common knowledge, but while Max grew tougher and stronger the longer he stayed awake, his body "reset" whenever he slept and it would take up to an hour for his skin to start steeling up.
Consequently, in order to go toe-to-toe with Tony in battle, Max would force himself to stay awake for days at a time. But I don't care how strong you are...
...sleep deprivation impairs your judgment.
It makes you forget things.
Like how someone with Tony's hearing could follow my screams through even the heaviest soundproof walls.
If Max had remembered that, maybe he wouldn't have tortured me.

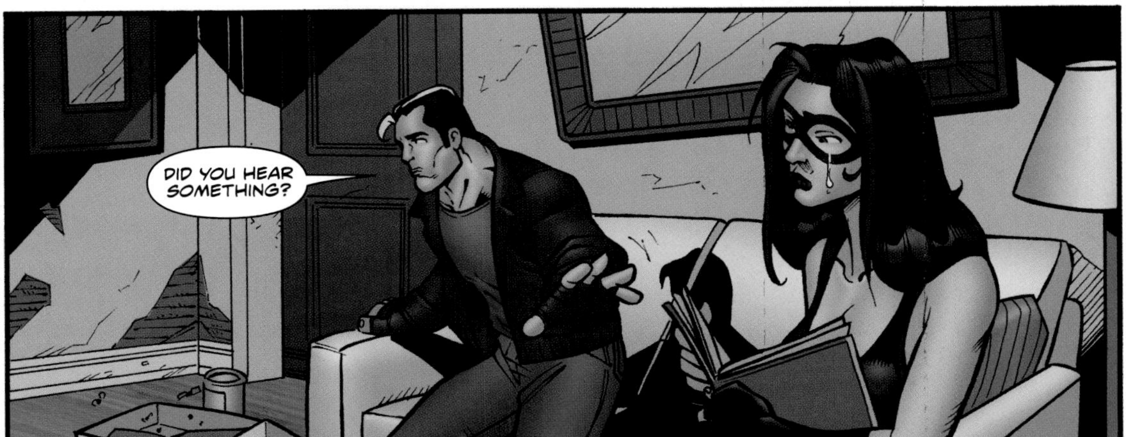
DID YOU HEAR SOMETHING?

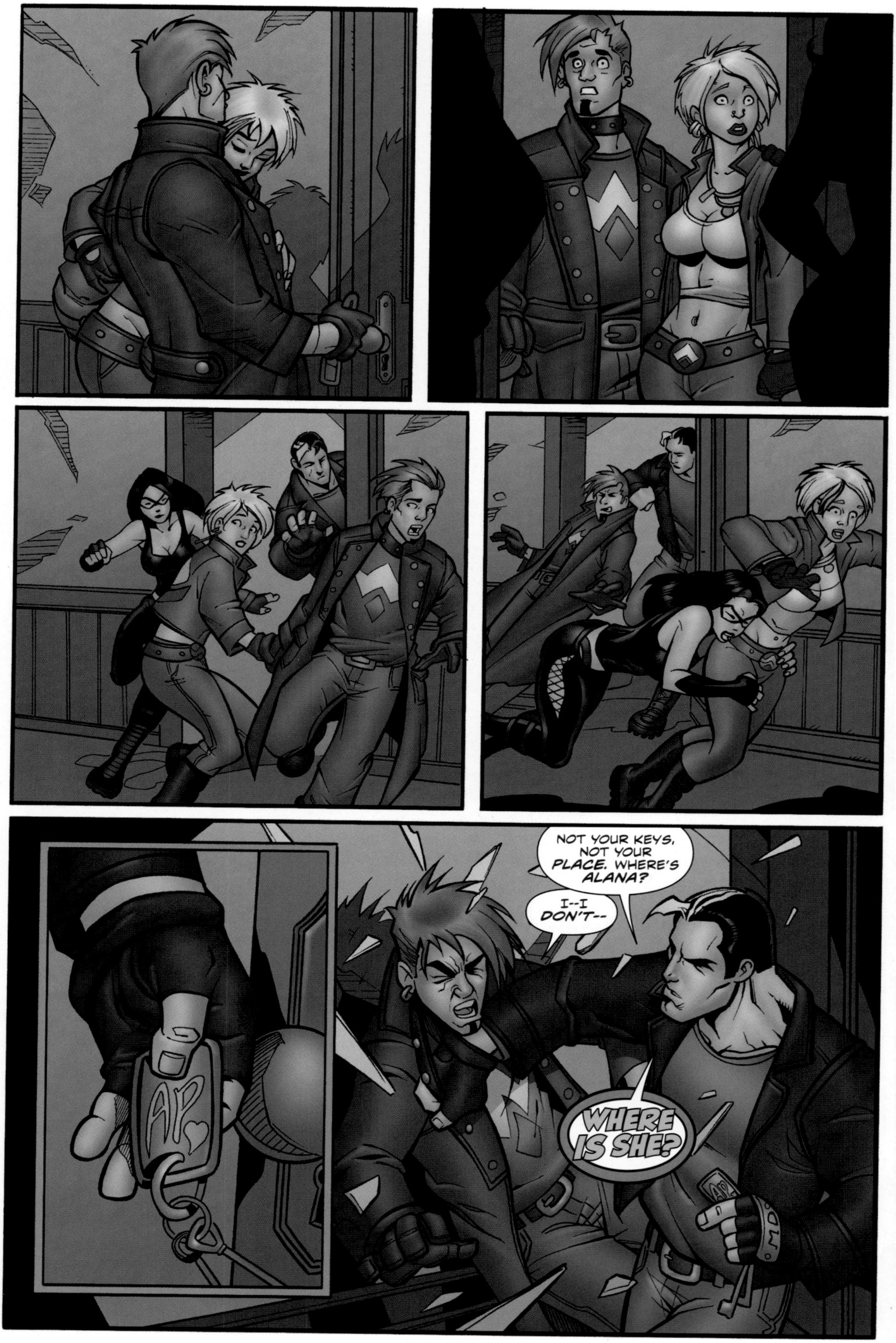
NOT YOUR KEYS, NOT YOUR PLACE. WHERE'S ALANA?
I--I DON'T--
WHERE IS SHE?

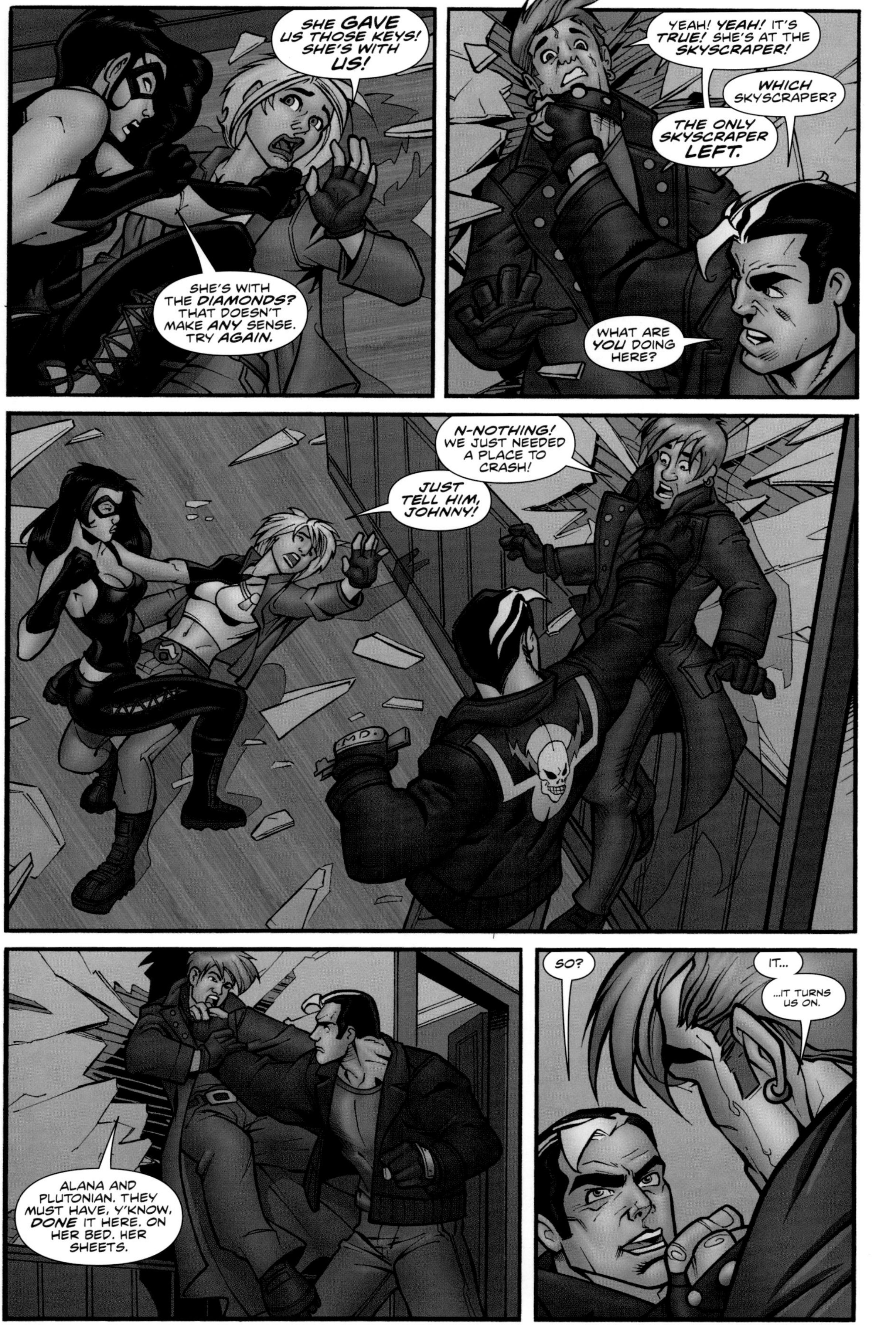
SHE GAVE US THOSE KEYS! SHE'S WITH US!
SHE'S WITH THE DIAMONDS? THAT DOESN'T MAKE ANY SENSE. TRY AGAIN.
YEAH! YEAH! IT'S TRUE! SHE'S AT THE SKYSCRAPER!
WHICH SKYSCRAPER?
THE ONLY SKYSCRAPER LEFT.
WHAT ARE YOU DOING HERE?
N-NOTHING! WE JUST NEEDED A PLACE TO CRASH!
JUST TELL HIM, JOHNNY!
M.D.
ALANA AND PLUTONIAN. THEY MUST HAVE, Y'KNOW, DONE IT HERE. ON HER BED. HER SHEETS.
SO?
IT...
...IT TURNS US ON.

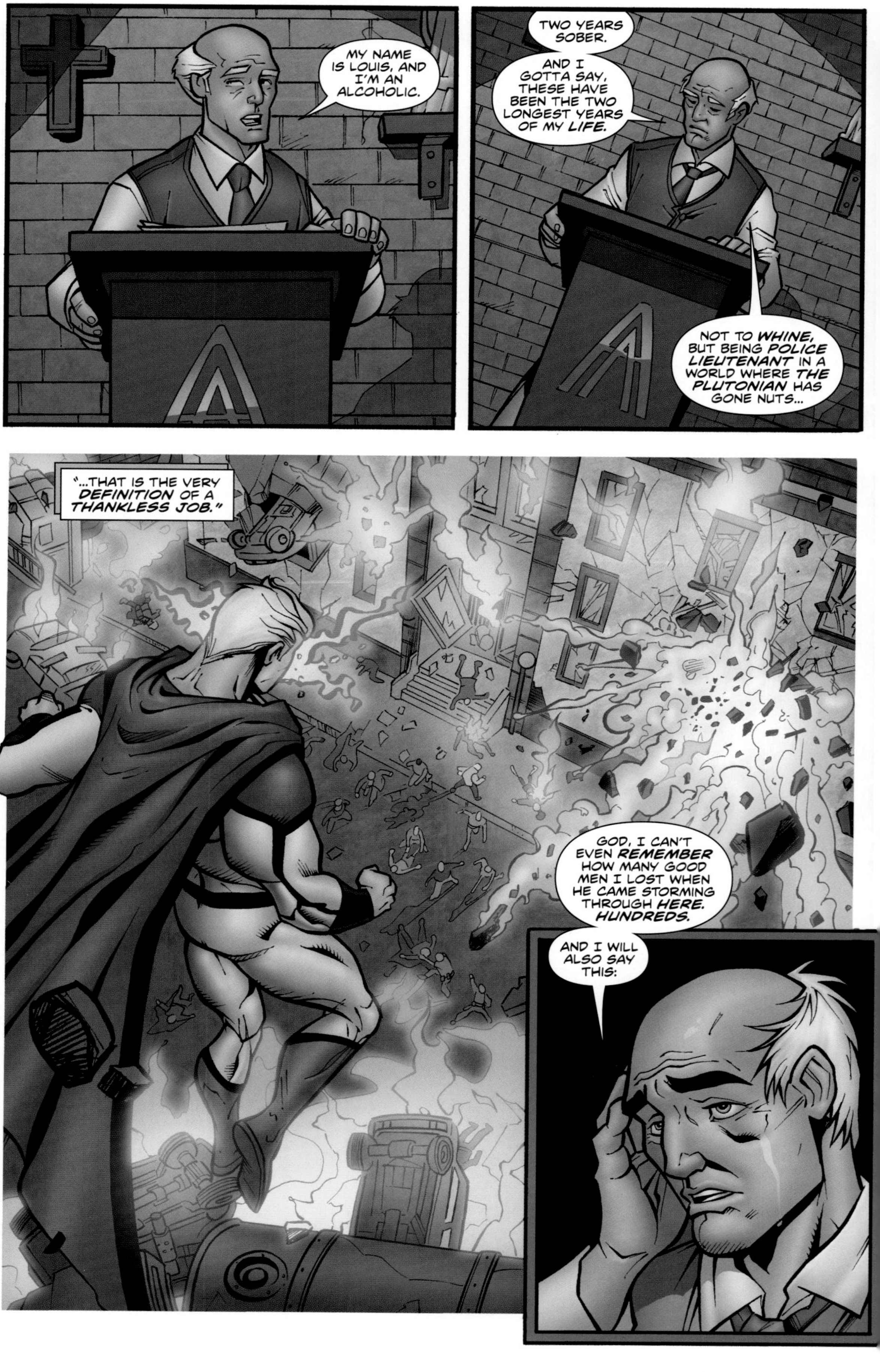
MY NAME IS LOUIS, AND I'M AN ALCOHOLIC.
TWO YEARS SOBER.
AND I GOTTA SAY, THESE HAVE BEEN THE TWO LONGEST YEARS OF MY *LIFE*.
NOT TO *WHINE*, BUT BEING *POLICE LIEUTENANT* IN A WORLD WHERE *THE PLUTONIAN* HAS GONE NUTS...
"...THAT IS THE VERY *DEFINITION* OF A *THANKLESS JOB*."
GOD, I CAN'T EVEN *REMEMBER* HOW MANY GOOD MEN I LOST WHEN HE CAME STORMING THROUGH *HERE*. *HUNDREDS*.
AND I WILL ALSO SAY THIS:

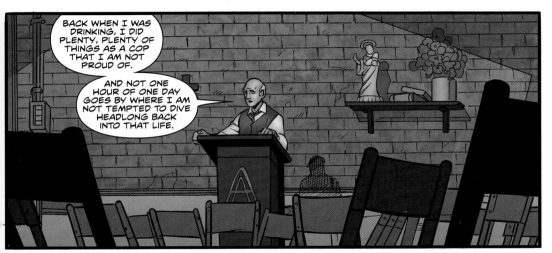

BACK WHEN I WAS DRINKING, I DID PLENTY, PLENTY OF THINGS AS A COP THAT I AM NOT PROUD OF.

AND NOT ONE HOUR OF ONE DAY GOES BY WHERE I AM NOT TEMPTED TO DIVE HEADLONG BACK INTO THAT LIFE.

... BUT I HAVE THIS FRIEND. GUY I HATED FOR A LONG TIME. MADE MY LIFE MISERABLE. WORST OF THE WORST.

AND I'VE SEEN HIM TURN OVER A NEW LEAF.

BECOME A NEW MAN. SO IT CAN BE DONE. I'VE SEEN IT.

THE ONLY THING IS, I DON'T KNOW HOW LONG HE CAN STAY ON THE HIGH ROAD.

I HOPE FOREVER.

BECAUSE IF HE FALLS, THERE IS NO ONE ELSE IN THIS WORLD I CAN COUNT ON TO KEEP ME HOPEFUL BUT YOU.

AND YOU SUCK.

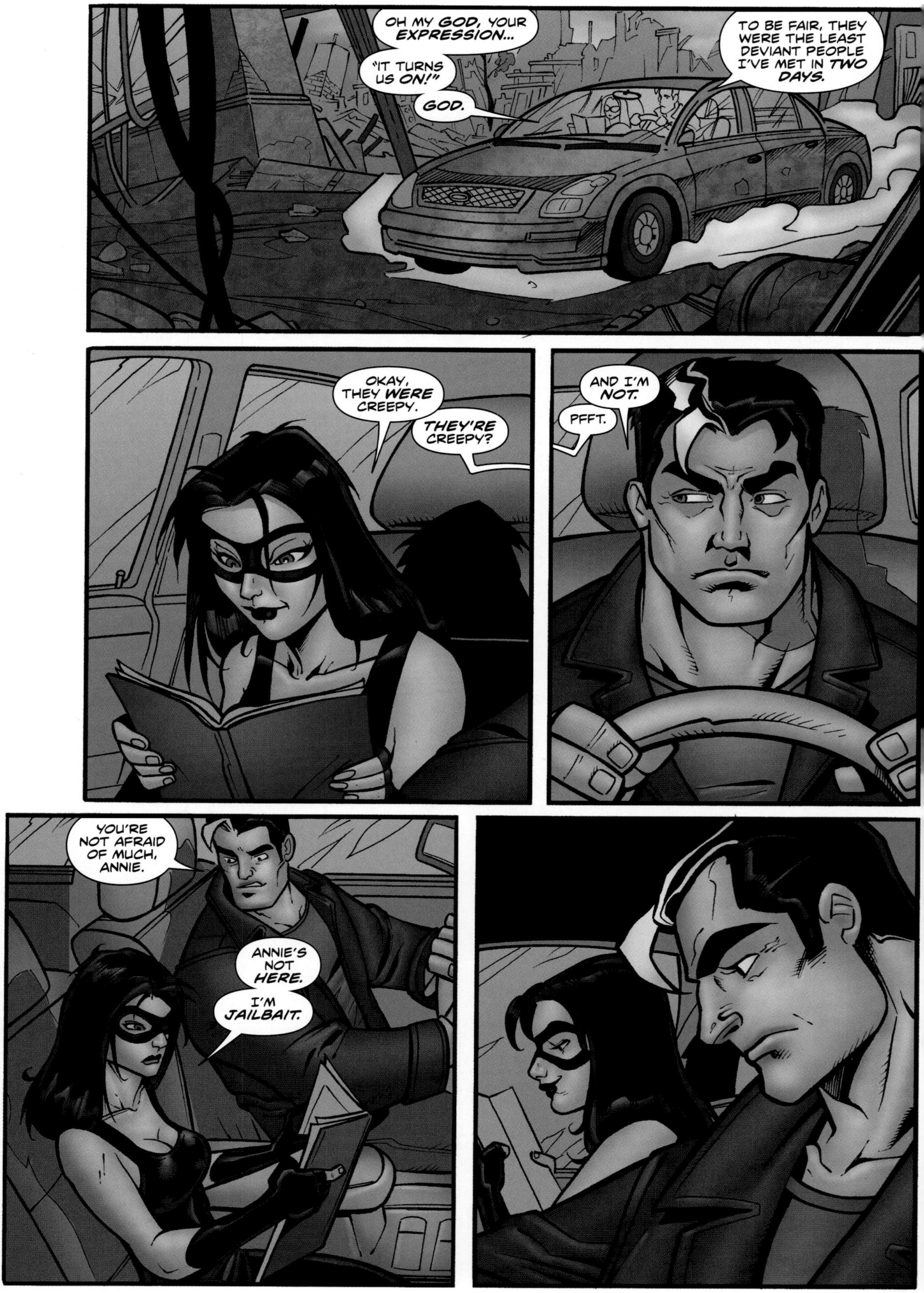
OH MY GOD, YOUR EXPRESSION...
"IT TURNS US ON!"
GOD.
TO BE FAIR, THEY WERE THE LEAST DEVIANT PEOPLE I'VE MET IN TWO DAYS.
OKAY, THEY WERE CREEPY.
THEY'RE CREEPY?
AND I'M NOT.
PFFT.
YOU'RE NOT AFRAID OF MUCH, ANNIE.
ANNIE'S NOT HERE.
I'M JAILBAIT.

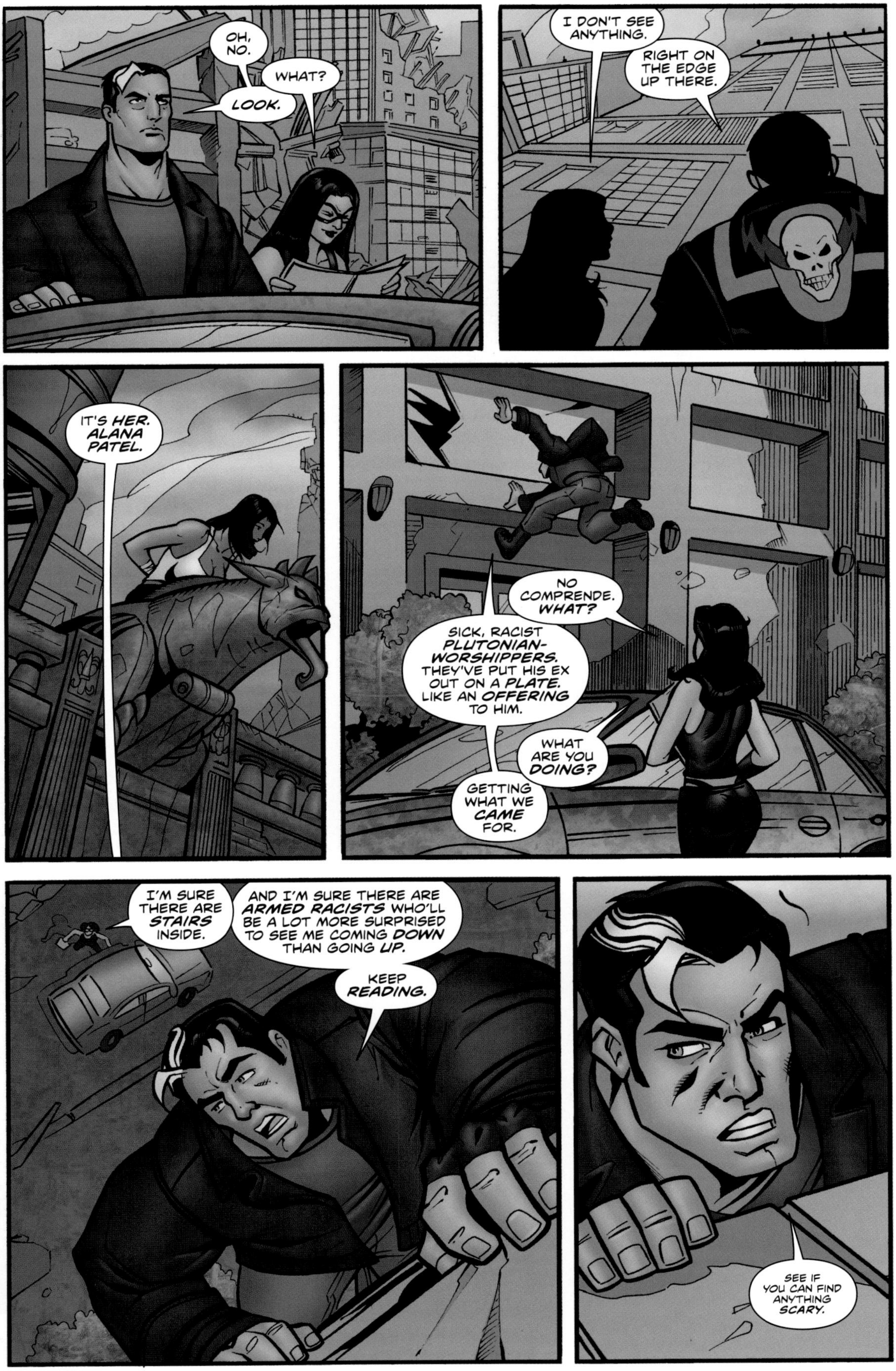
OH, NO.
WHAT?
LOOK.
I DON'T SEE ANYTHING.
RIGHT ON THE EDGE UP THERE.
IT'S HER. ALANA PATEL.
NO COMPRENDE. WHAT?
SICK, RACIST PLUTONIAN-WORSHIPPERS. THEY'VE PUT HIS EX OUT ON A PLATE. LIKE AN OFFERING TO HIM.
WHAT ARE YOU DOING?
GETTING WHAT WE CAME FOR.
I'M SURE THERE ARE STAIRS INSIDE.
AND I'M SURE THERE ARE ARMED RACISTS WHO'LL BE A LOT MORE SURPRISED TO SEE ME COMING DOWN THAN GOING UP.
KEEP READING.
SEE IF YOU CAN FIND ANYTHING SCARY.

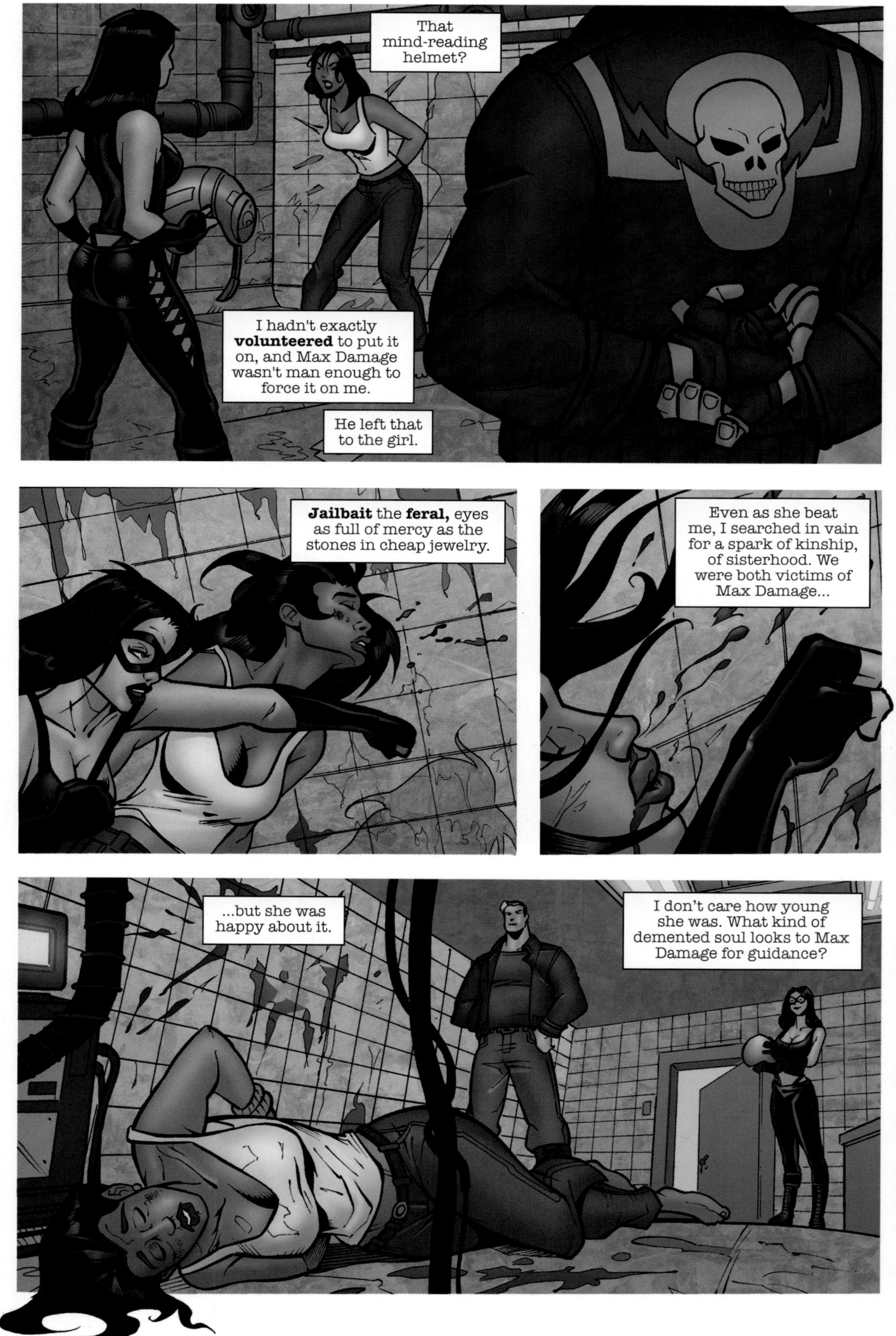
That mind-reading helmet?
I hadn't exactly **volunteered** to put it on, and Max Damage wasn't man enough to force it on me.
He left that to the girl.
Jailbait the **feral,** eyes as full of mercy as the stones in cheap jewelry.
Even as she beat me, I searched in vain for a spark of kinship, of sisterhood. We were both victims of Max Damage...
...but she was happy about it.
I don't care how young she was. What kind of demented soul looks to Max Damage for guidance?

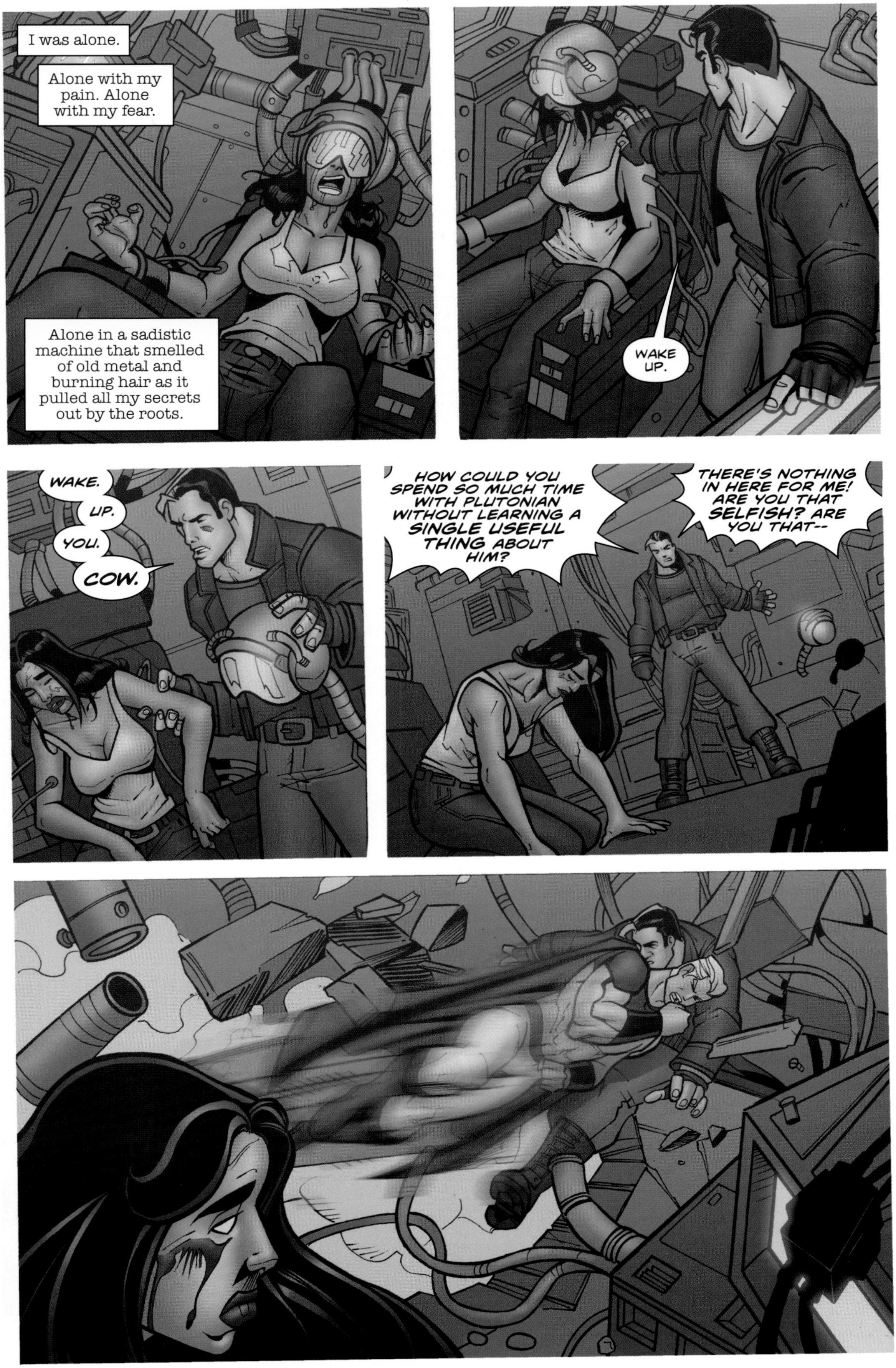
I was alone.
Alone with my pain. Alone with my fear.
Alone in a sadistic machine that smelled of old metal and burning hair as it pulled all my secrets out by the roots.
WAKE UP.
WAKE.
UP.
YOU.
COW.
HOW COULD YOU SPEND SO MUCH TIME WITH PLUTONIAN WITHOUT LEARNING A SINGLE USEFUL THING ABOUT HIM?
THERE'S NOTHING IN HERE FOR ME! ARE YOU THAT SELFISH? ARE YOU THAT--

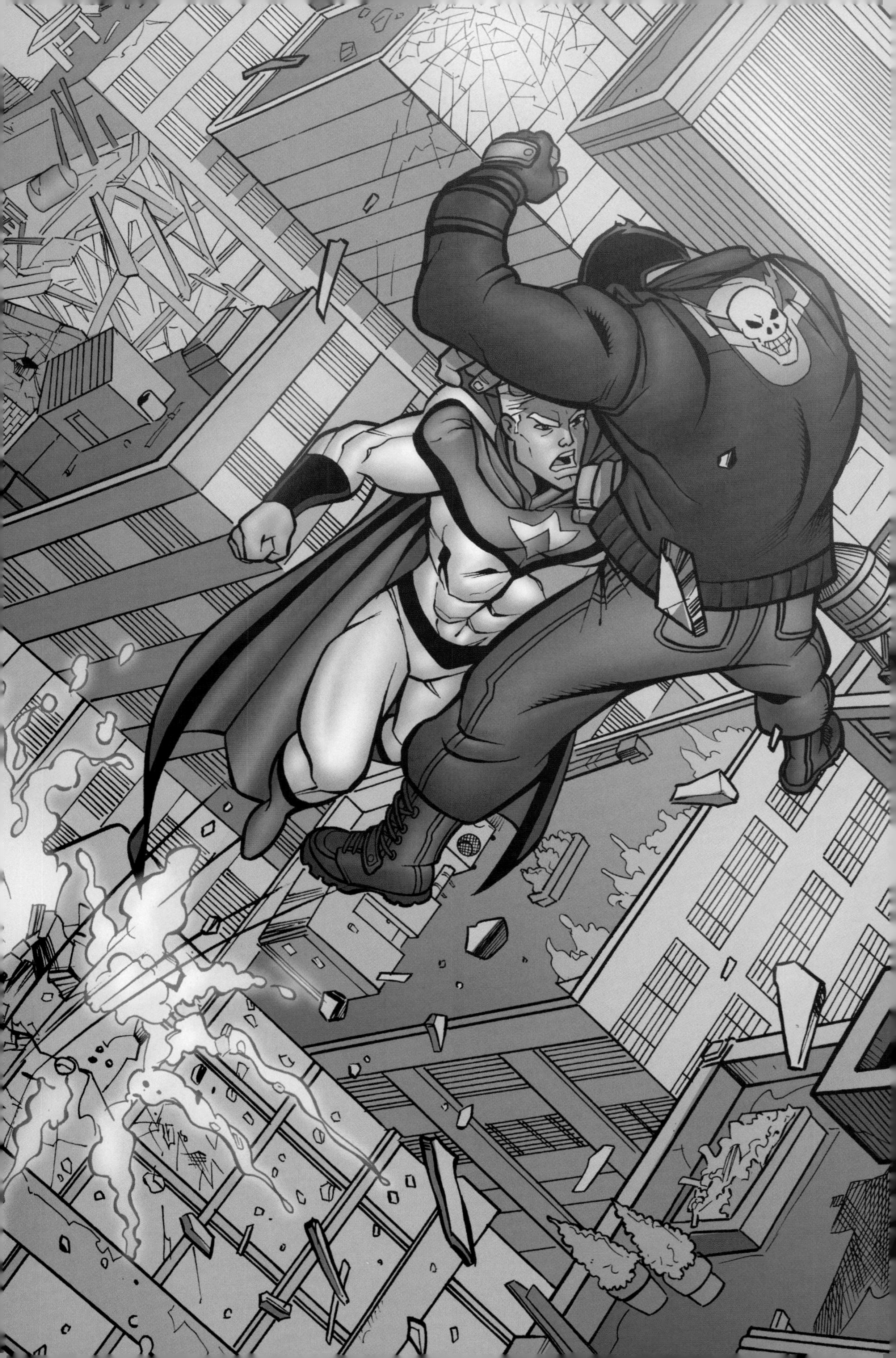

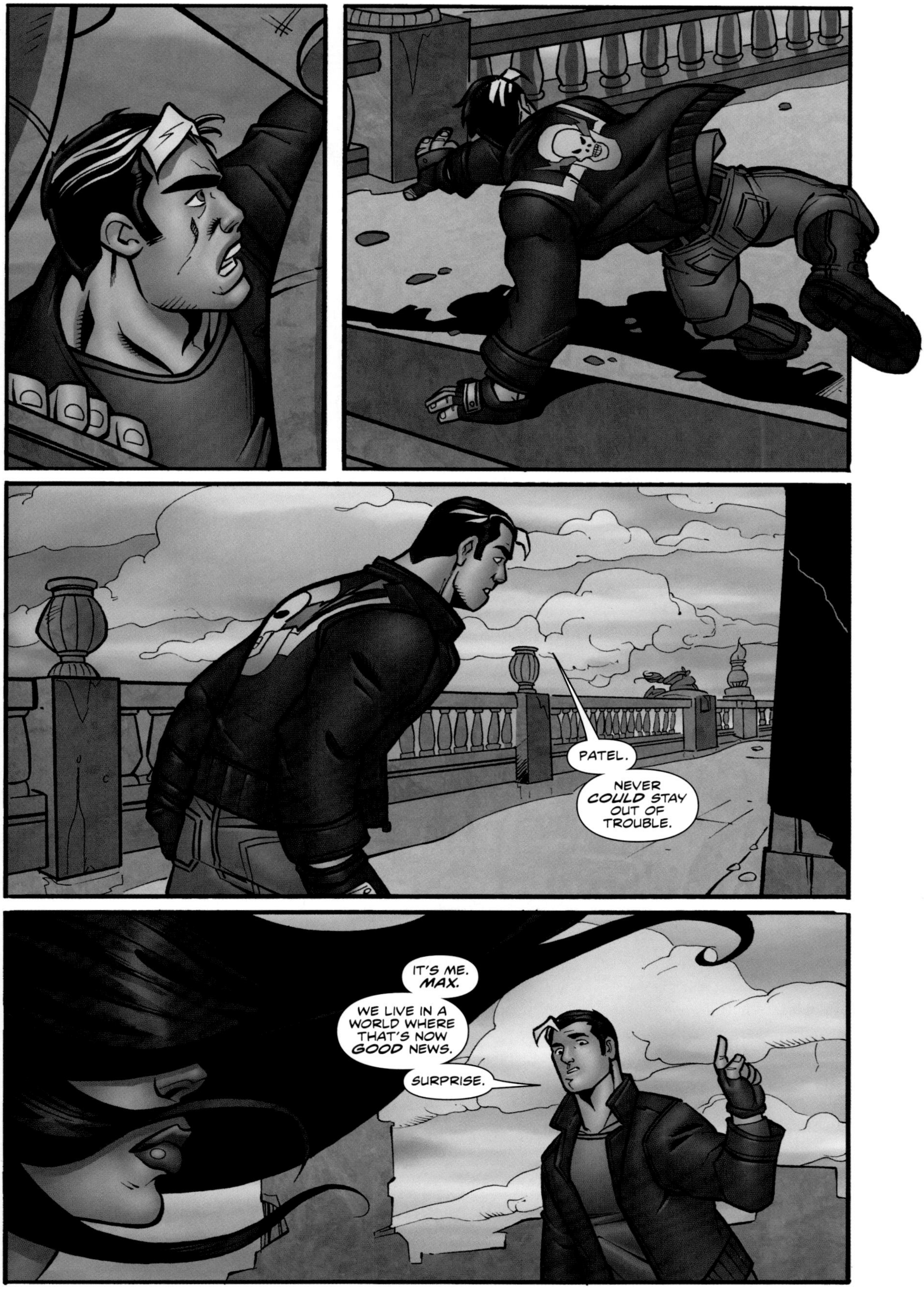
PATEL.
NEVER COULD STAY OUT OF TROUBLE.
IT'S ME. MAX.
WE LIVE IN A WORLD WHERE THAT'S NOW GOOD NEWS.
SURPRISE.

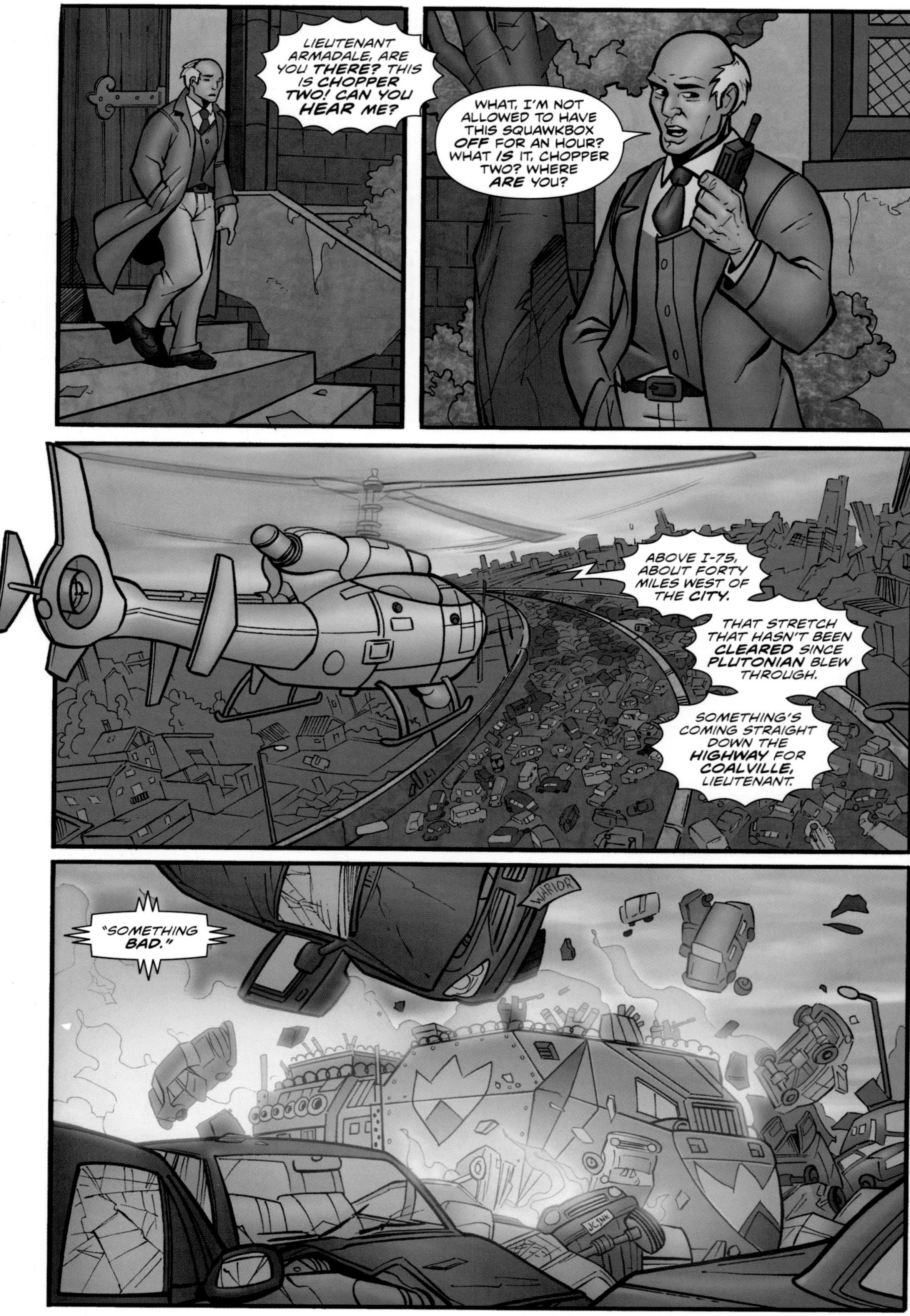
LIEUTENANT ARMADALE, ARE YOU THERE? THIS IS CHOPPER TWO! CAN YOU HEAR ME?
WHAT, I'M NOT ALLOWED TO HAVE THIS SQUAWKBOX OFF FOR AN HOUR? WHAT IS IT, CHOPPER TWO? WHERE ARE YOU?
ABOVE I-75, ABOUT FORTY MILES WEST OF THE CITY.
THAT STRETCH THAT HASN'T BEEN CLEARED SINCE PLUTONIAN BLEW THROUGH.
SOMETHING'S COMING STRAIGHT DOWN THE HIGHWAY FOR COALVILLE, LIEUTENANT.
"SOMETHING BAD."

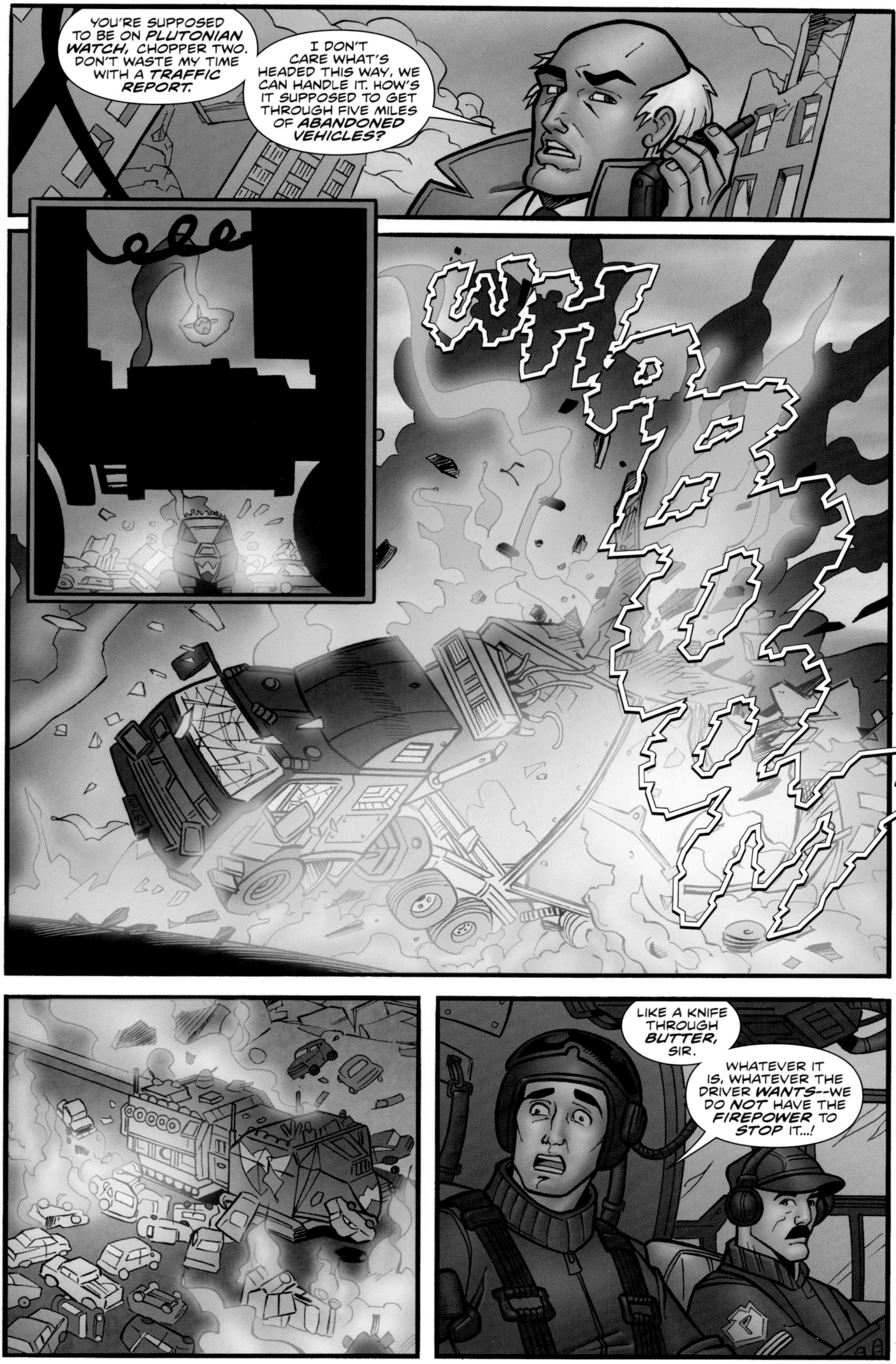
YOU'RE SUPPOSED TO BE ON *PLUTONIAN WATCH,* CHOPPER TWO. DON'T WASTE MY TIME WITH A *TRAFFIC REPORT.*
I DON'T CARE WHAT'S HEADED THIS WAY, WE CAN HANDLE IT. HOW'S IT SUPPOSED TO GET THROUGH FIVE MILES OF *ABANDONED VEHICLES?*
WHABOOM!
LIKE A KNIFE THROUGH *BUTTER,* SIR.
WHATEVER IT IS, WHATEVER THE DRIVER *WANTS*--WE DO *NOT* HAVE THE *FIREPOWER* TO *STOP* IT...!

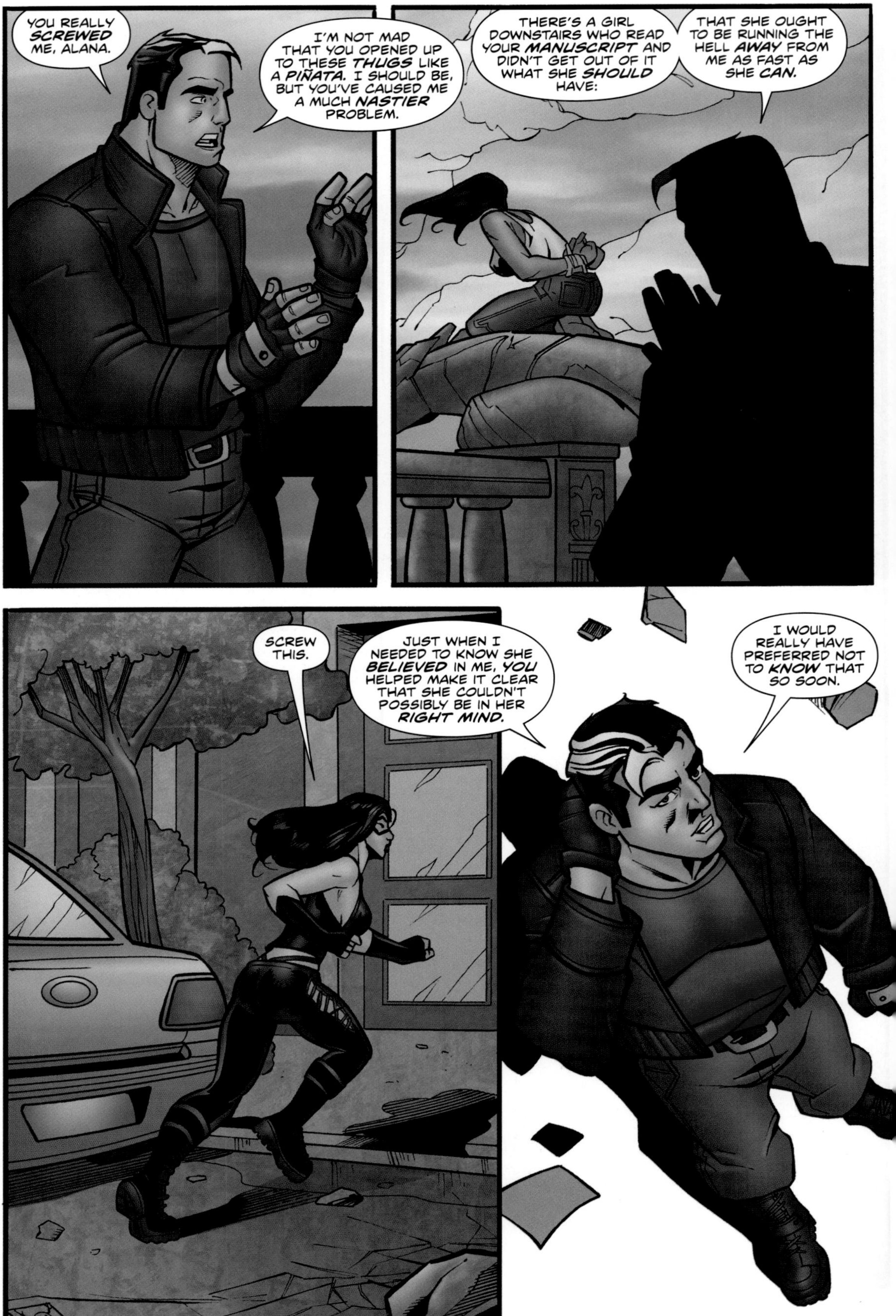
YOU REALLY SCREWED ME, ALANA.
I'M NOT MAD THAT YOU OPENED UP TO THESE THUGS LIKE A PIÑATA. I SHOULD BE, BUT YOU'VE CAUSED ME A MUCH NASTIER PROBLEM.
THERE'S A GIRL DOWNSTAIRS WHO READ YOUR MANUSCRIPT AND DIDN'T GET OUT OF IT WHAT SHE SHOULD HAVE:
THAT SHE OUGHT TO BE RUNNING THE HELL AWAY FROM ME AS FAST AS SHE CAN.
SCREW THIS.
JUST WHEN I NEEDED TO KNOW SHE BELIEVED IN ME, YOU HELPED MAKE IT CLEAR THAT SHE COULDN'T POSSIBLY BE IN HER RIGHT MIND.
I WOULD REALLY HAVE PREFERRED NOT TO KNOW THAT SO SOON.

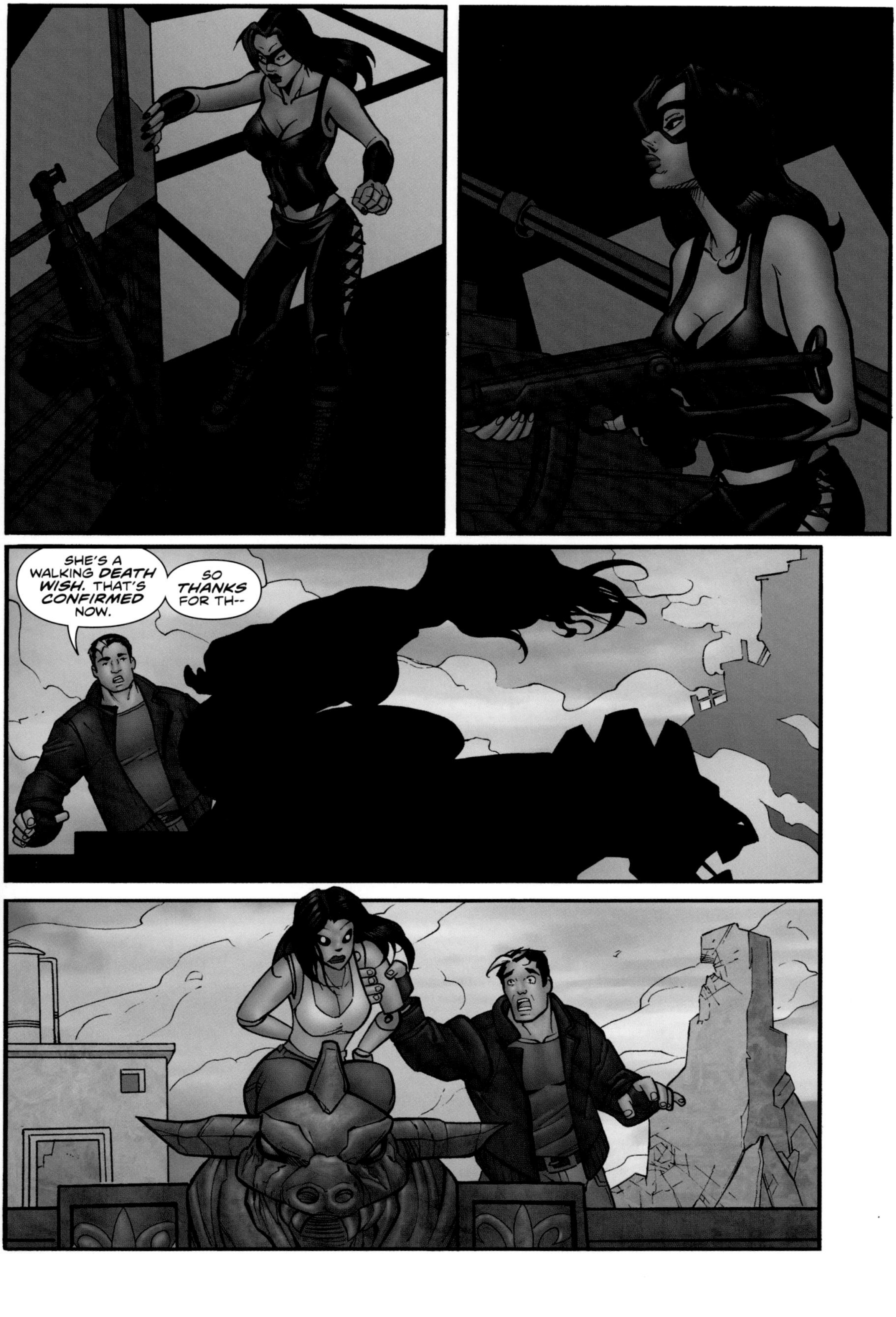
SHE'S A WALKING DEATH WISH. THAT'S CONFIRMED NOW.
SO THANKS FOR TH--

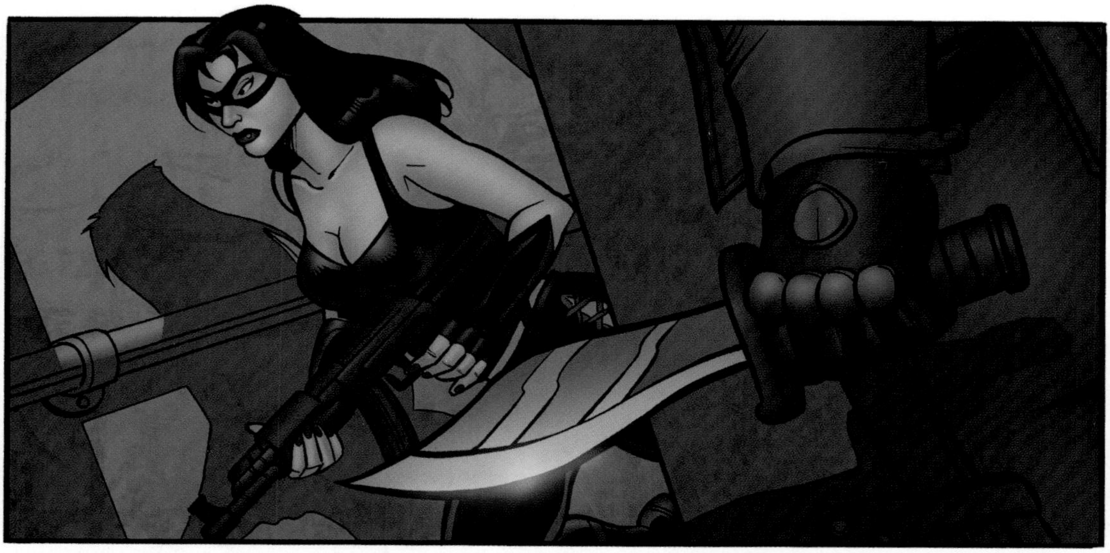

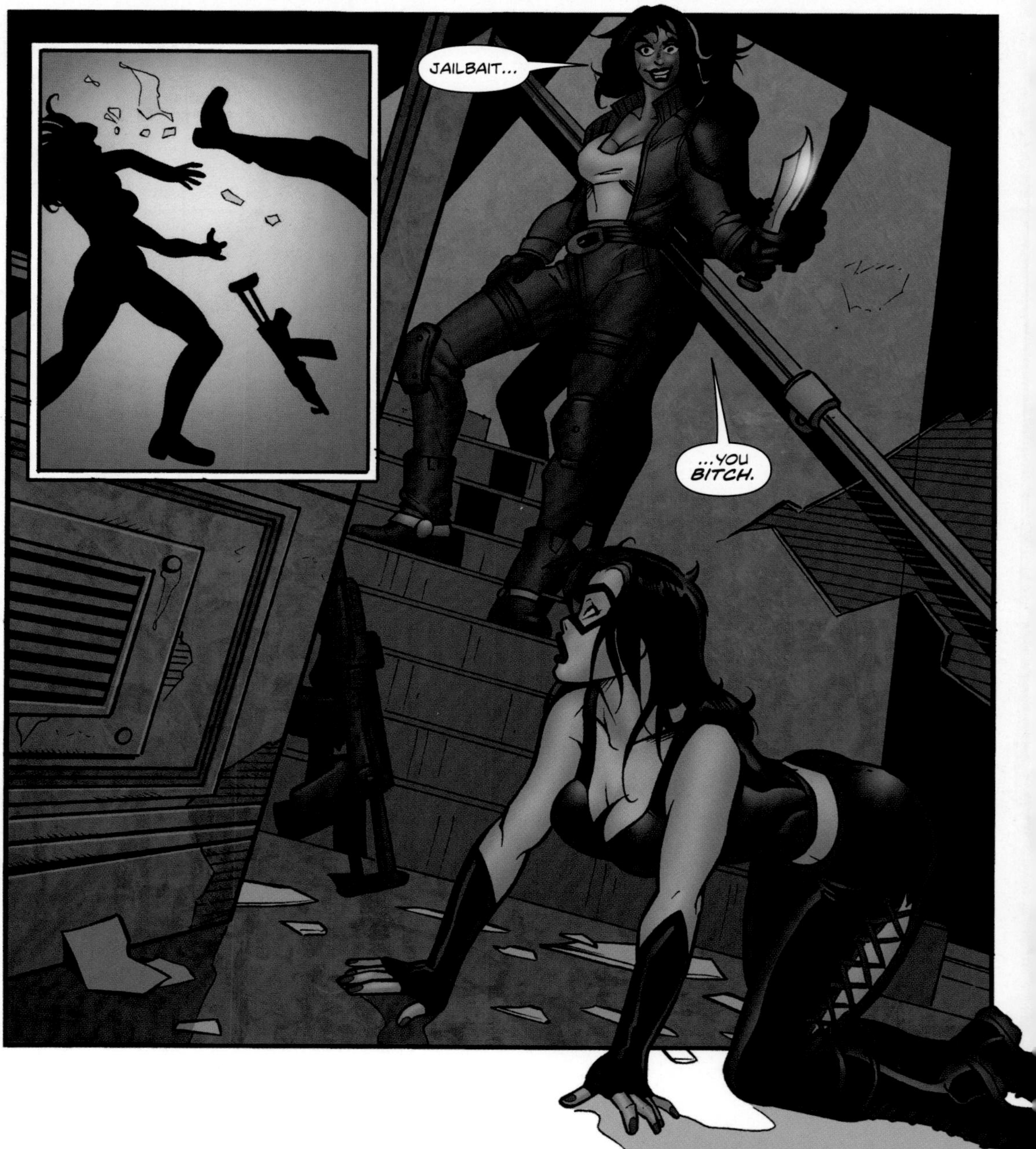
JAILBAIT...
...YOU BITCH.

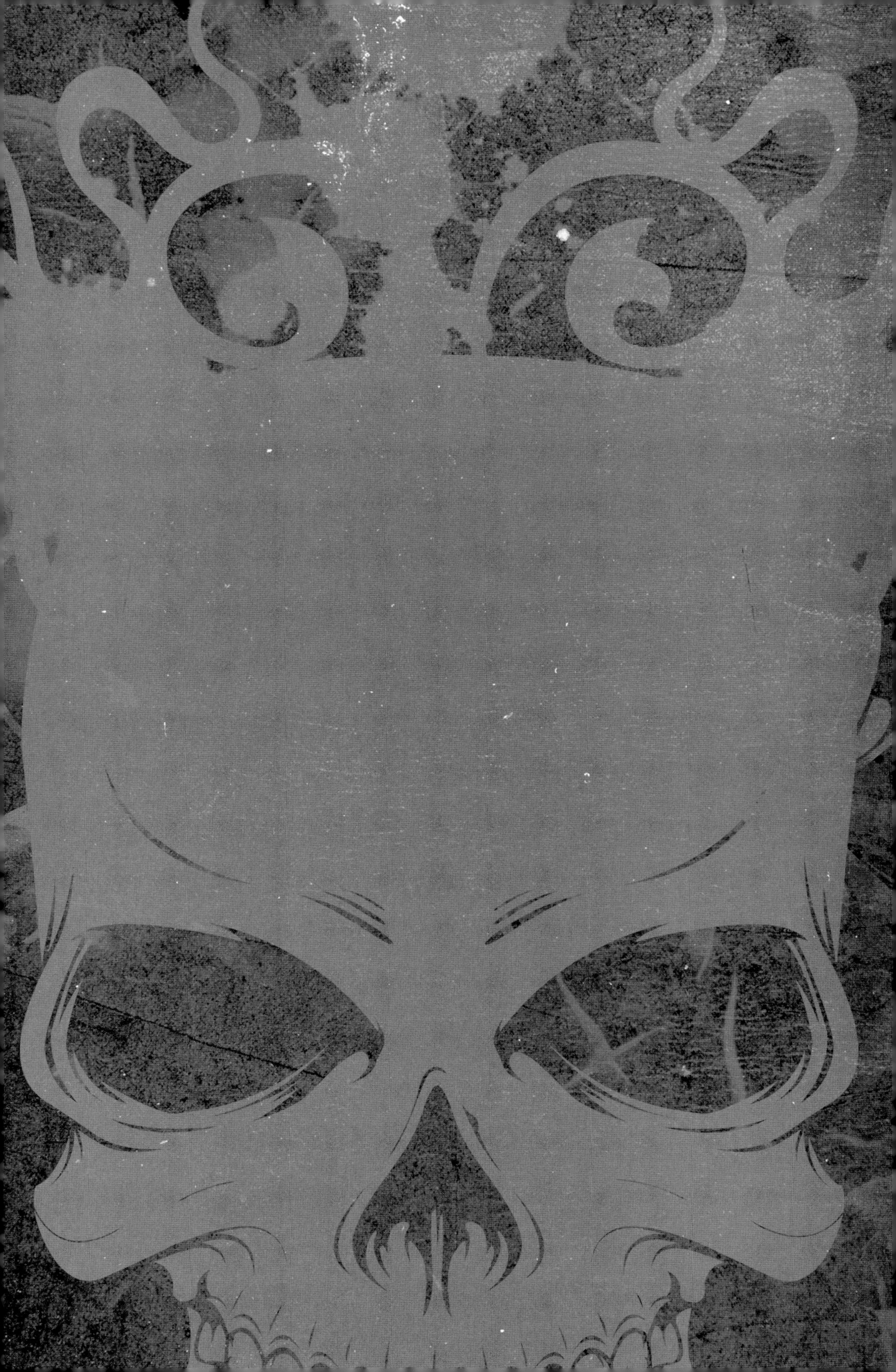

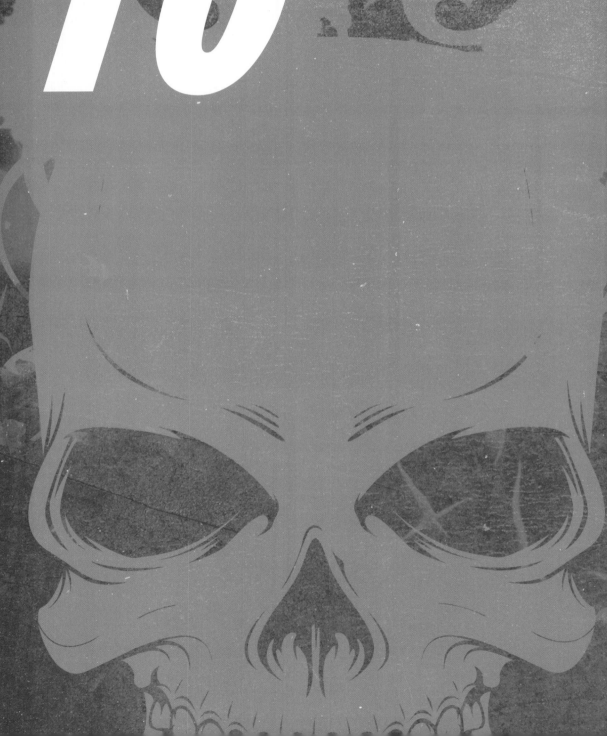

CHAPTER

10

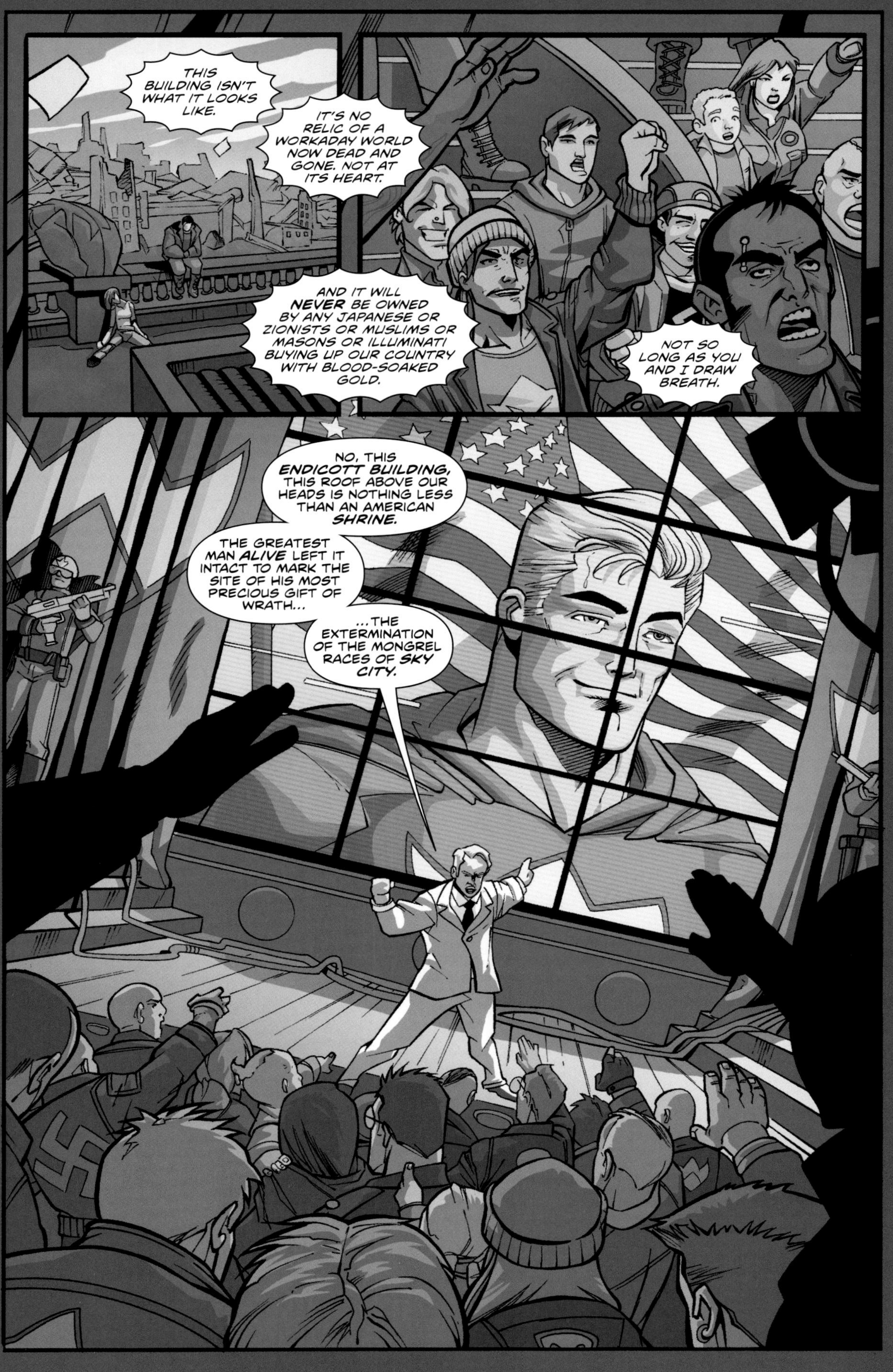
THIS BUILDING ISN'T WHAT IT LOOKS LIKE.
IT'S NO RELIC OF A WORKADAY WORLD NOW DEAD AND GONE. NOT AT ITS HEART.
AND IT WILL NEVER BE OWNED BY ANY JAPANESE OR ZIONISTS OR MUSLIMS OR MASONS OR ILLUMINATI BUYING UP OUR COUNTRY WITH BLOOD-SOAKED GOLD.
NOT SO LONG AS YOU AND I DRAW BREATH.
NO, THIS ENDICOTT BUILDING, THIS ROOF ABOVE OUR HEADS IS NOTHING LESS THAN AN AMERICAN SHRINE.
THE GREATEST MAN ALIVE LEFT IT INTACT TO MARK THE SITE OF HIS MOST PRECIOUS GIFT OF WRATH...
...THE EXTERMINATION OF THE MONGREL RACES OF SKY CITY.

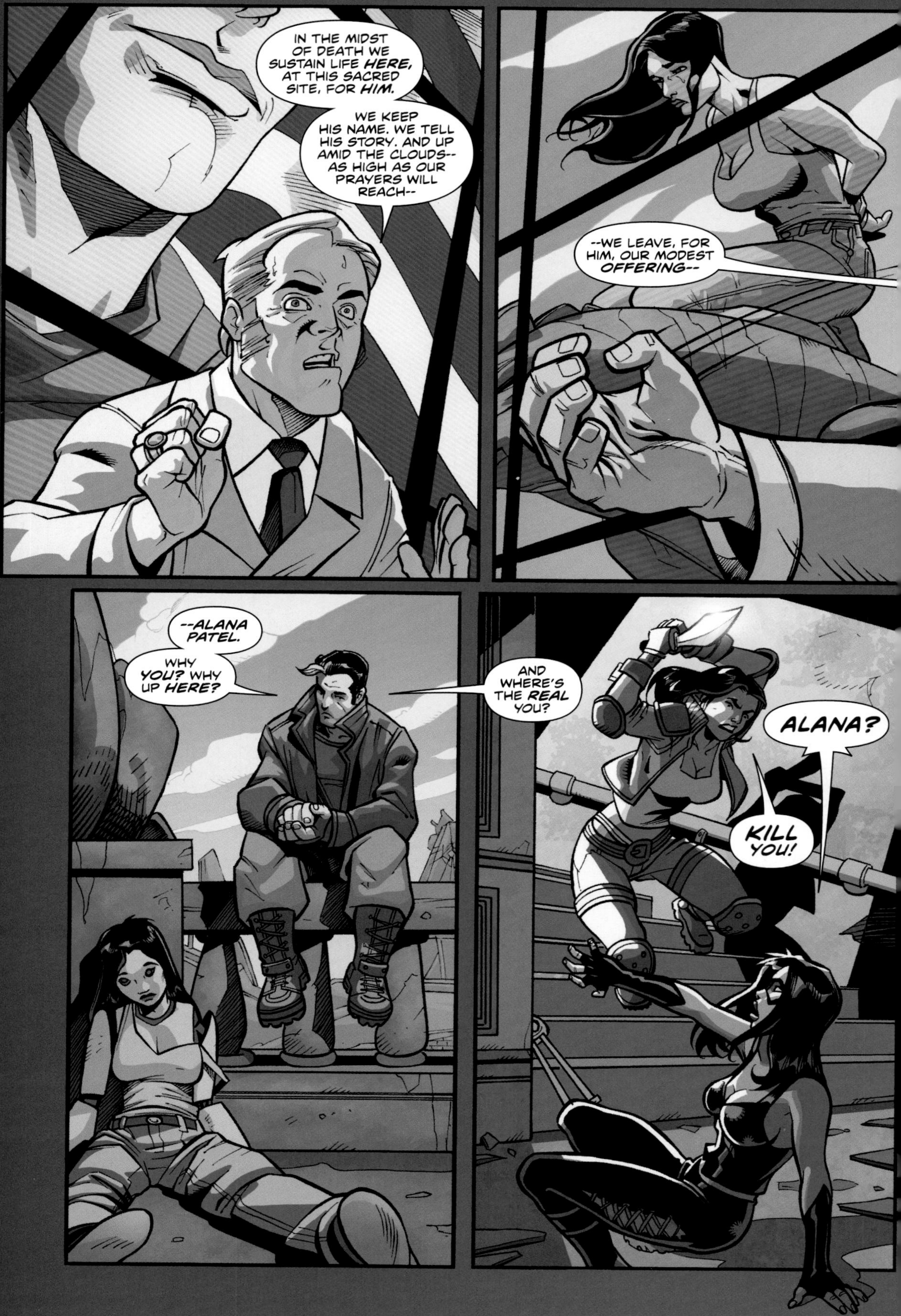
IN THE MIDST OF DEATH WE SUSTAIN LIFE HERE, AT THIS SACRED SITE, FOR HIM.
WE KEEP HIS NAME. WE TELL HIS STORY. AND UP AMID THE CLOUDS-- AS HIGH AS OUR PRAYERS WILL REACH--
--WE LEAVE, FOR HIM, OUR MODEST OFFERING--
--ALANA PATEL.
WHY YOU? WHY UP HERE?
AND WHERE'S THE REAL YOU?
ALANA?
KILL YOU!

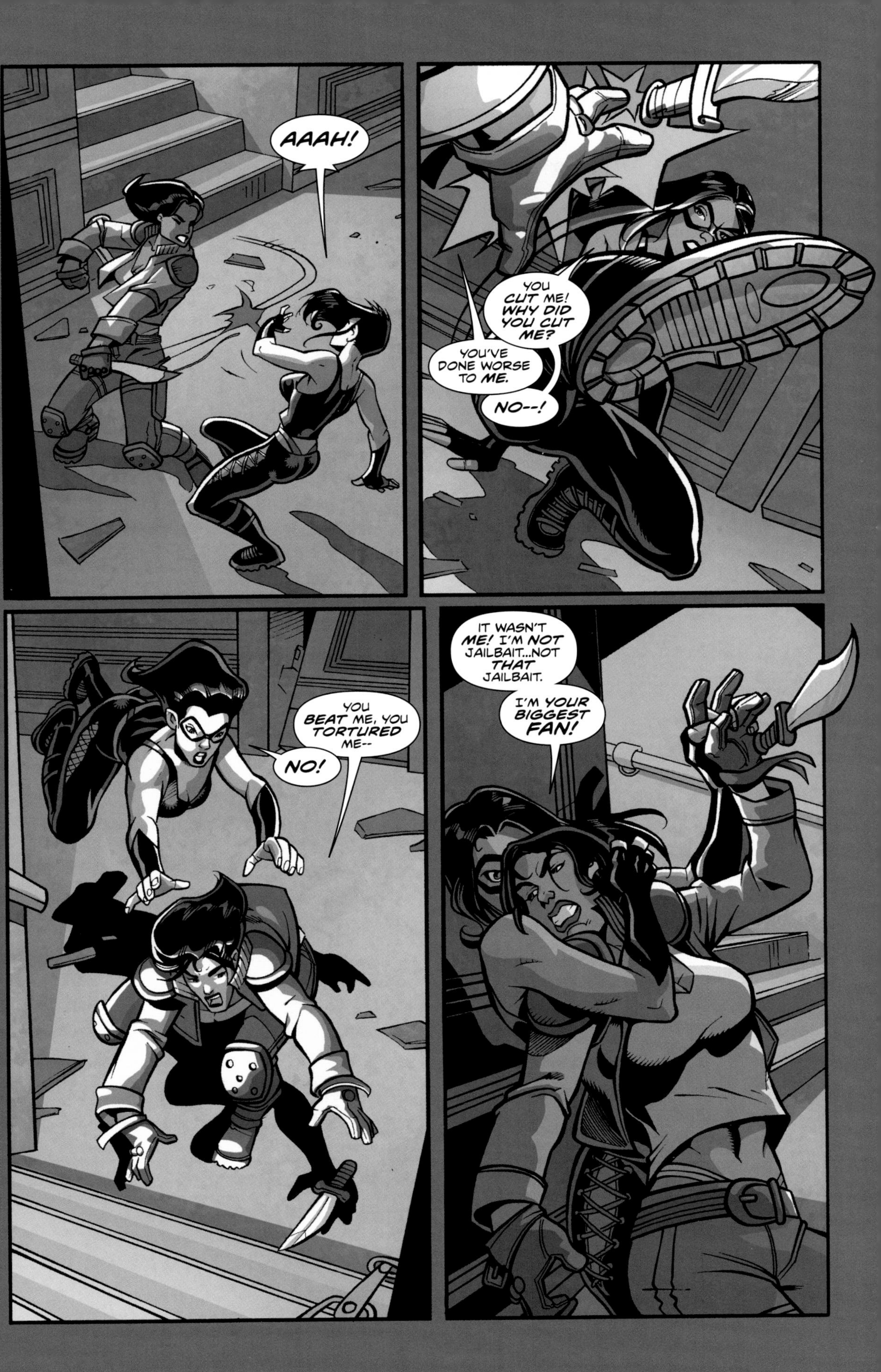

AAAH!
YOU CUT ME! WHY DID YOU CUT ME?
YOU'VE DONE WORSE TO ME.
NO--!
YOU BEAT ME, YOU TORTURED ME--
NO!
IT WASN'T ME! I'M NOT JAILBAIT...NOT THAT JAILBAIT.
I'M YOUR BIGGEST FAN!

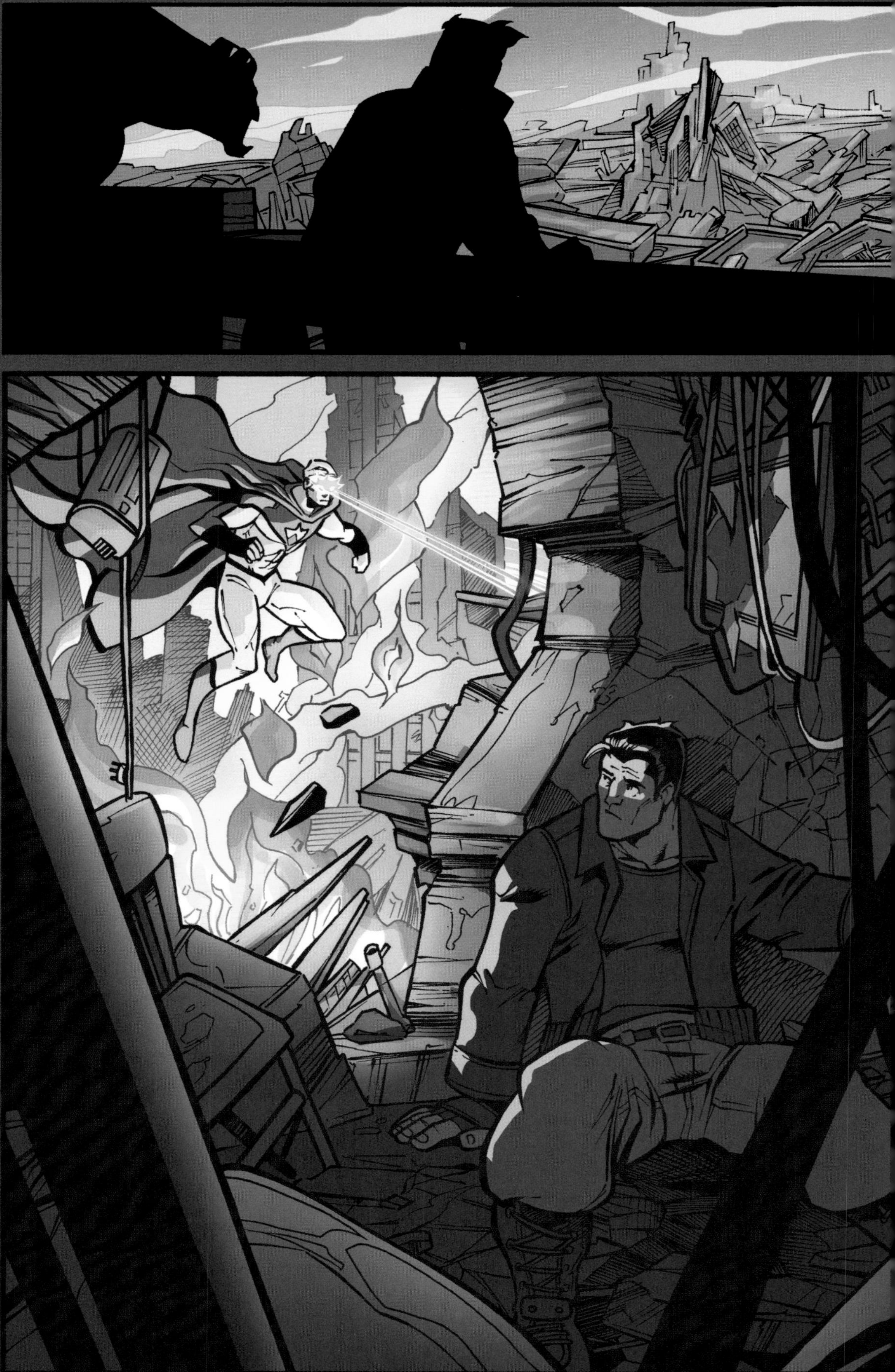

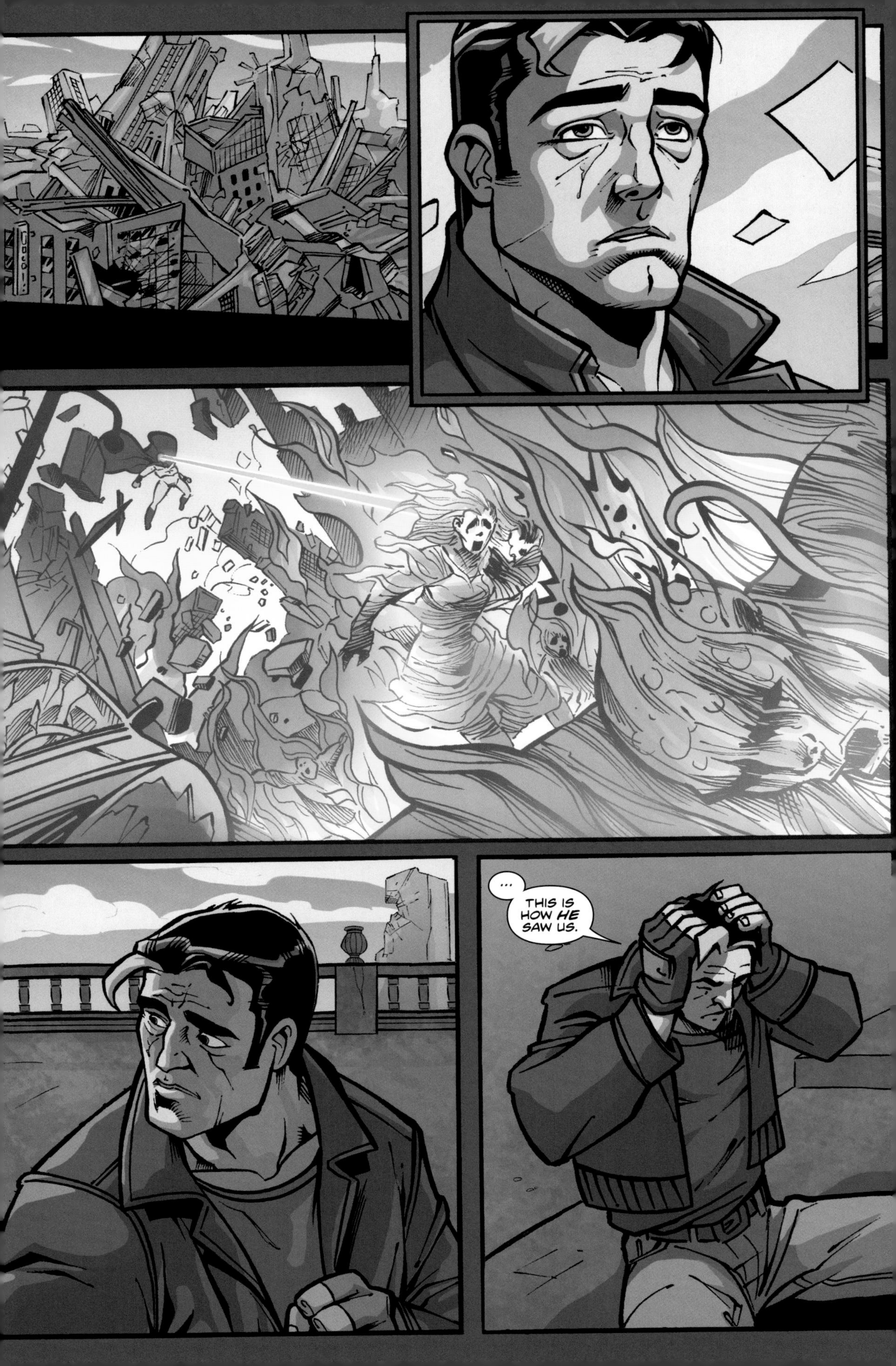
...
THIS IS HOW HE SAW US.

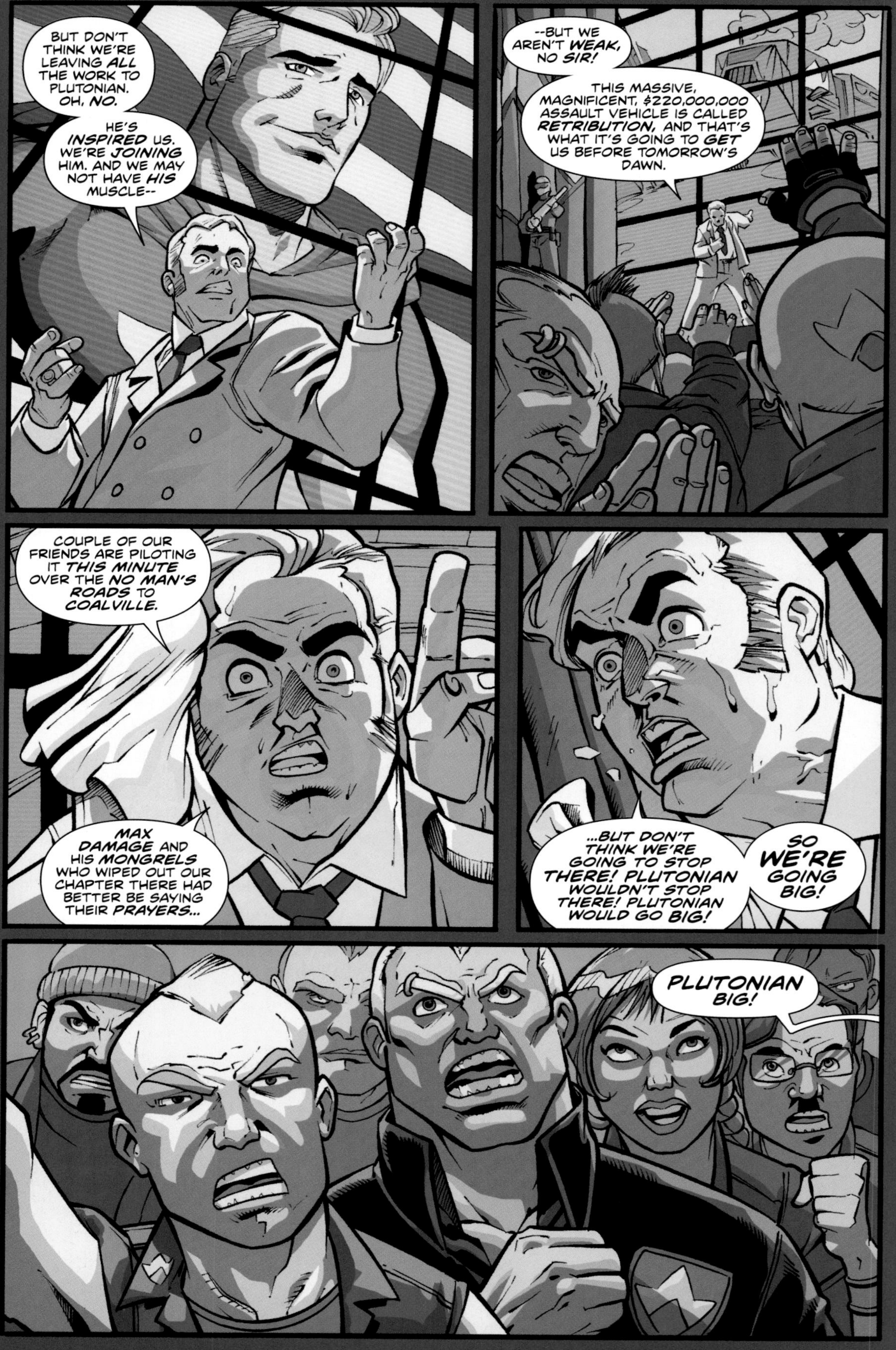
BUT DON'T THINK WE'RE LEAVING ALL THE WORK TO PLUTONIAN. OH, NO.
HE'S INSPIRED US. WE'RE JOINING HIM. AND WE MAY NOT HAVE HIS MUSCLE--
--BUT WE AREN'T WEAK, NO SIR!
THIS MASSIVE, MAGNIFICENT, $220,000,000 ASSAULT VEHICLE IS CALLED RETRIBUTION, AND THAT'S WHAT IT'S GOING TO GET US BEFORE TOMORROW'S DAWN.
COUPLE OF OUR FRIENDS ARE PILOTING IT THIS MINUTE OVER THE NO MAN'S ROADS TO COALVILLE.
MAX DAMAGE AND HIS MONGRELS WHO WIPED OUT OUR CHAPTER THERE HAD BETTER BE SAYING THEIR PRAYERS...
...BUT DON'T THINK WE'RE GOING TO STOP THERE! PLUTONIAN WOULDN'T STOP THERE! PLUTONIAN WOULD GO BIG!
SO WE'RE GOING BIG!
PLUTONIAN BIG!

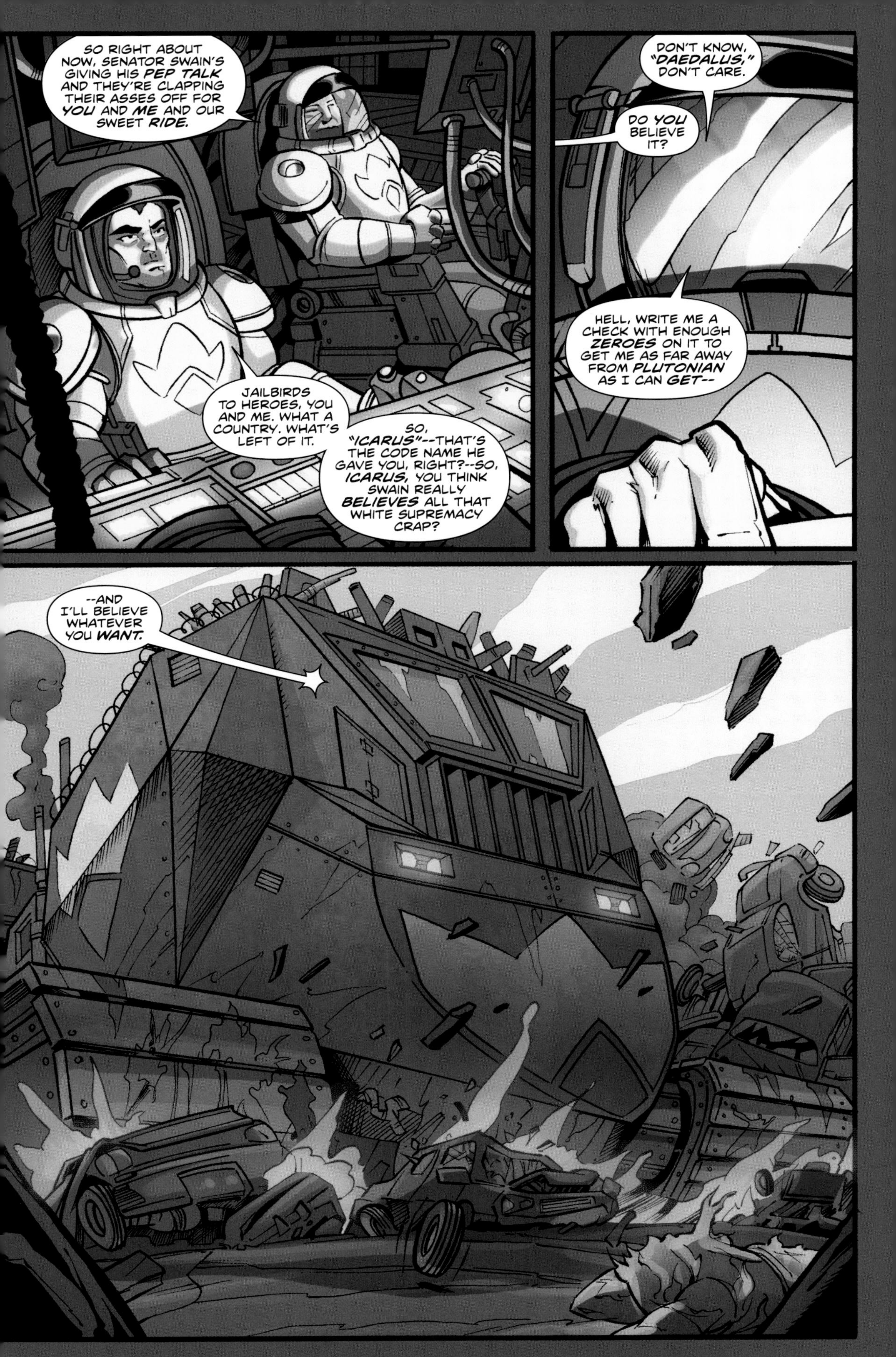
SO RIGHT ABOUT NOW, SENATOR SWAIN'S GIVING HIS PEP TALK AND THEY'RE CLAPPING THEIR ASSES OFF FOR YOU AND ME AND OUR SWEET RIDE.
JAILBIRDS TO HEROES, YOU AND ME. WHAT A COUNTRY. WHAT'S LEFT OF IT.
SO, "ICARUS"--THAT'S THE CODE NAME HE GAVE YOU, RIGHT?--SO, ICARUS, YOU THINK SWAIN REALLY BELIEVES ALL THAT WHITE SUPREMACY CRAP?
DON'T KNOW, "DAEDALUS," DON'T CARE.
DO YOU BELIEVE IT?
HELL, WRITE ME A CHECK WITH ENOUGH ZEROES ON IT TO GET ME AS FAR AWAY FROM PLUTONIAN AS I CAN GET--
--AND I'LL BELIEVE WHATEVER YOU WANT.

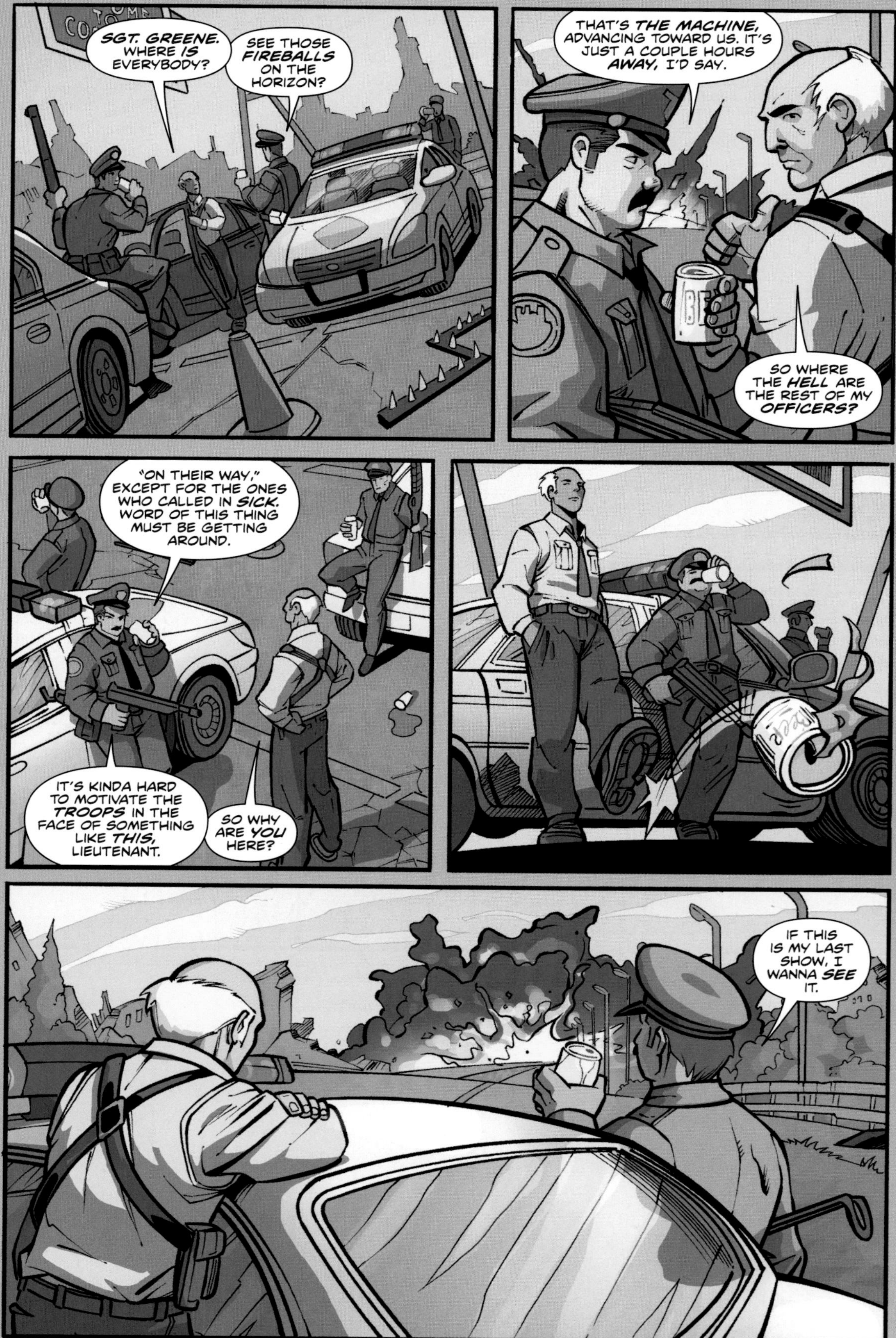
SGT. GREENE. WHERE IS EVERYBODY?
SEE THOSE FIREBALLS ON THE HORIZON?
THAT'S THE MACHINE, ADVANCING TOWARD US. IT'S JUST A COUPLE HOURS AWAY, I'D SAY.
SO WHERE THE HELL ARE THE REST OF MY OFFICERS?
"ON THEIR WAY," EXCEPT FOR THE ONES WHO CALLED IN SICK. WORD OF THIS THING MUST BE GETTING AROUND.
IT'S KINDA HARD TO MOTIVATE THE TROOPS IN THE FACE OF SOMETHING LIKE THIS, LIEUTENANT.
SO WHY ARE YOU HERE?
IF THIS IS MY LAST SHOW, I WANNA SEE IT.

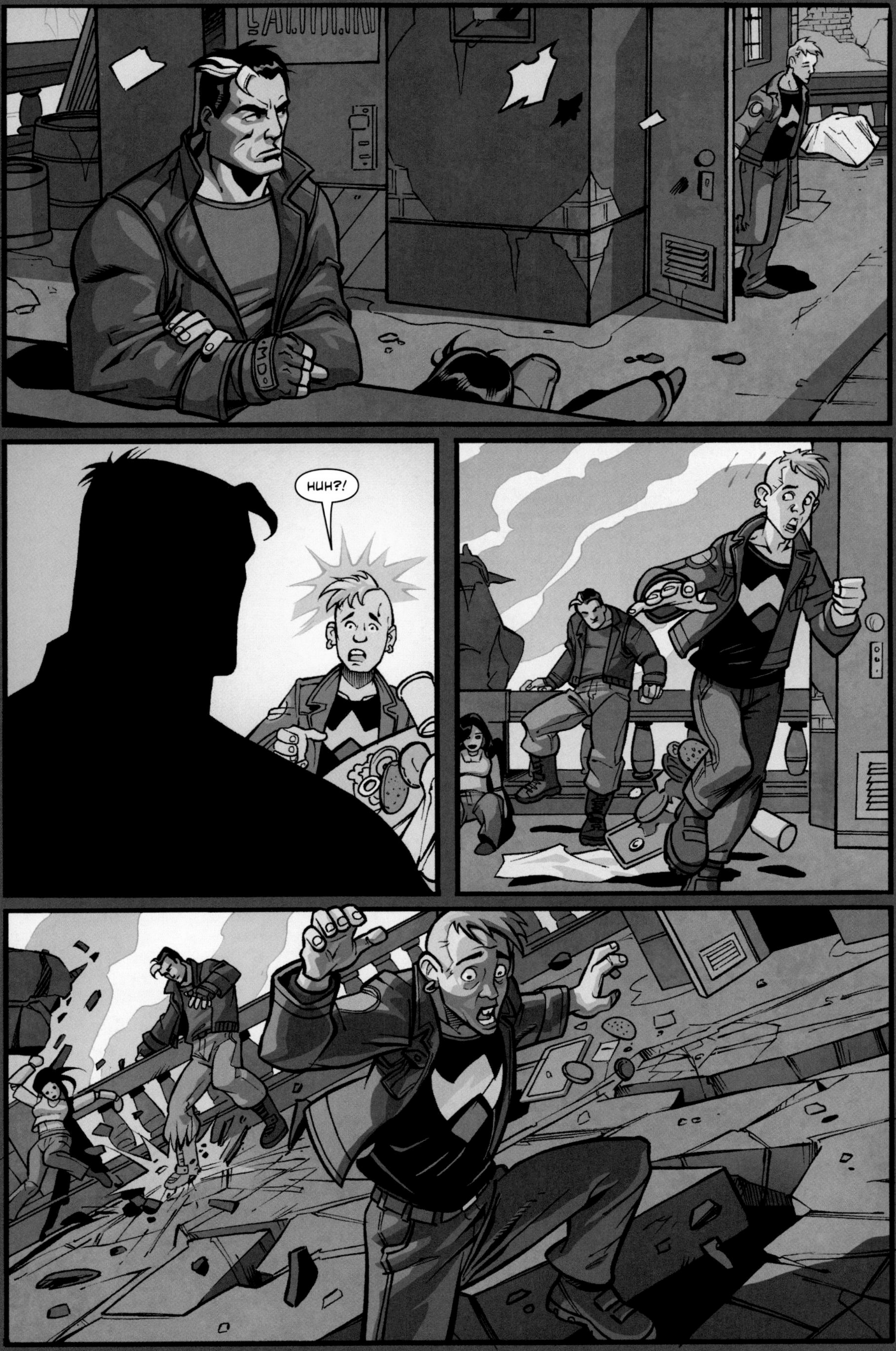
HUH?!

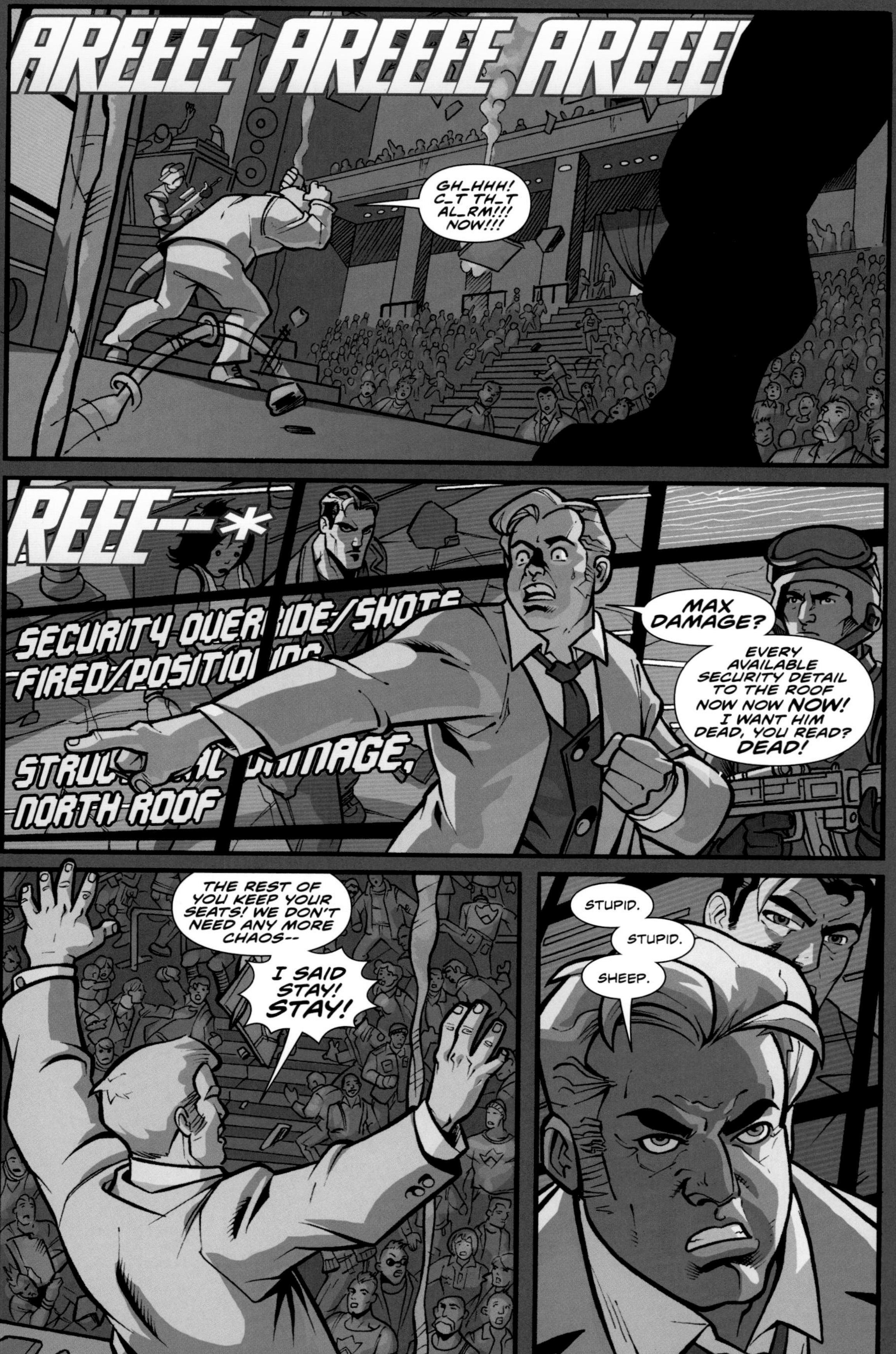
AREEEE AREEEE AREEE
GH_HHH! C_T TH_T AL_RM!!! NOW!!!
REEE--*
SECURITY OVERRIDE/SHOTS
FIRED/POSITIONING
STRUCTURAL DAMAGE, NORTH ROOF
MAX DAMAGE?
EVERY AVAILABLE SECURITY DETAIL TO THE ROOF NOW NOW NOW! I WANT HIM DEAD, YOU READ? DEAD!
THE REST OF YOU KEEP YOUR SEATS! WE DON'T NEED ANY MORE CHAOS--
I SAID STAY! STAY!
STUPID.
STUPID.
SHEEP.

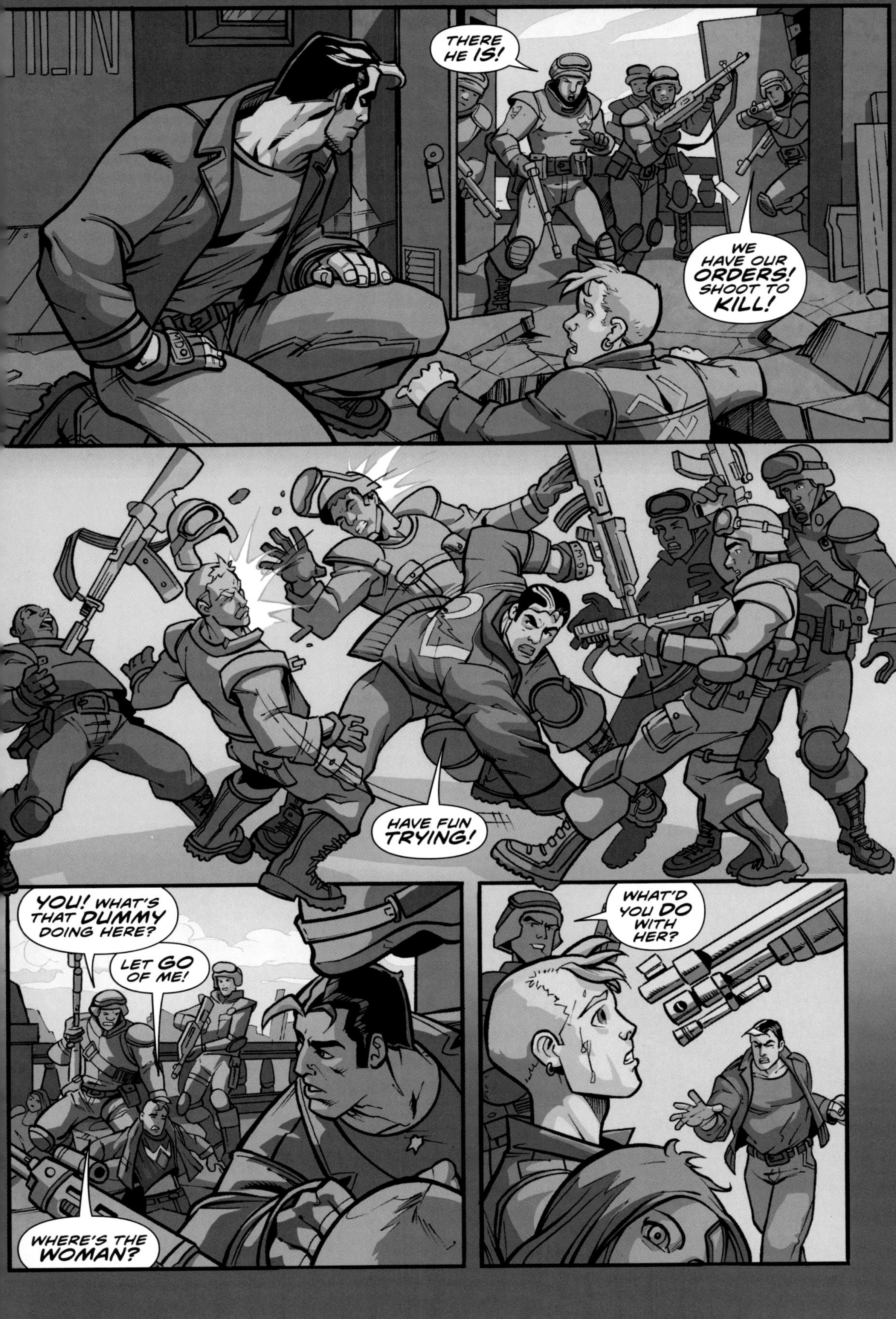
THERE HE IS!
WE HAVE OUR ORDERS! SHOOT TO KILL!
HAVE FUN TRYING!
YOU! WHAT'S THAT DUMMY DOING HERE?
LET GO OF ME!
WHERE'S THE WOMAN?
WHAT'D YOU DO WITH HER?

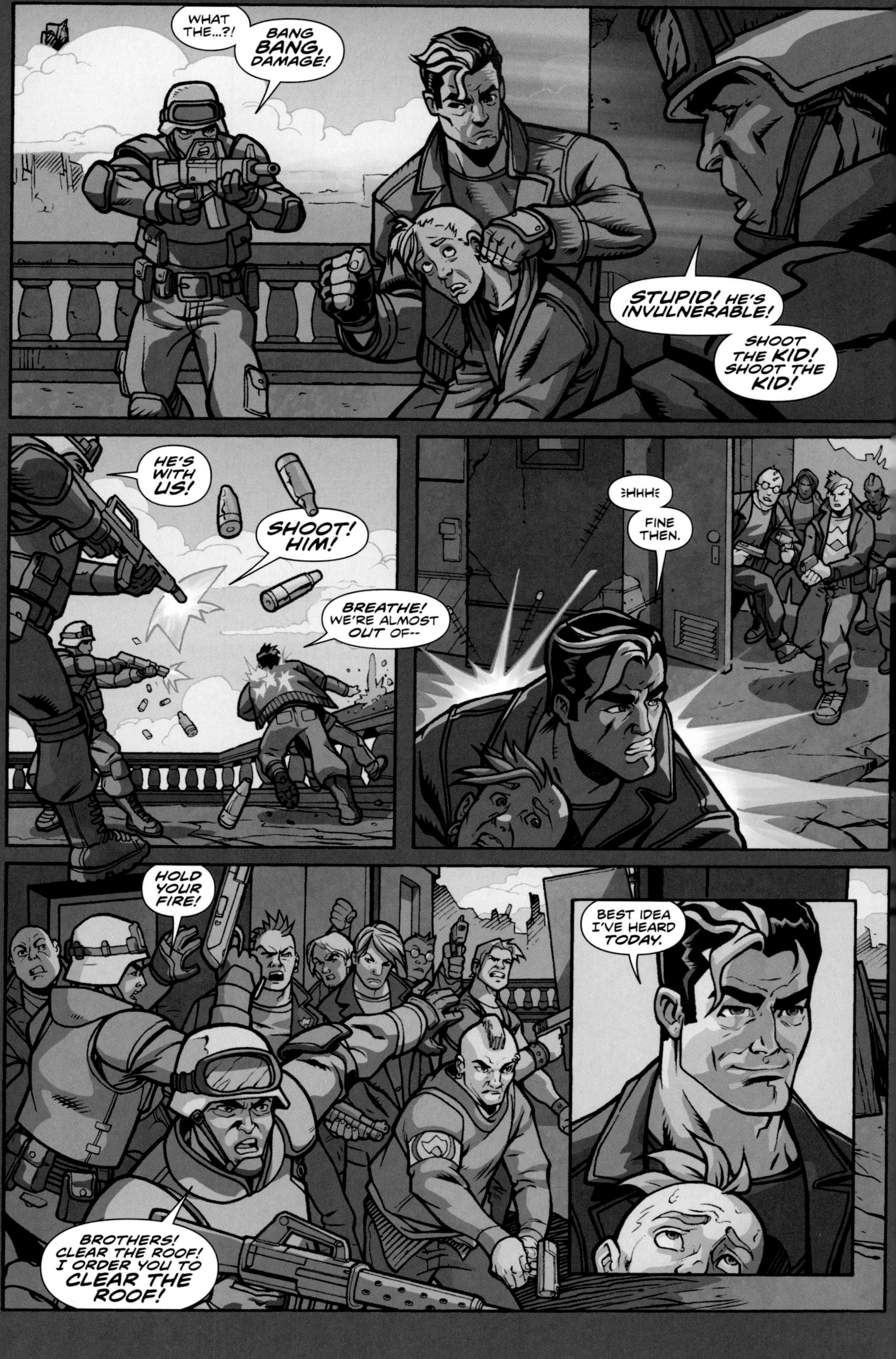
WHAT THE...?!
BANG BANG, DAMAGE!
STUPID! HE'S INVULNERABLE!
SHOOT THE KID! SHOOT THE KID!
HE'S WITH US!
SHOOT! HIM!
BREATHE! WE'RE ALMOST OUT OF--
HHH
FINE THEN.
HOLD YOUR FIRE!
BROTHERS! CLEAR THE ROOF! I ORDER YOU TO CLEAR THE ROOF!
BEST IDEA I'VE HEARD TODAY.

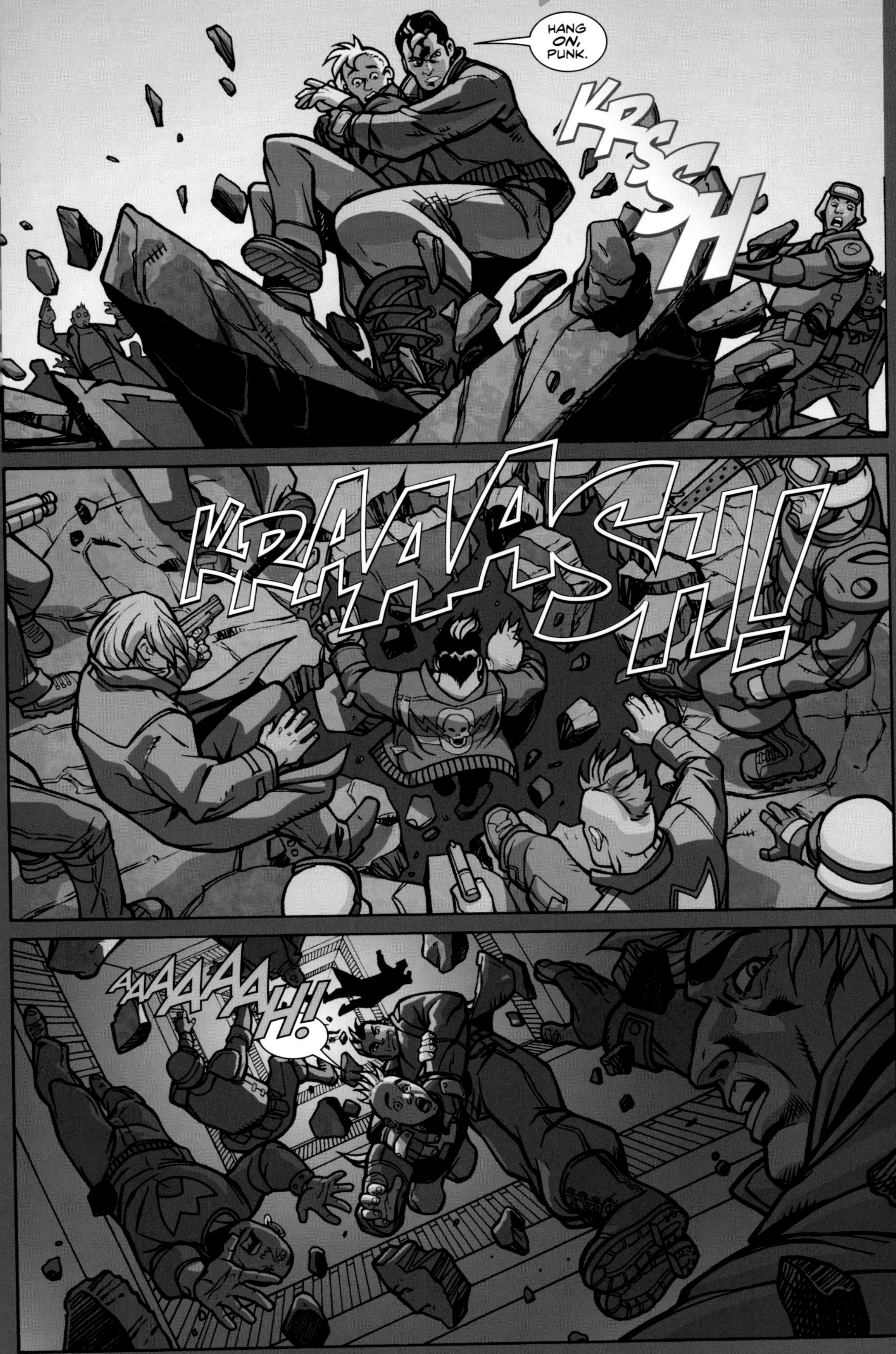
HANG ON, PUNK.
KRSSH
KRAAASH!
AAAAAAH!

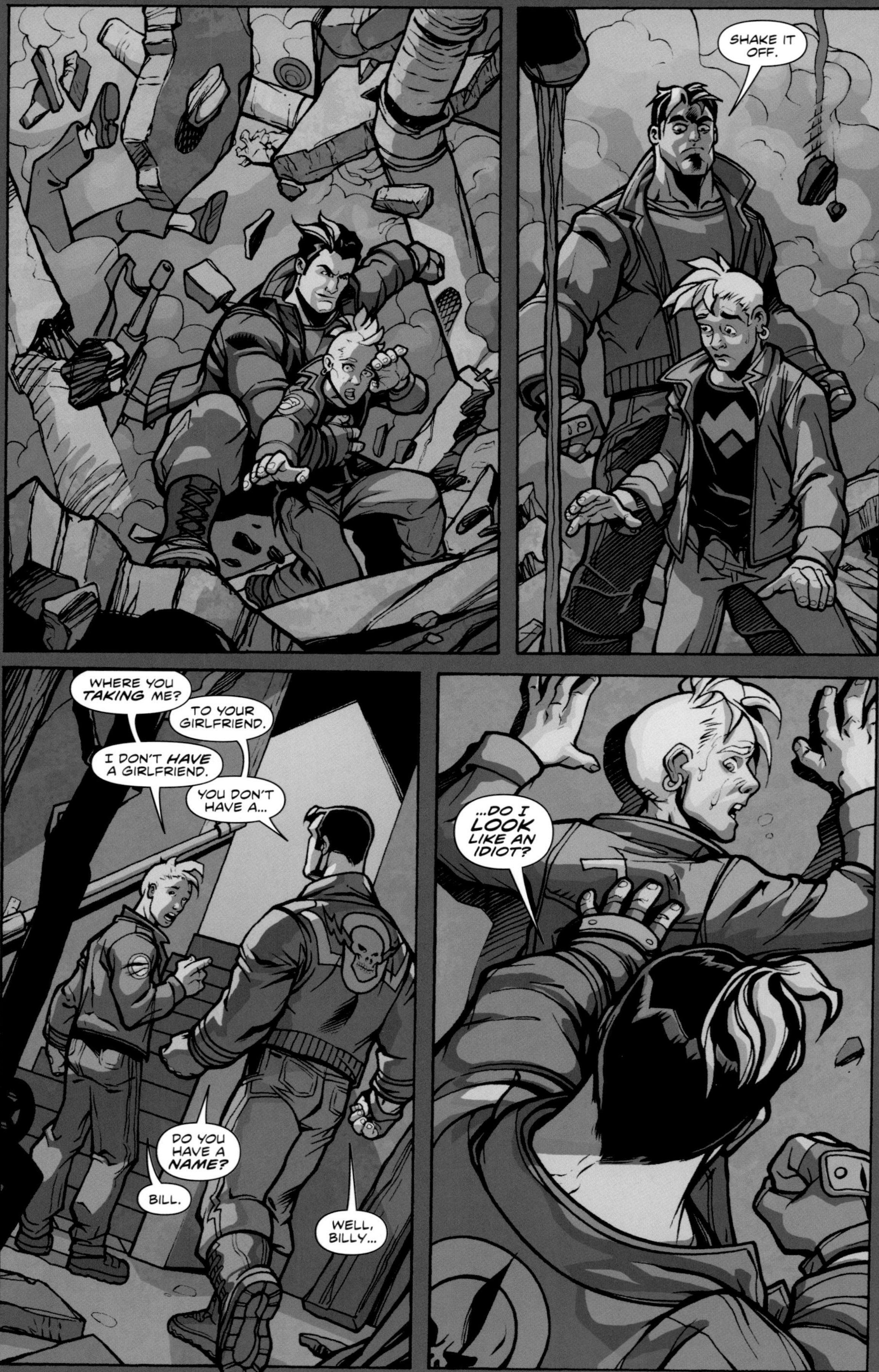
SHAKE IT OFF.
WHERE YOU TAKING ME?
TO YOUR GIRLFRIEND.
I DON'T HAVE A GIRLFRIEND.
YOU DON'T HAVE A...
DO YOU HAVE A NAME?
BILL.
WELL, BILLY...
...DO I LOOK LIKE AN IDIOT?

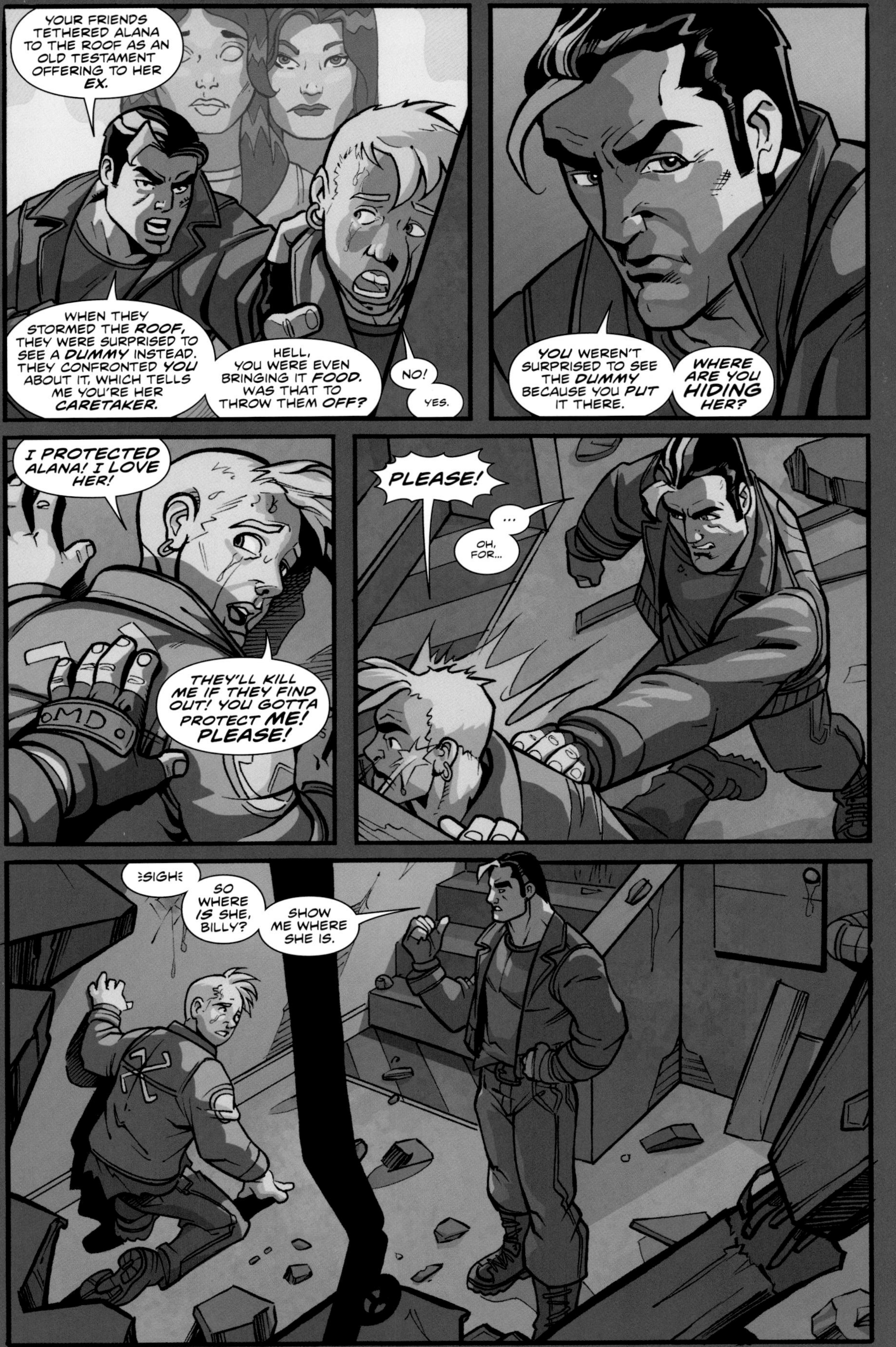
YOUR FRIENDS TETHERED ALANA TO THE ROOF AS AN OLD TESTAMENT OFFERING TO HER EX.
WHEN THEY STORMED THE ROOF, THEY WERE SURPRISED TO SEE A DUMMY INSTEAD. THEY CONFRONTED YOU ABOUT IT, WHICH TELLS ME YOU'RE HER CARETAKER.
HELL, YOU WERE EVEN BRINGING IT FOOD. WAS THAT TO THROW THEM OFF?
NO!
YES.
YOU WEREN'T SURPRISED TO SEE THE DUMMY BECAUSE YOU PUT IT THERE.
WHERE ARE YOU HIDING HER?
I PROTECTED ALANA! I LOVE HER!
THEY'LL KILL ME IF THEY FIND OUT! YOU GOTTA PROTECT ME! PLEASE!
PLEASE!
...
OH, FOR...
SIGH
SO WHERE IS SHE, BILLY?
SHOW ME WHERE SHE IS.

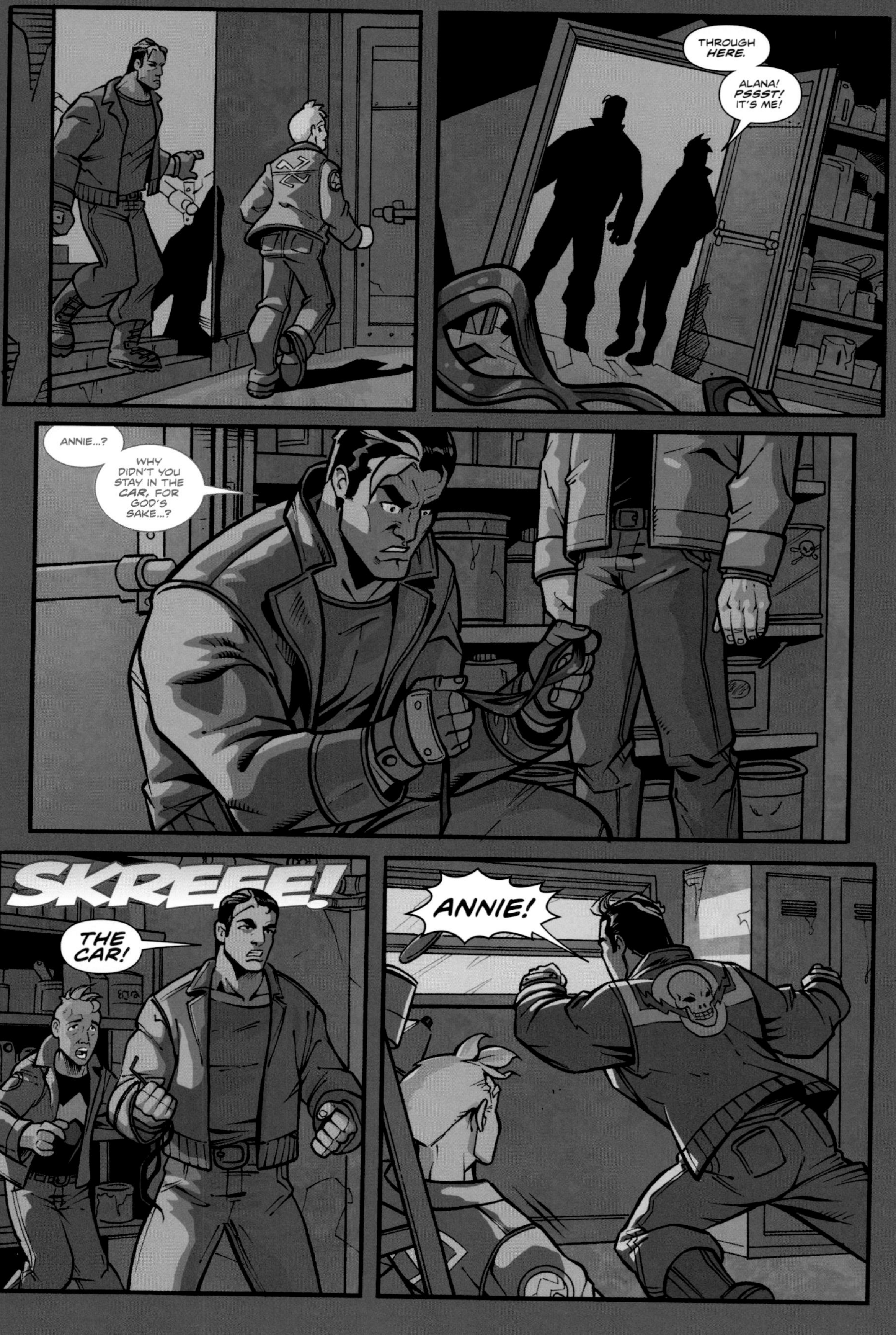
THROUGH HERE.
ALANA! PSSST! IT'S ME!
ANNIE...?
WHY DIDN'T YOU STAY IN THE CAR, FOR GOD'S SAKE...?
SKREEE!
THE CAR!
ANNIE!

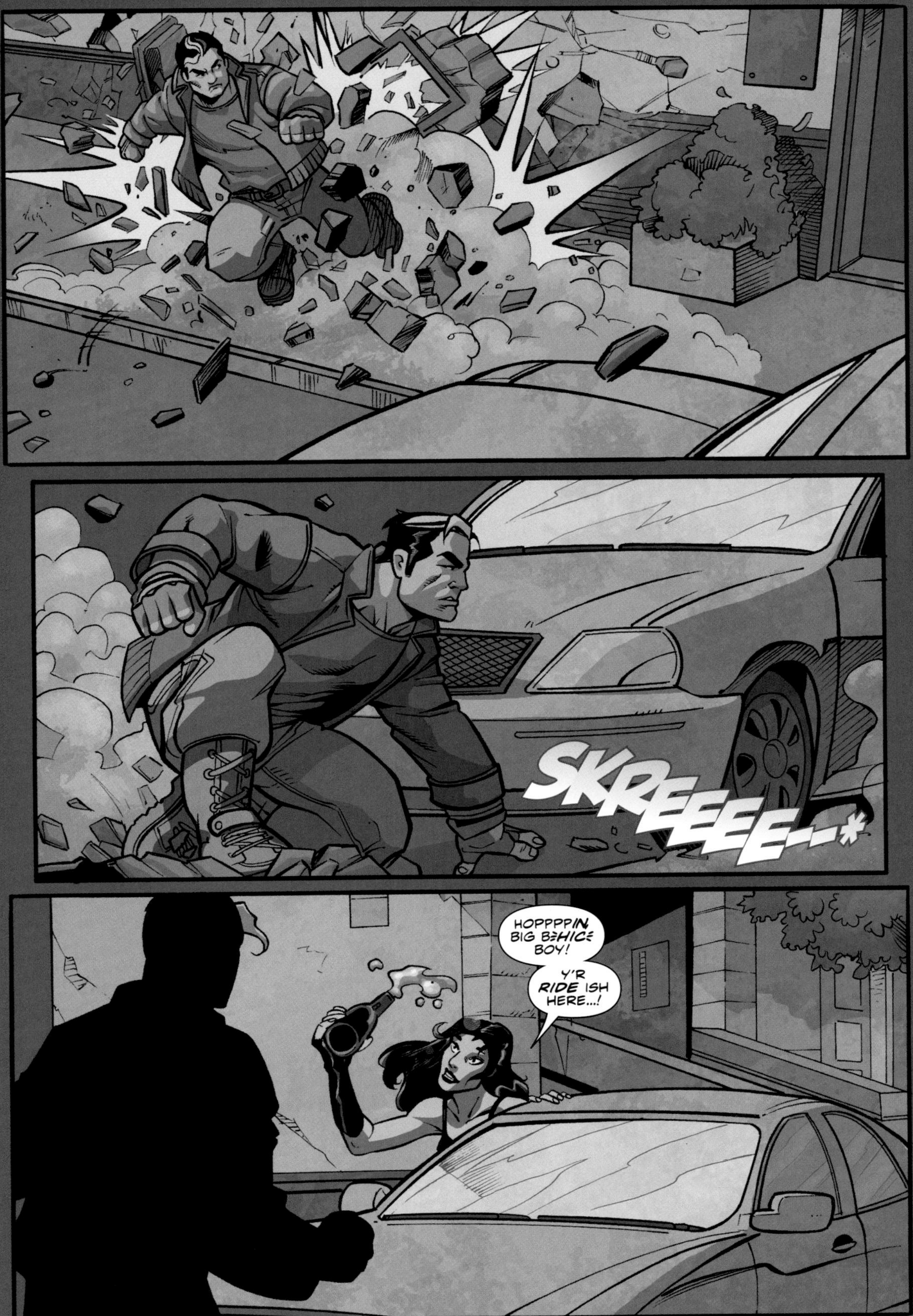
SKREEEEE--*
HOPPPPIN, BIG BEHICE BOY!
Y'R RIDE ISH HERE...!

MAX DAMAGE. STILL THE SAME SICK PERVO WHO RECRUITS OUTSIDE *CATHOLIC GIRLS' SCHOOLS.*

AREN'T *YOU* MOUTHY.

WHAT DO *I* HAVE TO LIVE FOR?

I DON'T KNOW. TRUE LOVE? HERE COMES YOUR *BOYFRIEND.*

ALANA!

THAT *BILLY* KID?

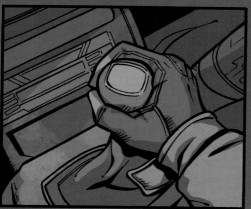

HNNGHH!

FTHUMP!

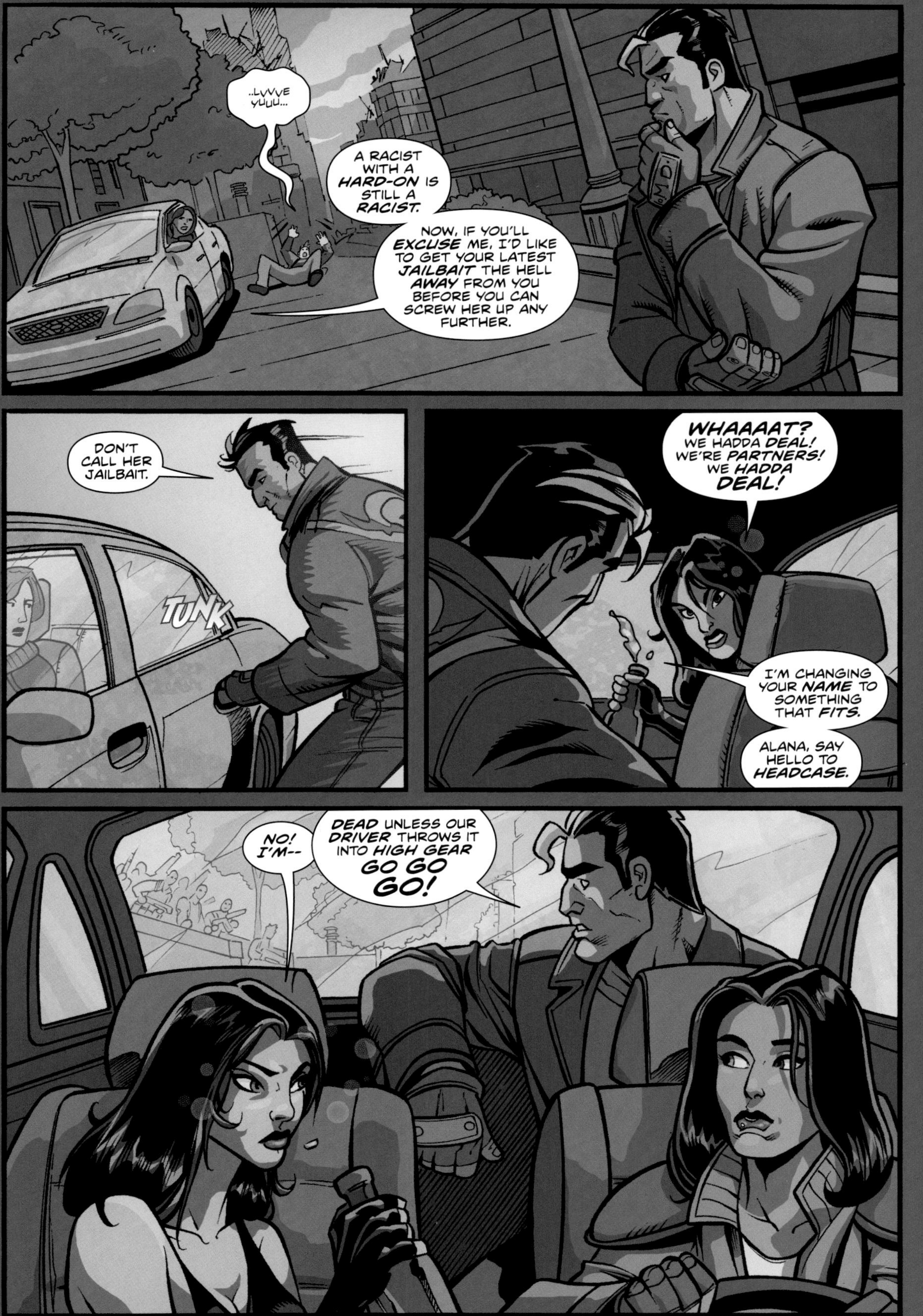
..LVVVE YUUU...
A RACIST WITH A HARD-ON IS STILL A RACIST.
NOW, IF YOU'LL EXCUSE ME, I'D LIKE TO GET YOUR LATEST JAILBAIT THE HELL AWAY FROM YOU BEFORE YOU CAN SCREW HER UP ANY FURTHER.
DON'T CALL HER JAILBAIT.
TUNK
WHAAAAT? WE HADDA DEAL! WE'RE PARTNERS! WE HADDA DEAL!
I'M CHANGING YOUR NAME TO SOMETHING THAT FITS.
ALANA, SAY HELLO TO HEADCASE.
NO! I'M--
DEAD UNLESS OUR DRIVER THROWS IT INTO HIGH GEAR GO GO GO!

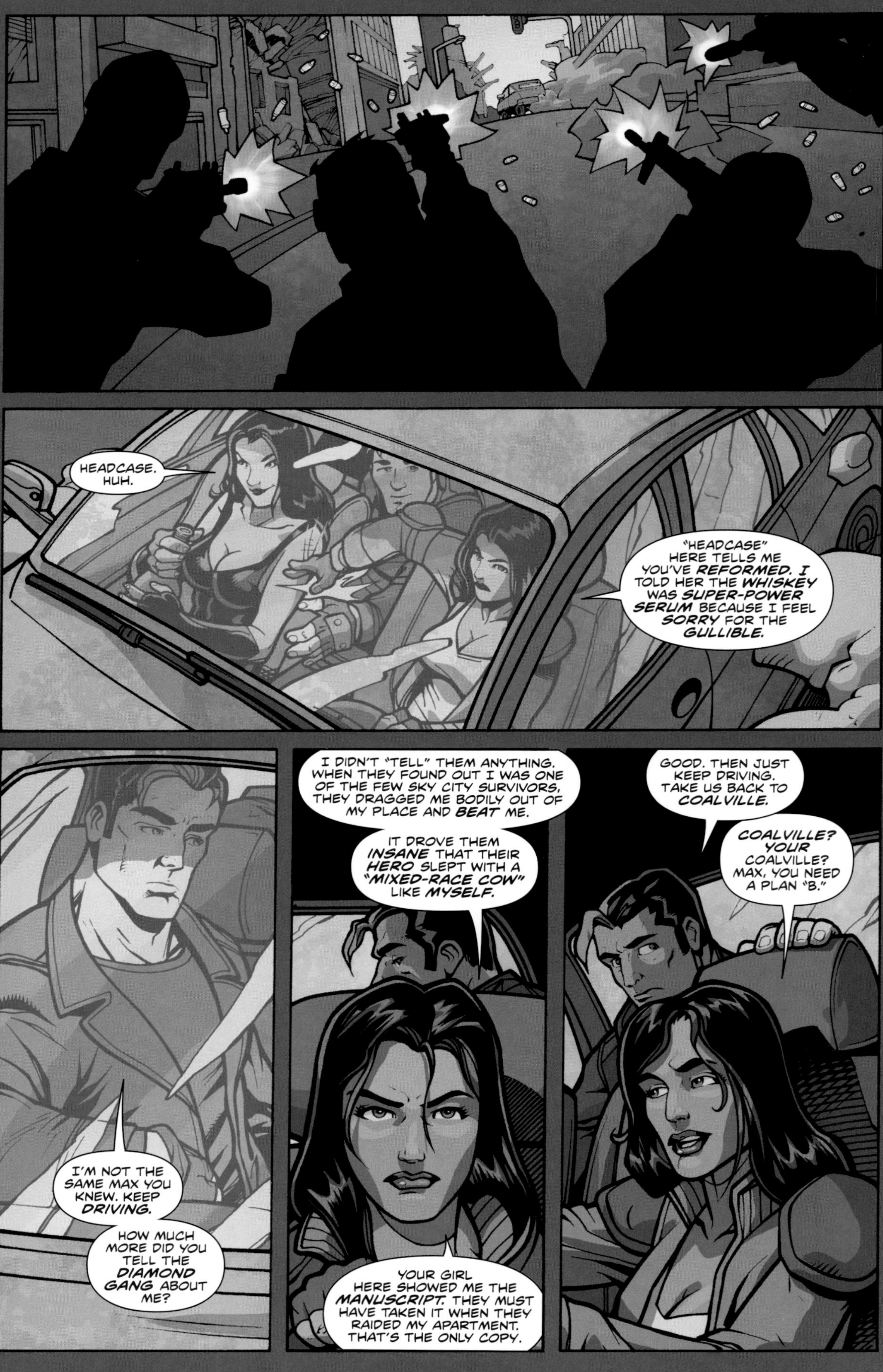
HEADCASE. HUH.
"HEADCASE" HERE TELLS ME YOU'VE REFORMED. I TOLD HER THE WHISKEY WAS SUPER-POWER SERUM BECAUSE I FEEL SORRY FOR THE GULLIBLE.
I'M NOT THE SAME MAX YOU KNEW. KEEP DRIVING.
HOW MUCH MORE DID YOU TELL THE DIAMOND GANG ABOUT ME?
I DIDN'T "TELL" THEM ANYTHING. WHEN THEY FOUND OUT I WAS ONE OF THE FEW SKY CITY SURVIVORS, THEY DRAGGED ME BODILY OUT OF MY PLACE AND BEAT ME.
IT DROVE THEM INSANE THAT THEIR HERO SLEPT WITH A "MIXED-RACE COW" LIKE MYSELF.
YOUR GIRL HERE SHOWED ME THE MANUSCRIPT. THEY MUST HAVE TAKEN IT WHEN THEY RAIDED MY APARTMENT. THAT'S THE ONLY COPY.
GOOD. THEN JUST KEEP DRIVING. TAKE US BACK TO COALVILLE.
COALVILLE? YOUR COALVILLE? MAX, YOU NEED A PLAN "B."

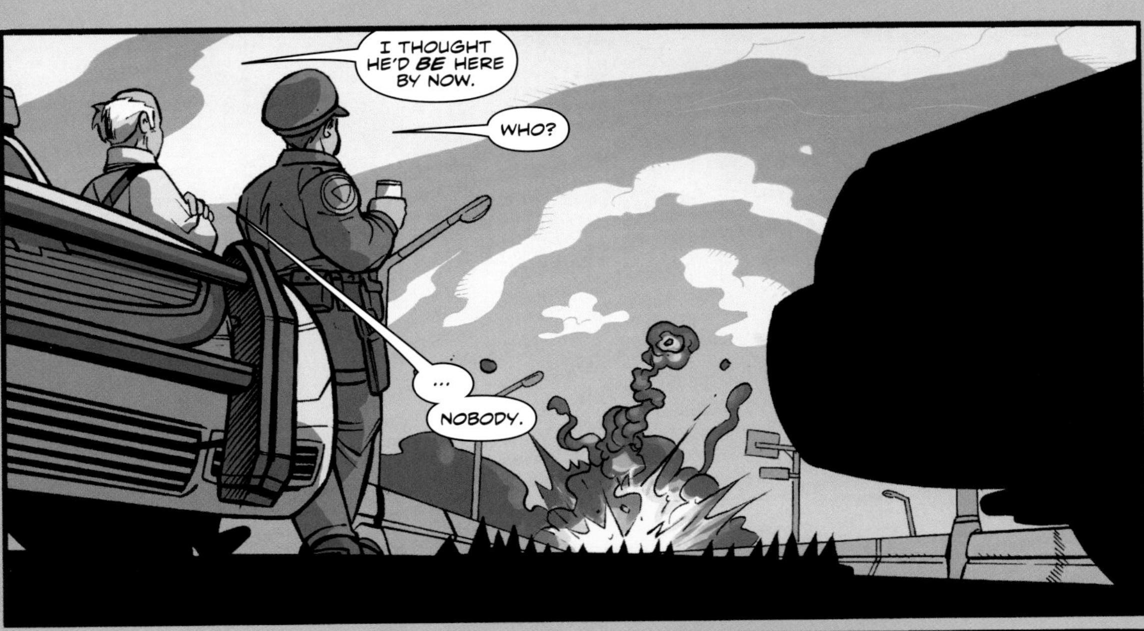
I THOUGHT HE'D *BE* HERE BY NOW.
WHO?
... NOBODY.

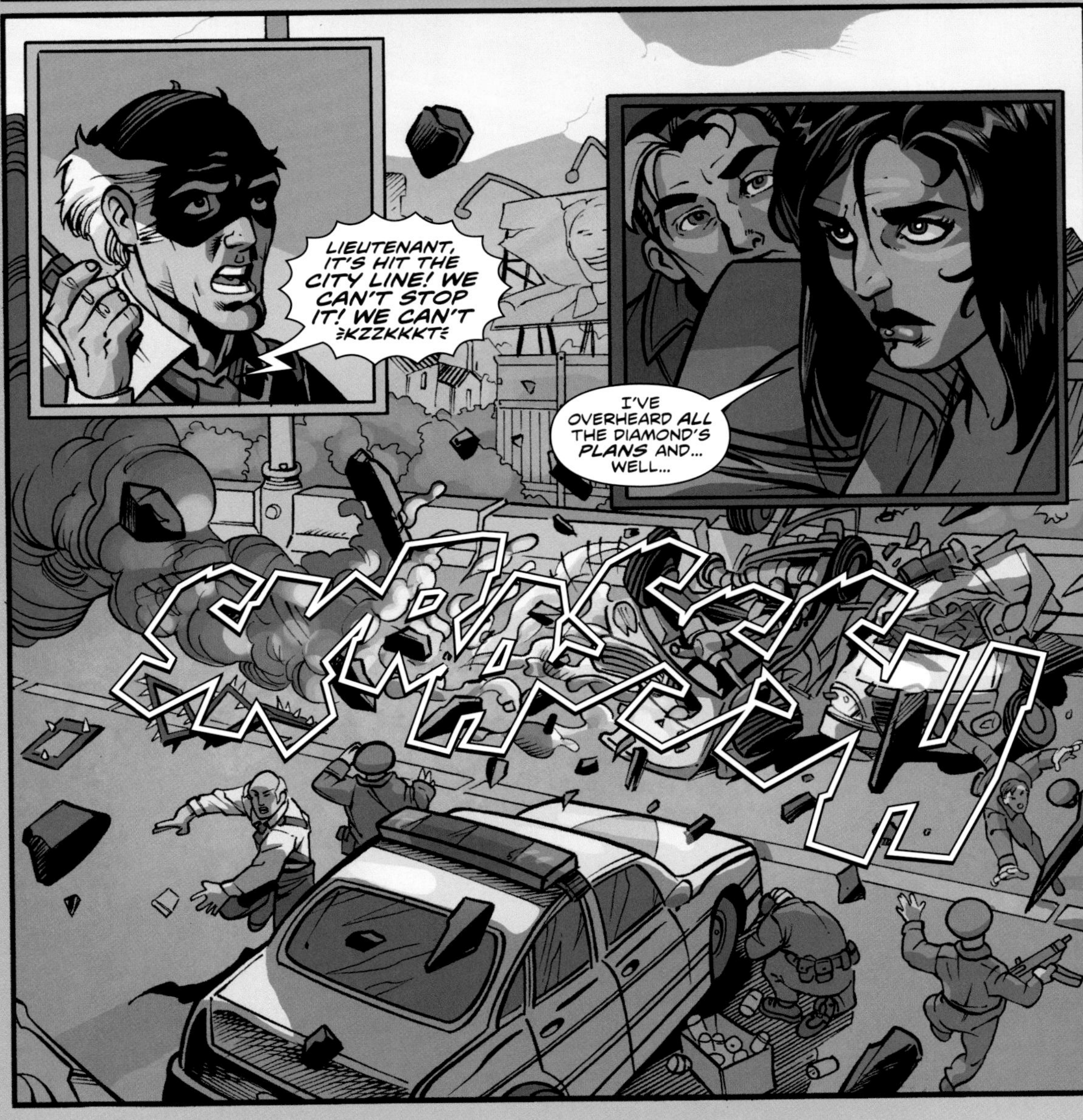
LIEUTENANT, IT'S HIT THE *CITY LINE!* WE *CAN'T* STOP IT! WE CAN'T KZZKKKT
I'VE OVERHEARD *ALL* THE DIAMOND'S *PLANS* AND... WELL...

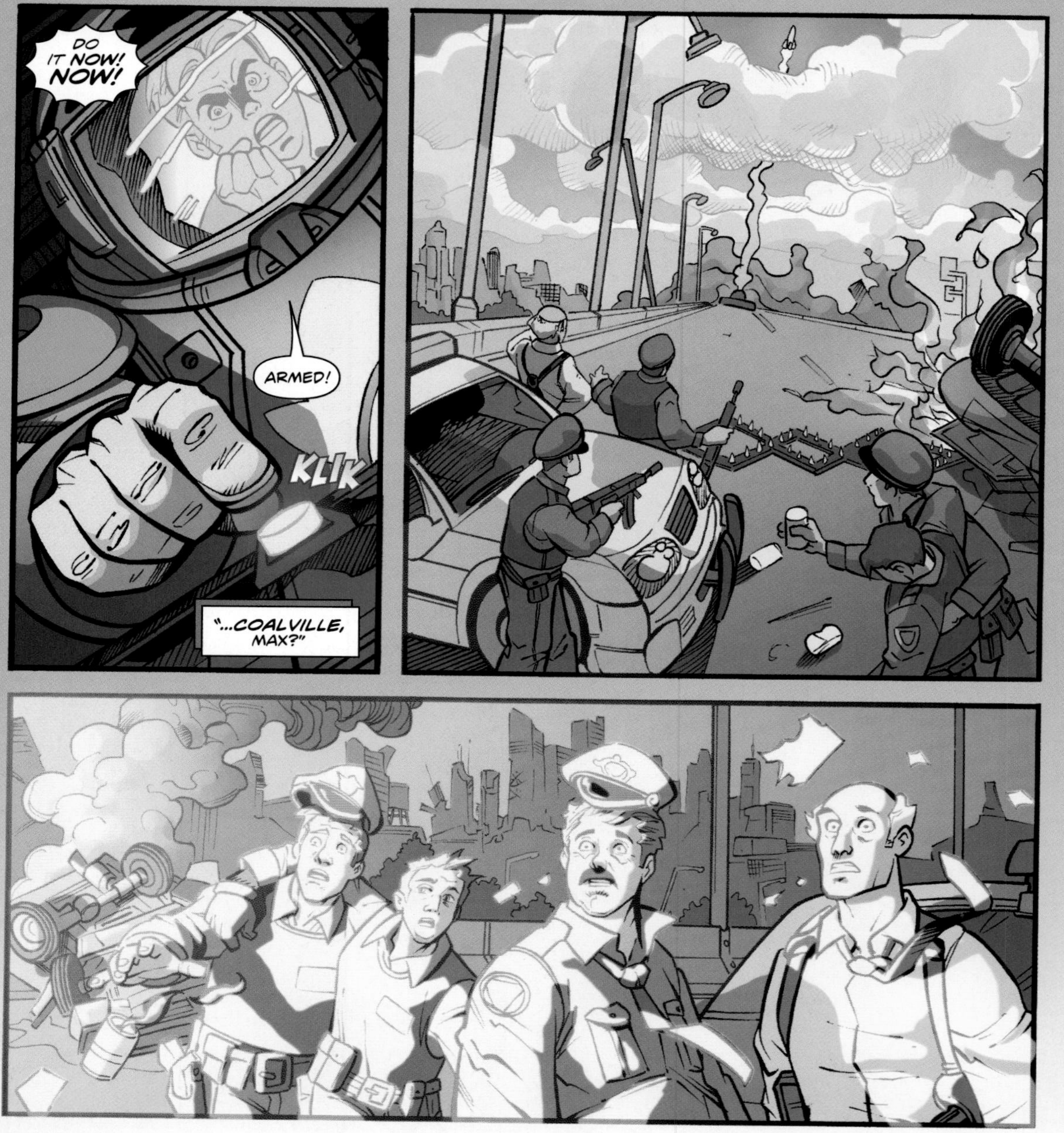
DO IT NOW! NOW!
ARMED!
KLIK
"...COALVILLE, MAX?"

"THERE *ISN'T* ANY MORE COALVILLE."

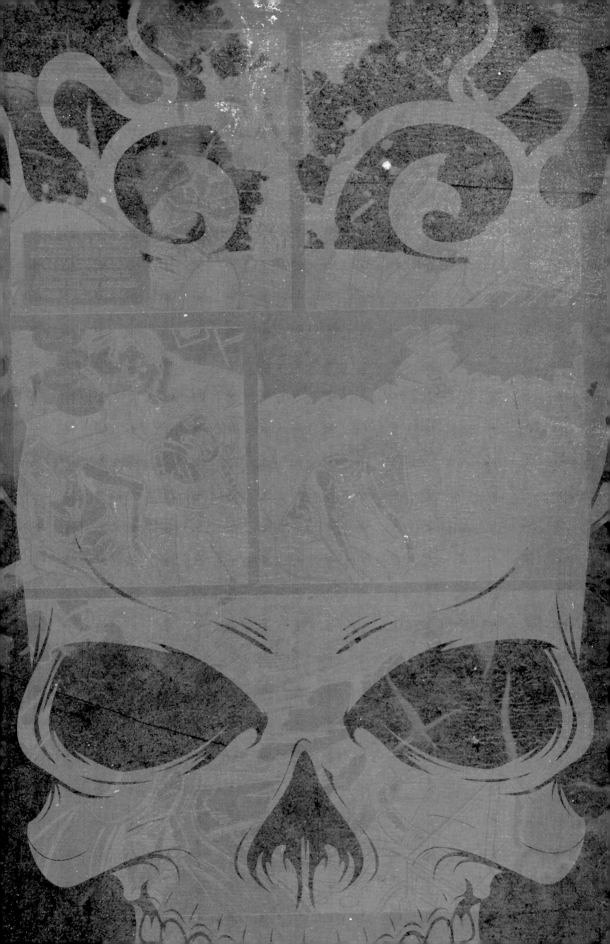

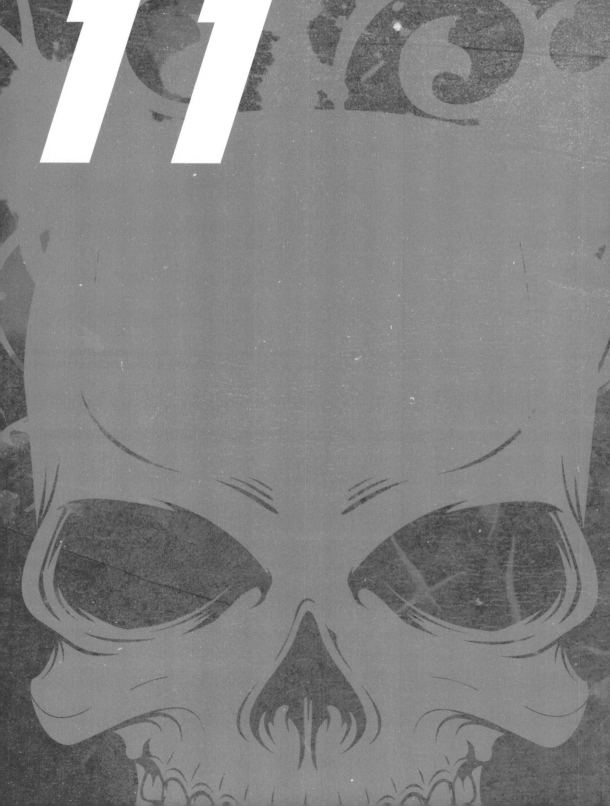

CHAPTER
11

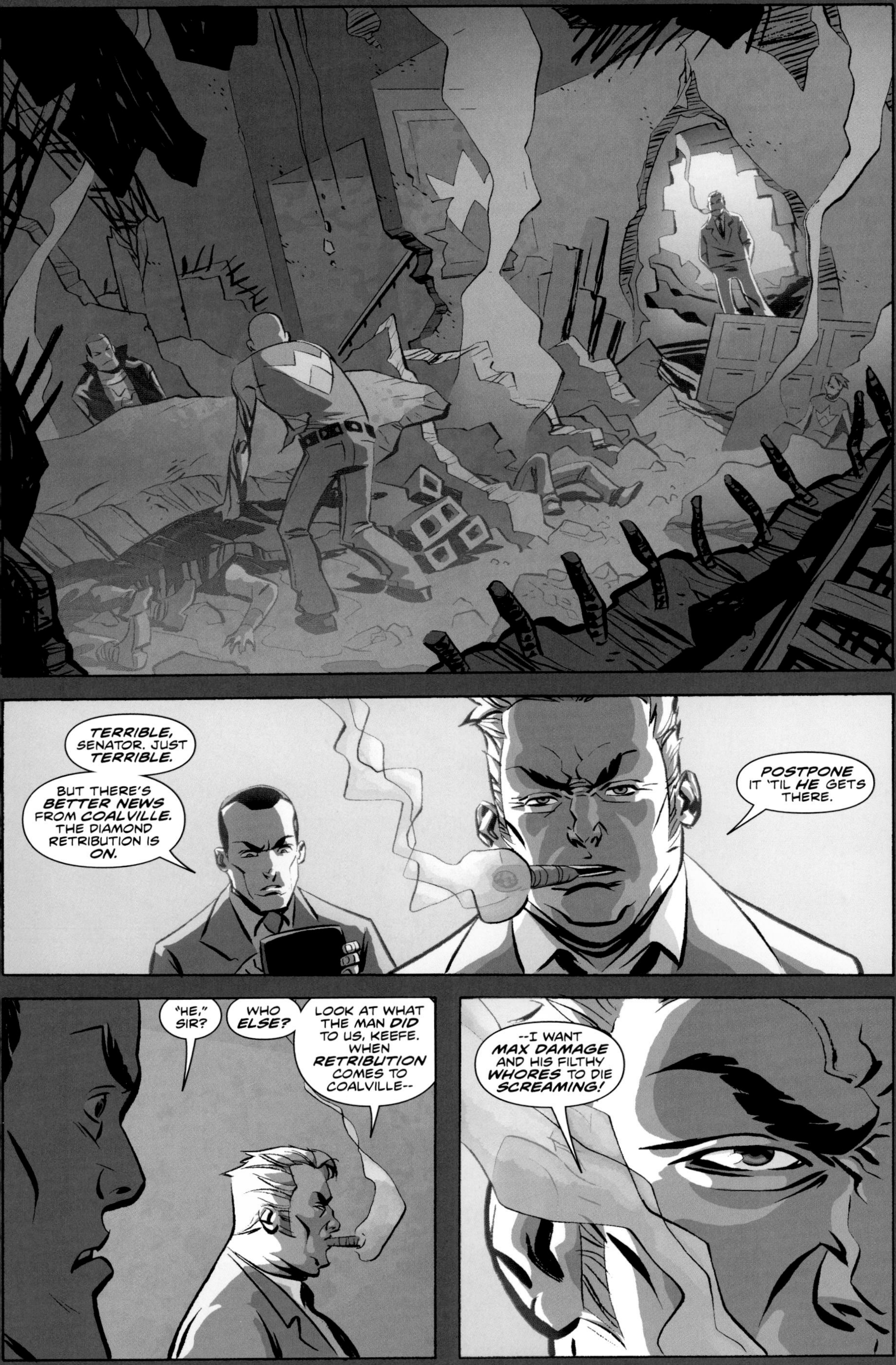
TERRIBLE, SENATOR. JUST TERRIBLE.
BUT THERE'S BETTER NEWS FROM COALVILLE. THE DIAMOND RETRIBUTION IS ON.
POSTPONE IT 'TIL HE GETS THERE.
"HE," SIR?
WHO ELSE?
LOOK AT WHAT THE MAN DID TO US, KEEFE. WHEN RETRIBUTION COMES TO COALVILLE--
--I WANT MAX DAMAGE AND HIS FILTHY WHORES TO DIE SCREAMING!

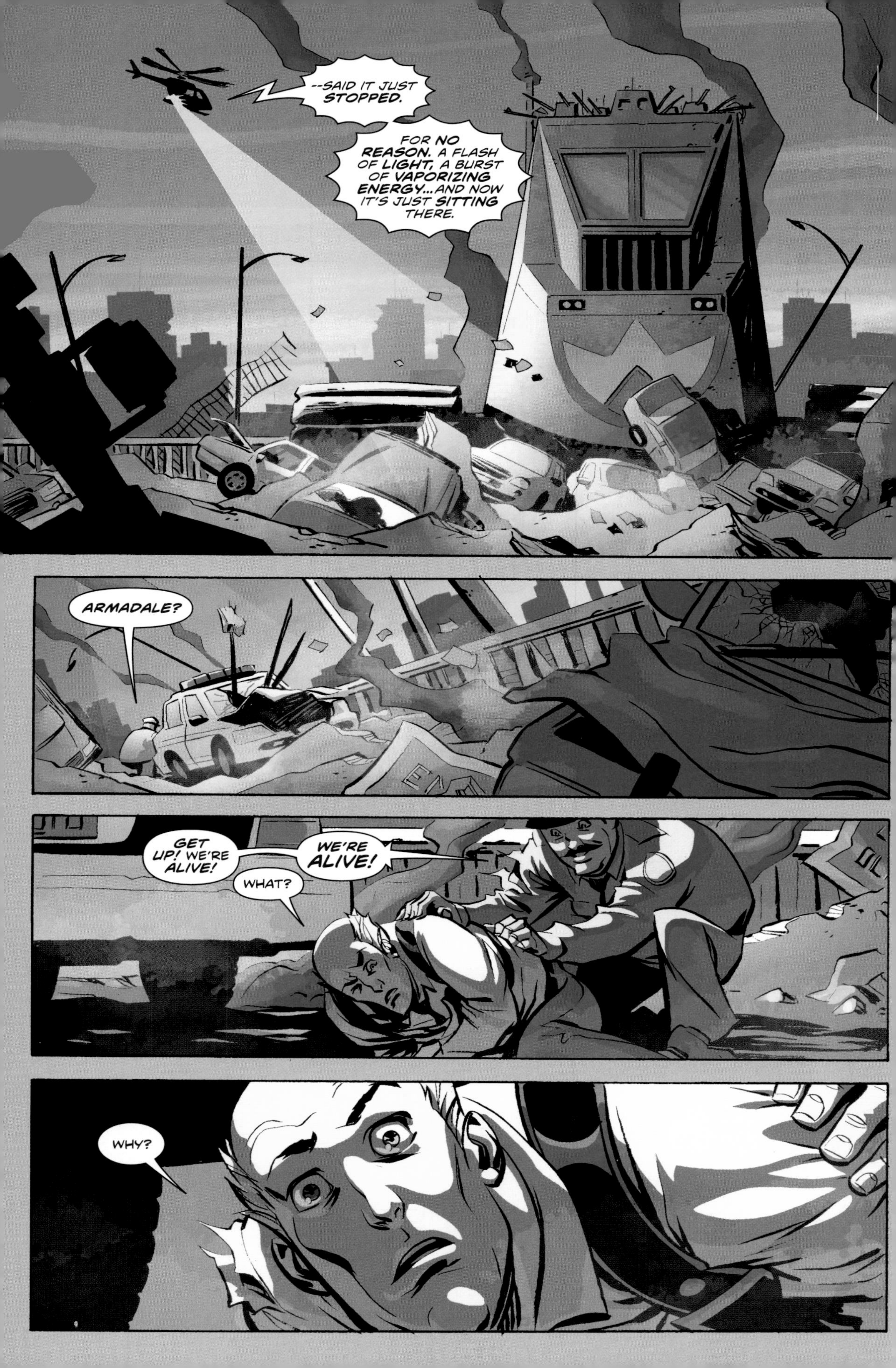
--SAID IT JUST STOPPED.
FOR NO REASON. A FLASH OF LIGHT, A BURST OF VAPORIZING ENERGY...AND NOW IT'S JUST SITTING THERE.
ARMADALE?
GET UP! WE'RE ALIVE!
WE'RE ALIVE!
WHAT?
WHY?

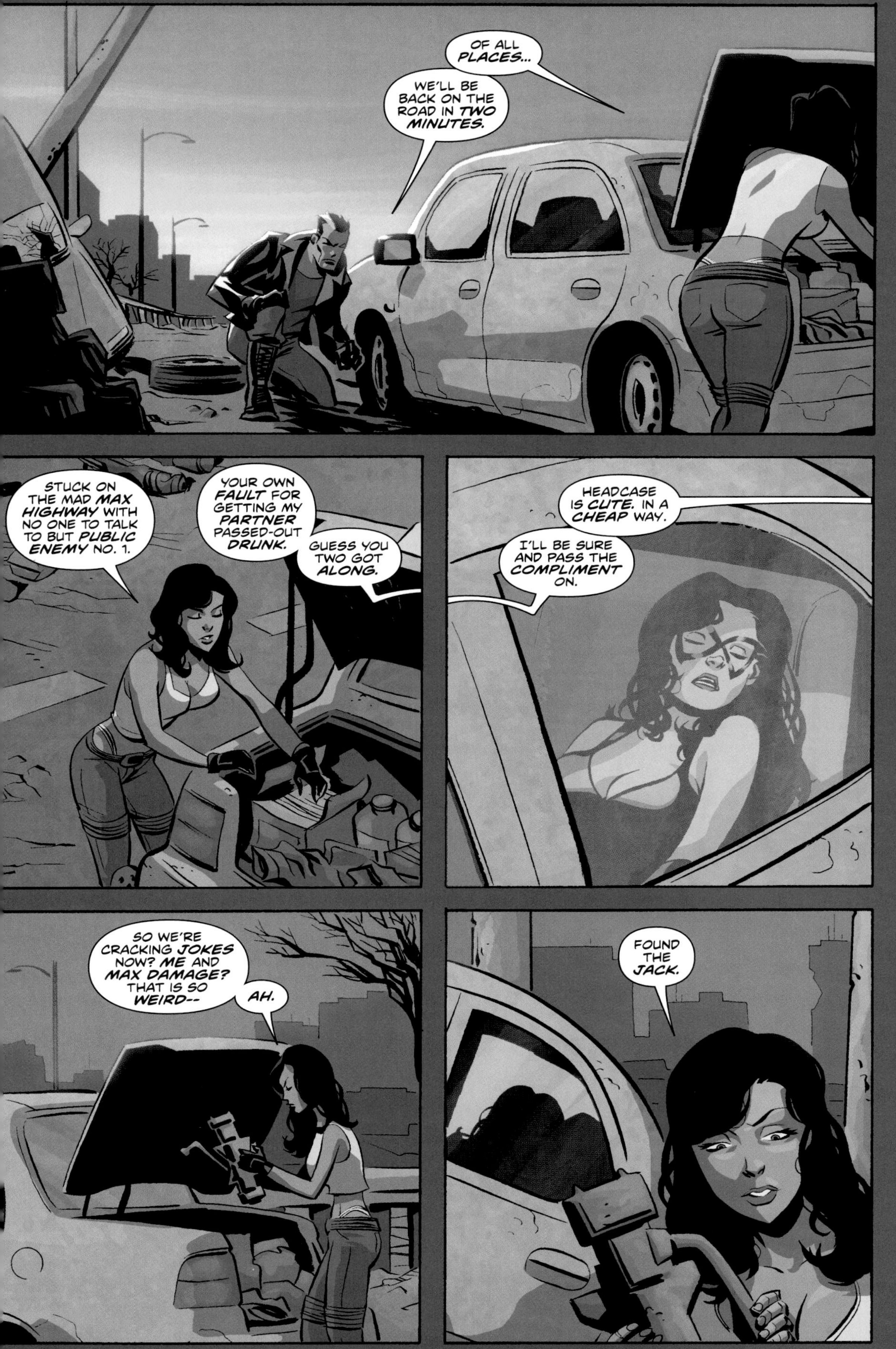
OF ALL PLACES...
WE'LL BE BACK ON THE ROAD IN TWO MINUTES.
STUCK ON THE MAD MAX HIGHWAY WITH NO ONE TO TALK TO BUT PUBLIC ENEMY NO. 1.
YOUR OWN FAULT FOR GETTING MY PARTNER PASSED-OUT DRUNK.
GUESS YOU TWO GOT ALONG.
HEADCASE IS CUTE. IN A CHEAP WAY.
I'LL BE SURE AND PASS THE COMPLIMENT ON.
SO WE'RE CRACKING JOKES NOW? ME AND MAX DAMAGE? THAT IS SO WEIRD--
AH.
FOUND THE JACK.

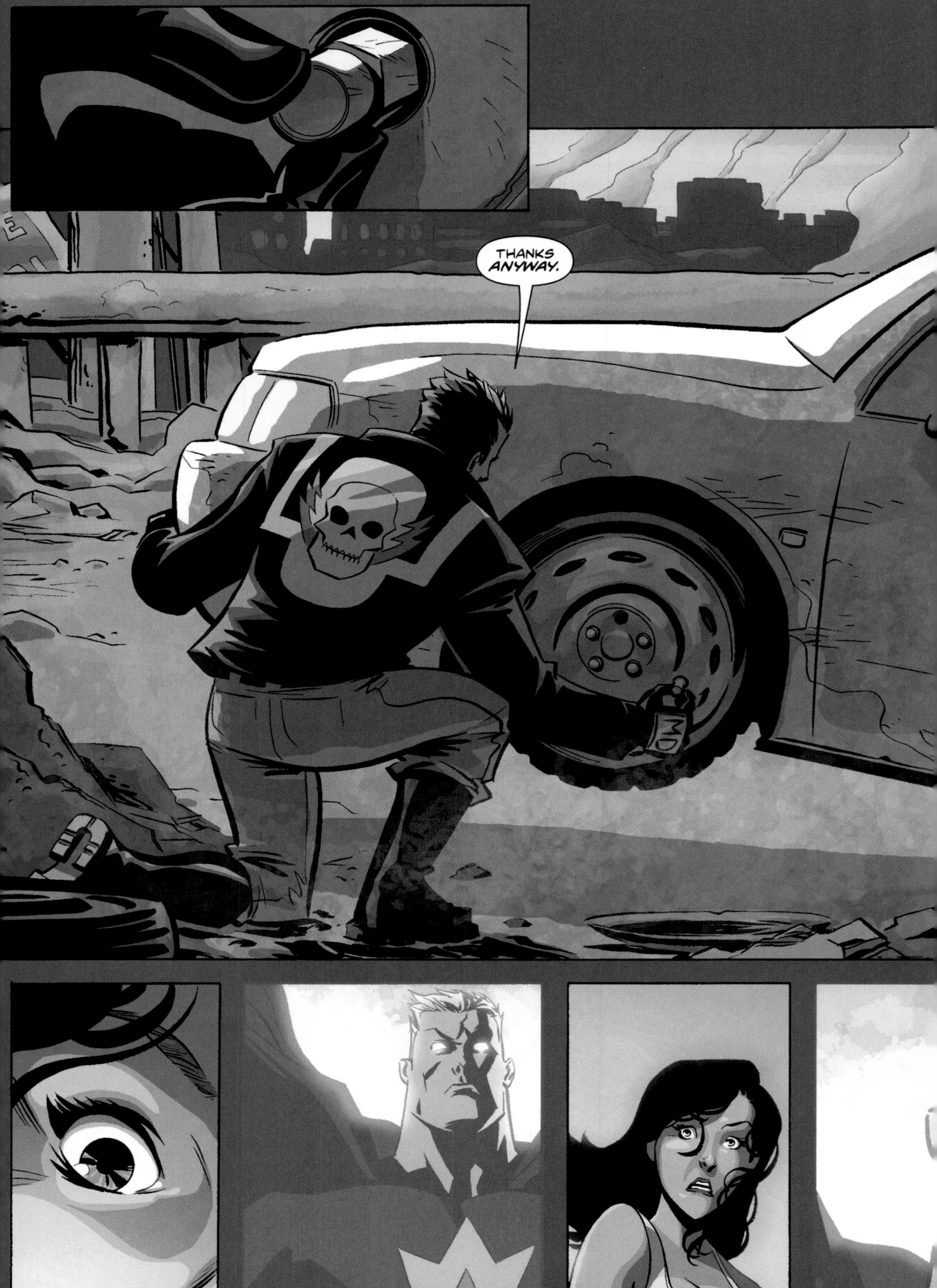
THANKS ANYWAY.

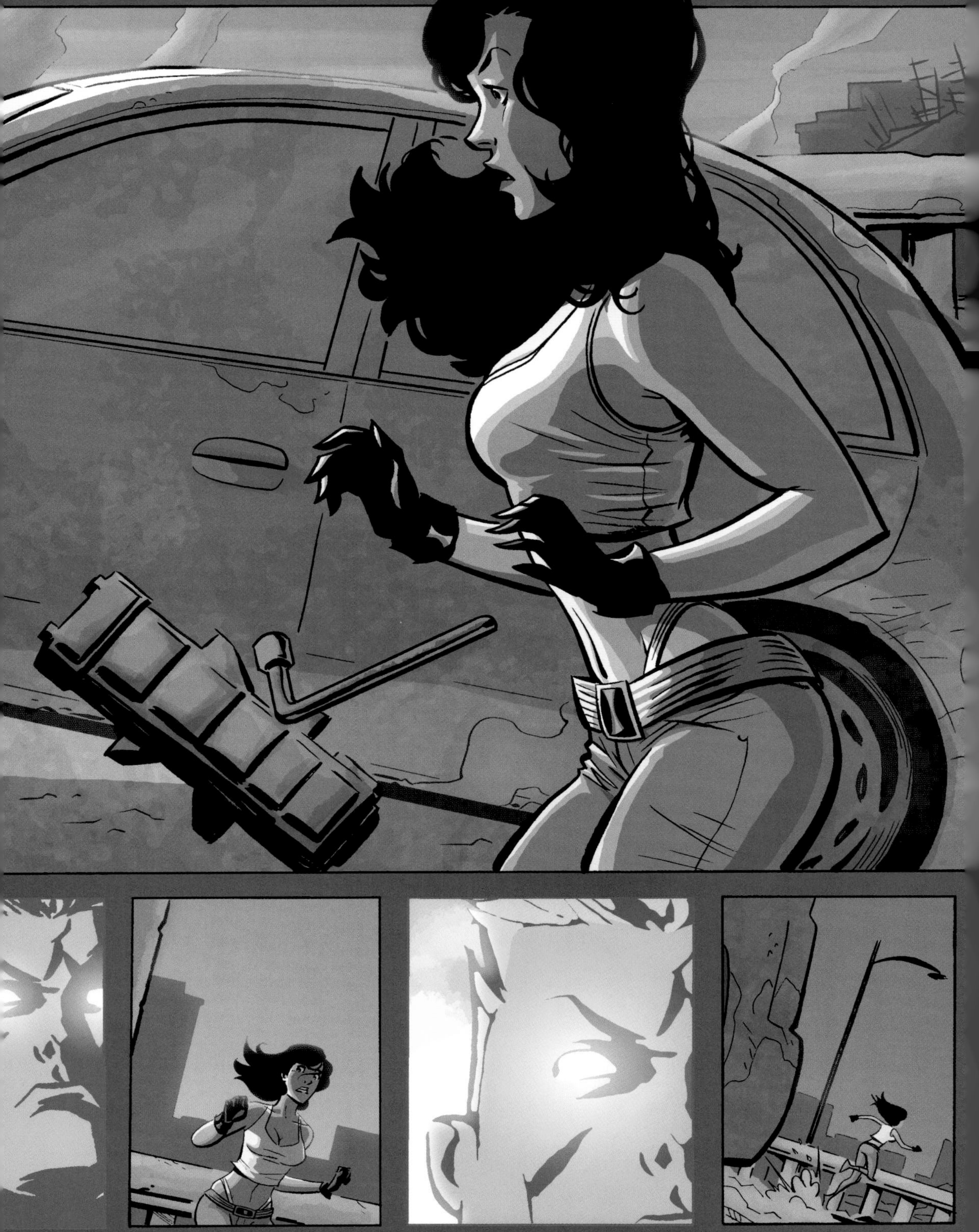

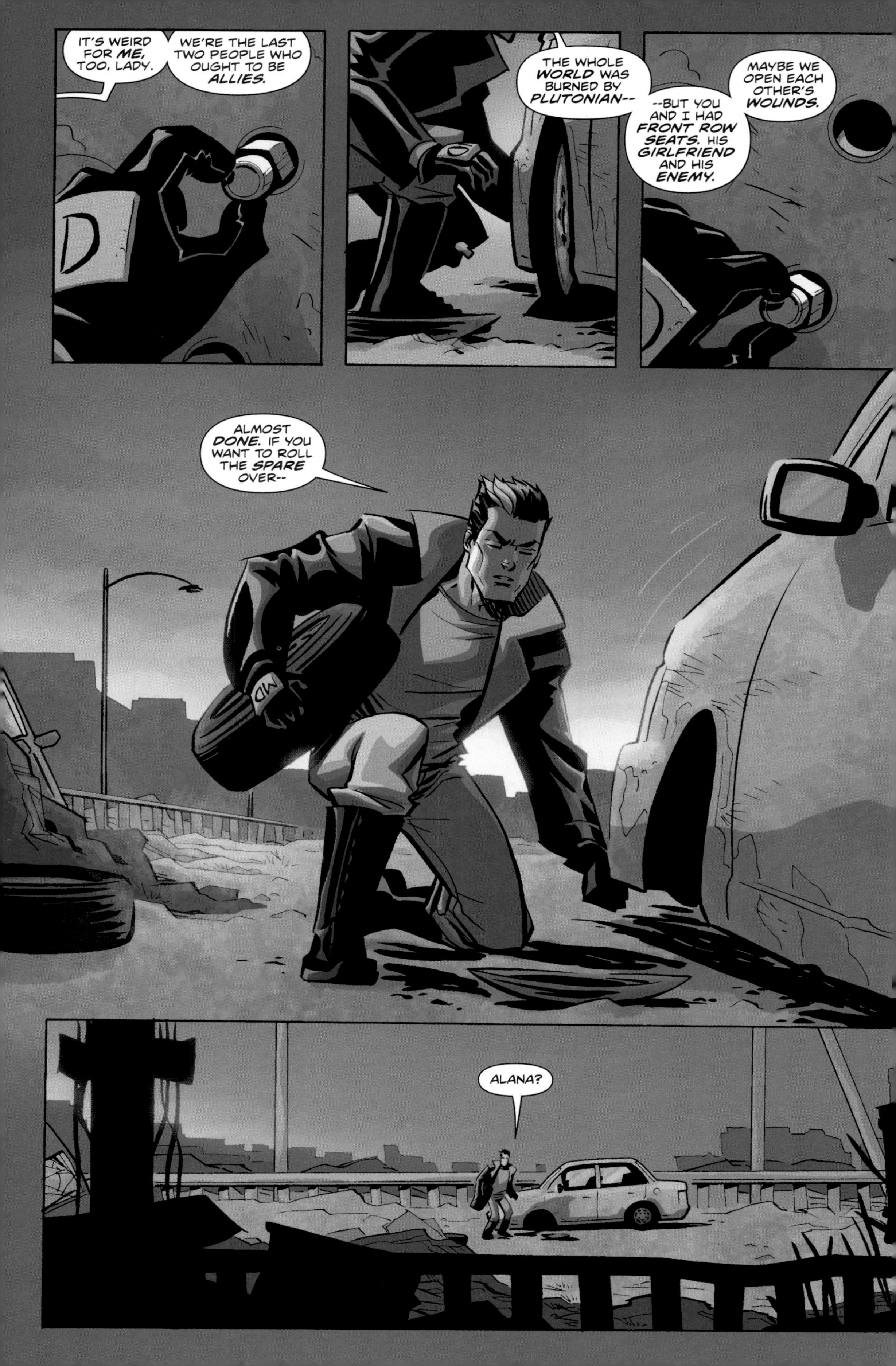
IT'S WEIRD FOR ME, TOO, LADY.
WE'RE THE LAST TWO PEOPLE WHO OUGHT TO BE ALLIES.
THE WHOLE WORLD WAS BURNED BY PLUTONIAN--
--BUT YOU AND I HAD FRONT ROW SEATS. HIS GIRLFRIEND AND HIS ENEMY.
MAYBE WE OPEN EACH OTHER'S WOUNDS.
ALMOST DONE. IF YOU WANT TO ROLL THE SPARE OVER--
ALANA?

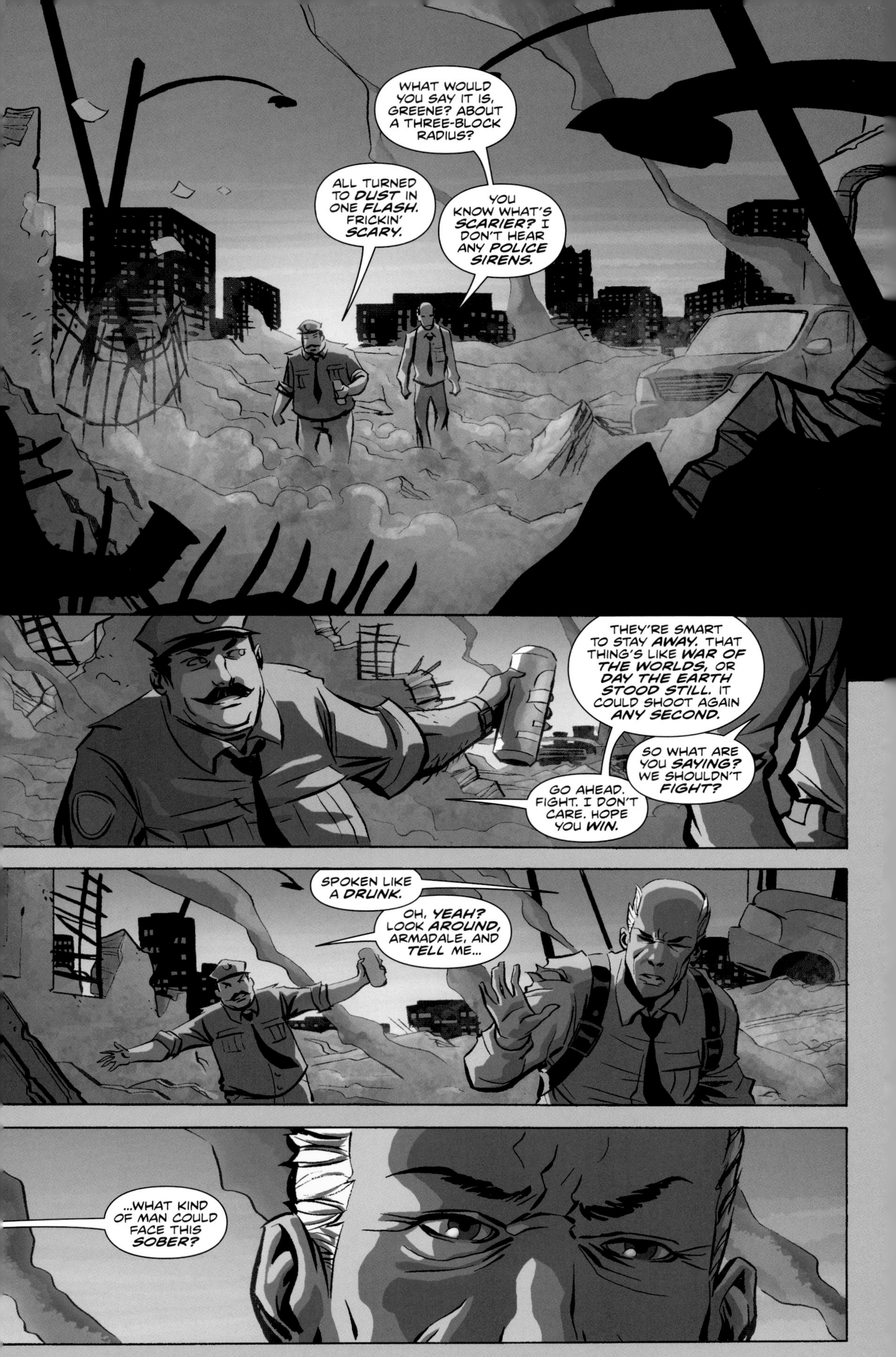
WHAT WOULD YOU SAY IT IS, GREENE? ABOUT A THREE-BLOCK RADIUS?
ALL TURNED TO DUST IN ONE FLASH. FRICKIN' SCARY.
YOU KNOW WHAT'S SCARIER? I DON'T HEAR ANY POLICE SIRENS.
THEY'RE SMART TO STAY AWAY. THAT THING'S LIKE WAR OF THE WORLDS, OR DAY THE EARTH STOOD STILL. IT COULD SHOOT AGAIN ANY SECOND.
SO WHAT ARE YOU SAYING? WE SHOULDN'T FIGHT?
GO AHEAD. FIGHT. I DON'T CARE. HOPE YOU WIN.
SPOKEN LIKE A DRUNK.
OH, YEAH? LOOK AROUND, ARMADALE, AND TELL ME...
...WHAT KIND OF MAN COULD FACE THIS SOBER?

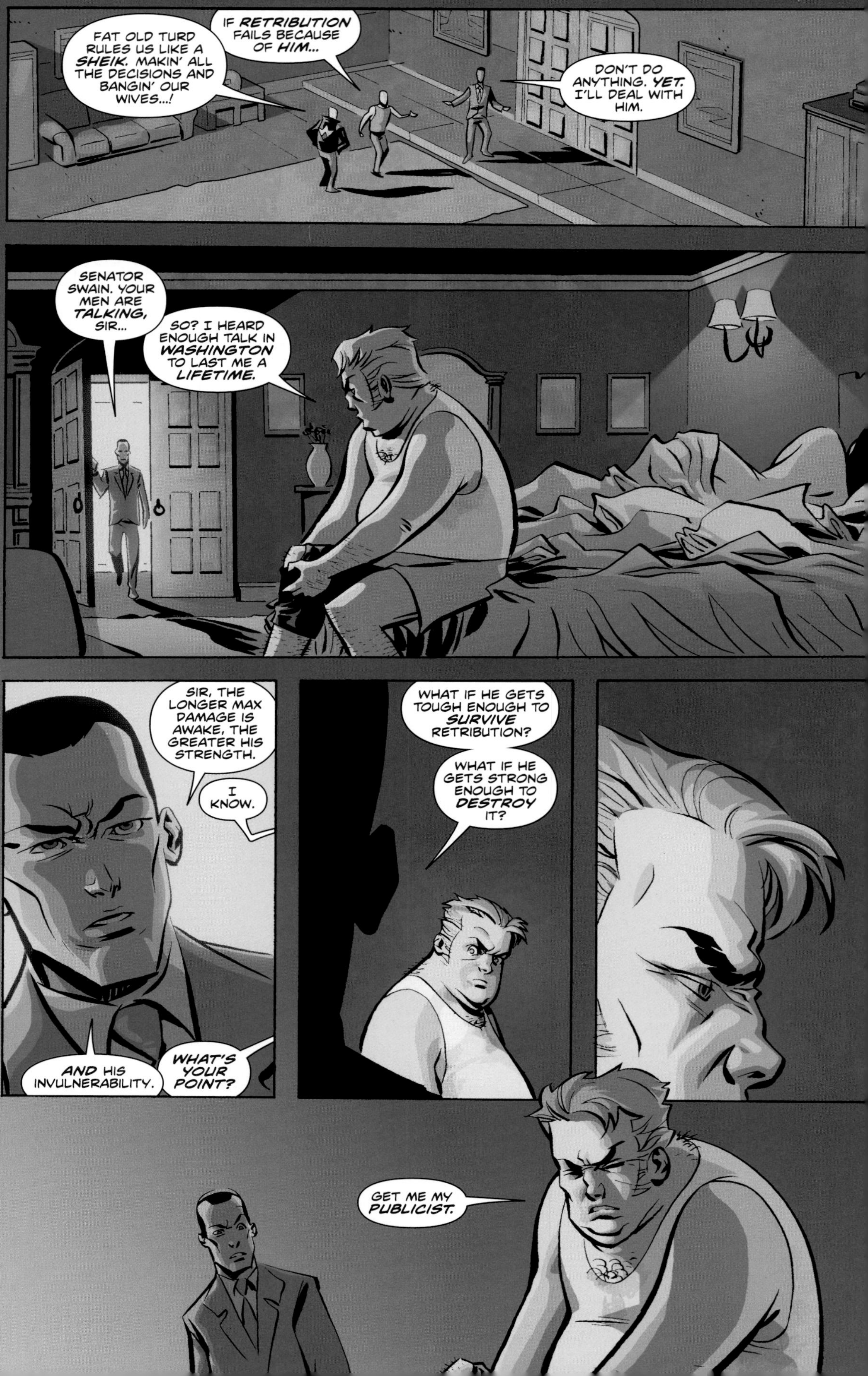
FAT OLD TURD RULES US LIKE A SHEIK. MAKIN' ALL THE DECISIONS AND BANGIN' OUR WIVES...!
IF RETRIBUTION FAILS BECAUSE OF HIM...
DON'T DO ANYTHING. YET. I'LL DEAL WITH HIM.
SENATOR SWAIN. YOUR MEN ARE TALKING, SIR...
SO? I HEARD ENOUGH TALK IN WASHINGTON TO LAST ME A LIFETIME.
SIR, THE LONGER MAX DAMAGE IS AWAKE, THE GREATER HIS STRENGTH.
I KNOW.
AND HIS INVULNERABILITY.
WHAT'S YOUR POINT?
WHAT IF HE GETS TOUGH ENOUGH TO SURVIVE RETRIBUTION?
WHAT IF HE GETS STRONG ENOUGH TO DESTROY IT?
GET ME MY PUBLICIST.

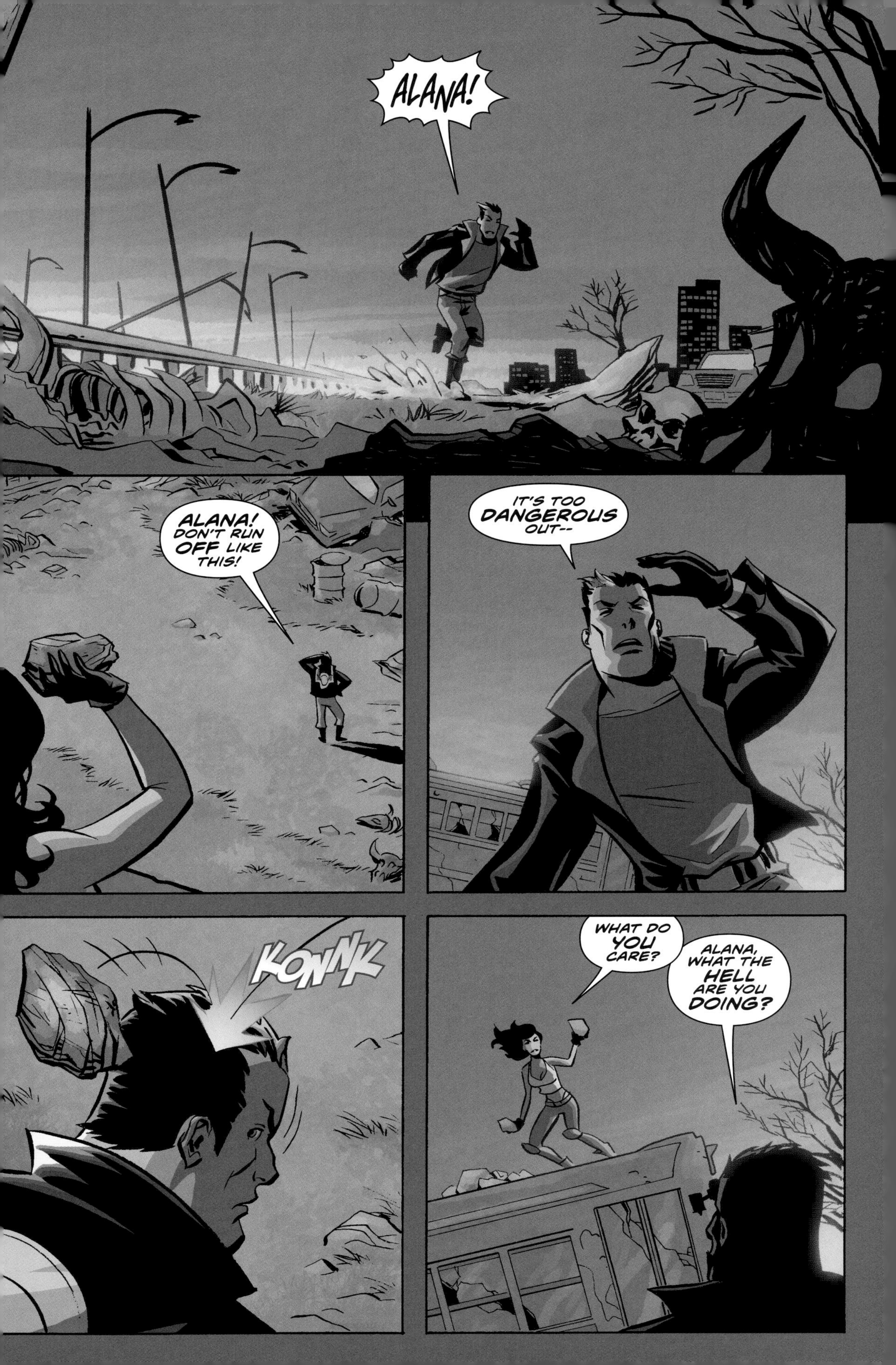
ALANA!
ALANA! DON'T RUN OFF LIKE THIS!
IT'S TOO DANGEROUS OUT--
KONNK
WHAT DO YOU CARE?
ALANA, WHAT THE HELL ARE YOU DOING?

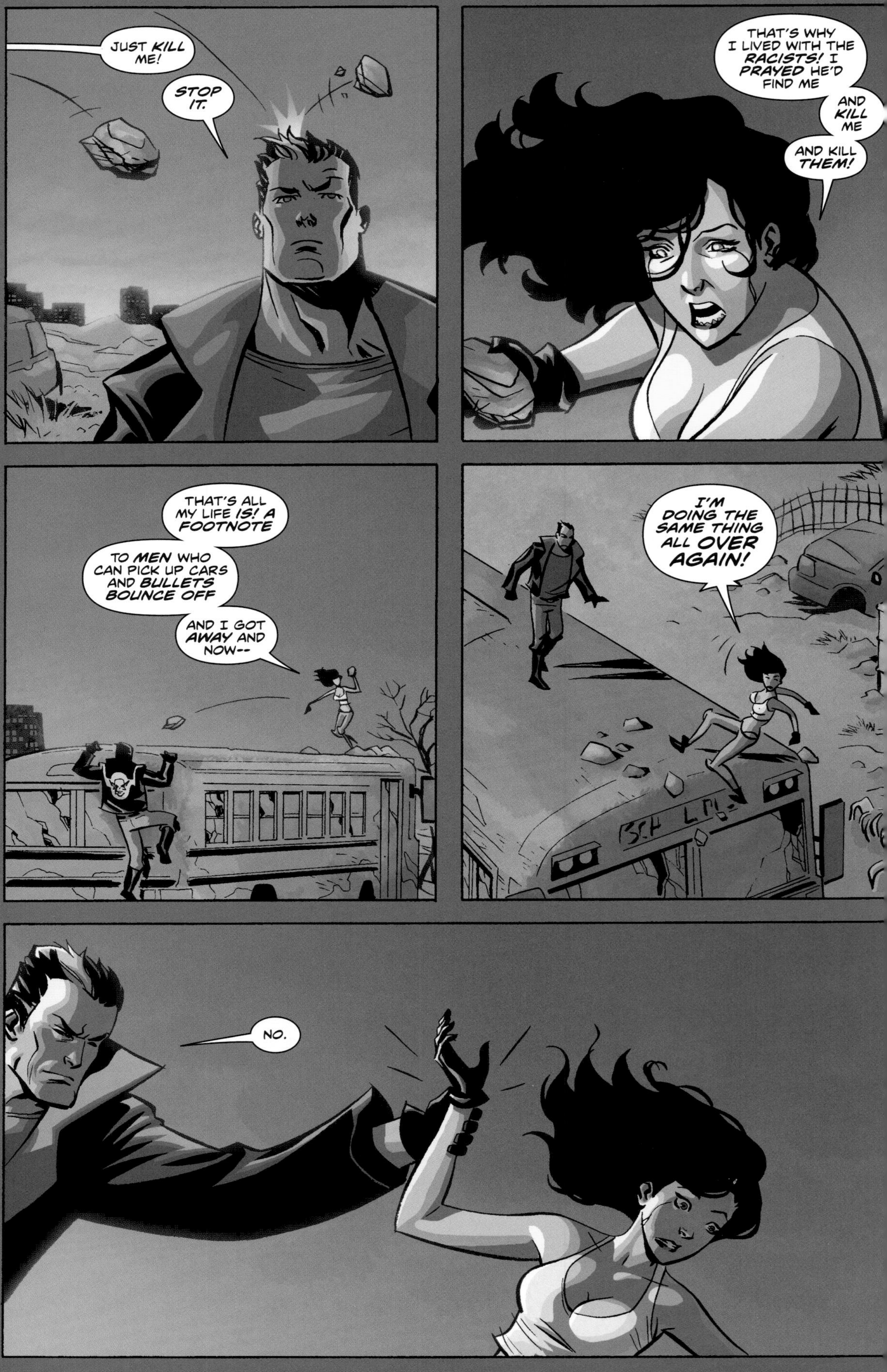
JUST KILL ME!
STOP IT.
THAT'S WHY I LIVED WITH THE RACISTS! I PRAYED HE'D FIND ME
AND KILL ME
AND KILL THEM!
THAT'S ALL MY LIFE IS! A FOOTNOTE
TO MEN WHO CAN PICK UP CARS AND BULLETS BOUNCE OFF
AND I GOT AWAY AND NOW--
I'M DOING THE SAME THING ALL OVER AGAIN!
NO.

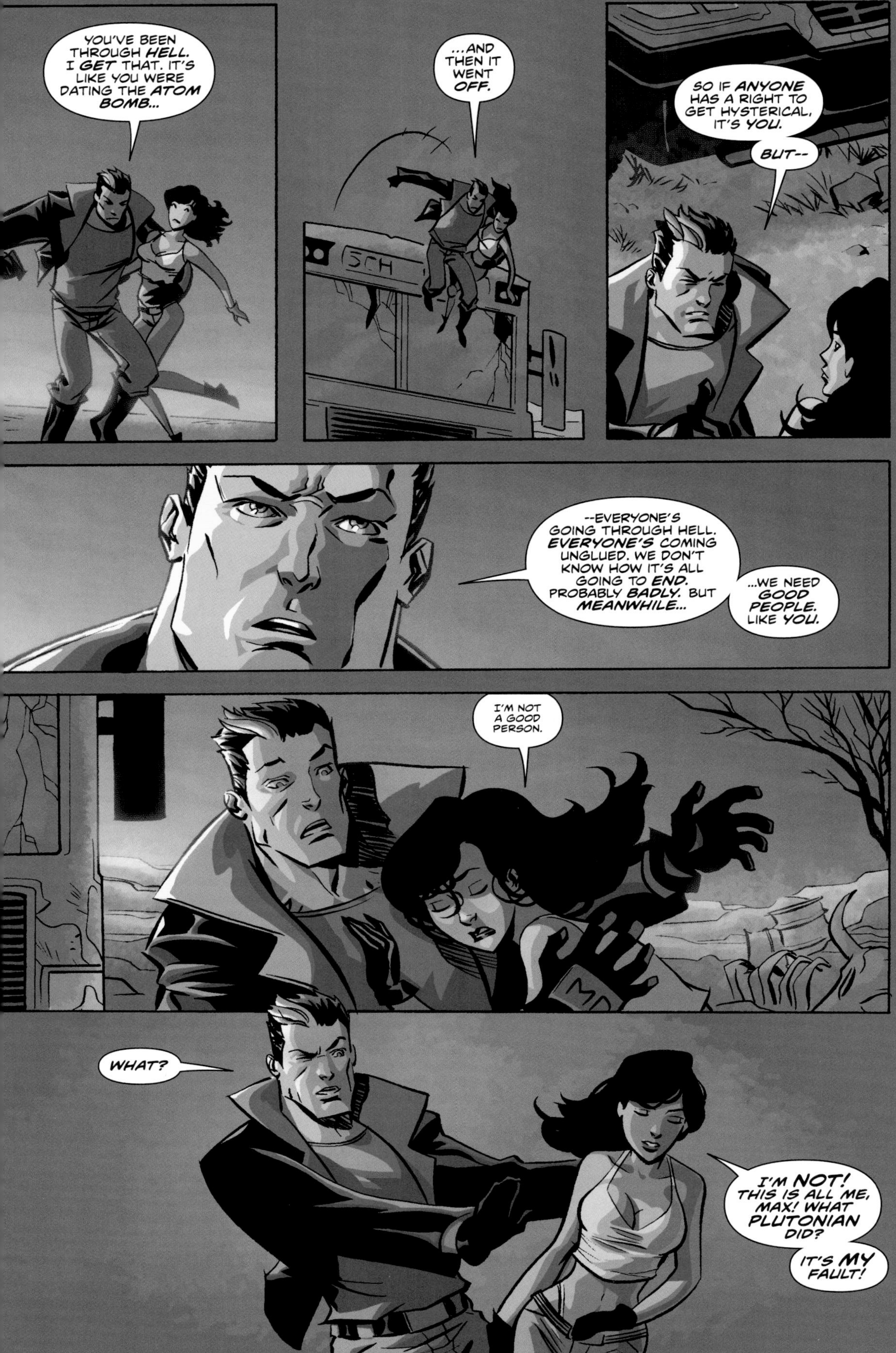

YOU'VE BEEN THROUGH HELL. I GET THAT. IT'S LIKE YOU WERE DATING THE ATOM BOMB...
...AND THEN IT WENT OFF.
SO IF ANYONE HAS A RIGHT TO GET HYSTERICAL, IT'S YOU.
BUT--
--EVERYONE'S GOING THROUGH HELL. EVERYONE'S COMING UNGLUED. WE DON'T KNOW HOW IT'S ALL GOING TO END. PROBABLY BADLY. BUT MEANWHILE...
...WE NEED GOOD PEOPLE. LIKE YOU.
I'M NOT A GOOD PERSON.
WHAT?
I'M NOT! THIS IS ALL ME, MAX! WHAT PLUTONIAN DID?
IT'S MY FAULT!

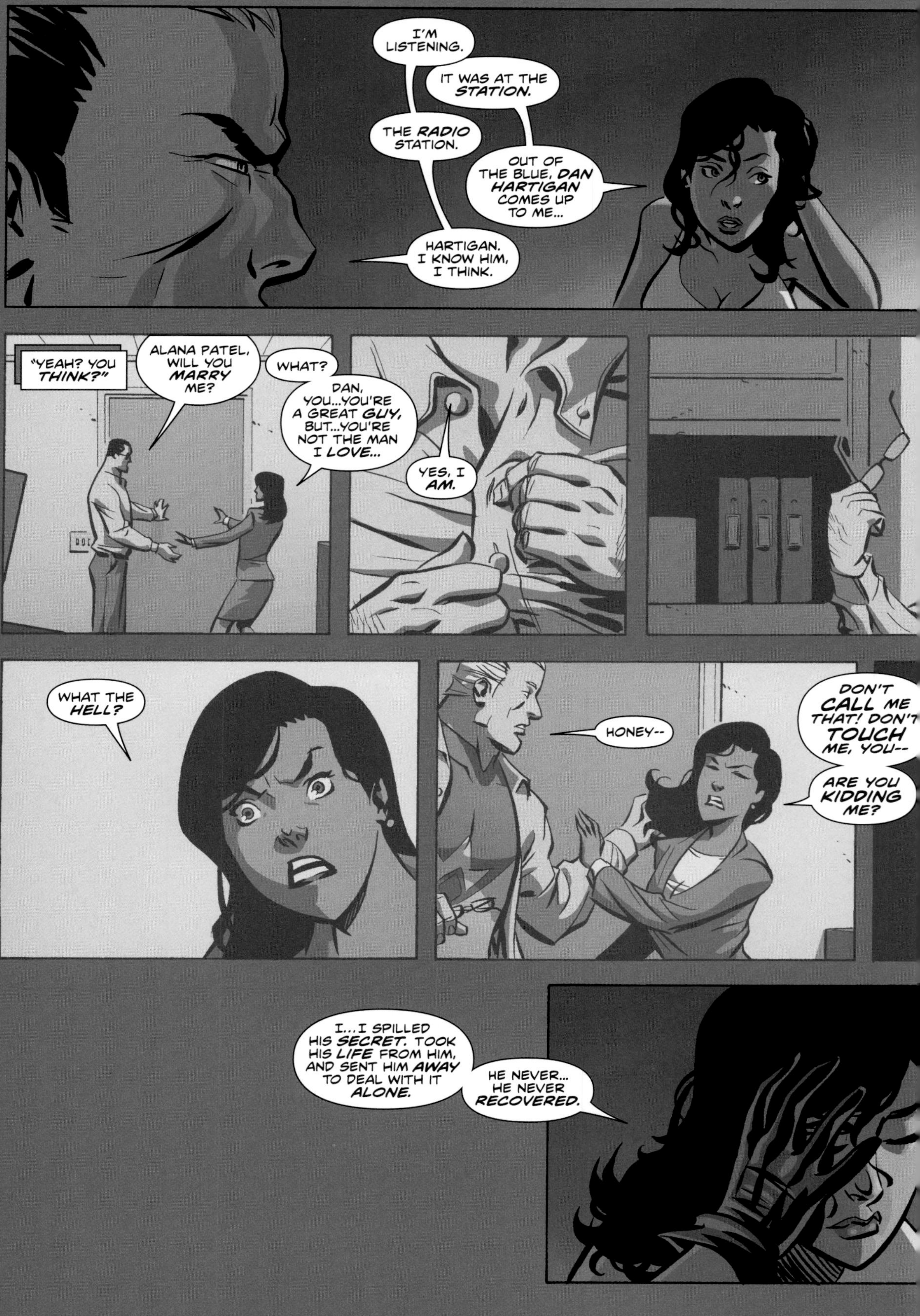

I'M LISTENING.
IT WAS AT THE STATION.
THE RADIO STATION.
OUT OF THE BLUE, DAN HARTIGAN COMES UP TO ME...
HARTIGAN. I KNOW HIM, I THINK.
"YEAH? YOU THINK?"
ALANA PATEL, WILL YOU MARRY ME?
WHAT?
DAN, YOU...YOU'RE A GREAT GUY, BUT...YOU'RE NOT THE MAN I LOVE...
YES, I AM.
WHAT THE HELL?
HONEY--
DON'T CALL ME THAT! DON'T TOUCH ME, YOU--
ARE YOU KIDDING ME?
I...I SPILLED HIS SECRET. TOOK HIS LIFE FROM HIM, AND SENT HIM AWAY TO DEAL WITH IT ALONE.
HE NEVER... HE NEVER RECOVERED.

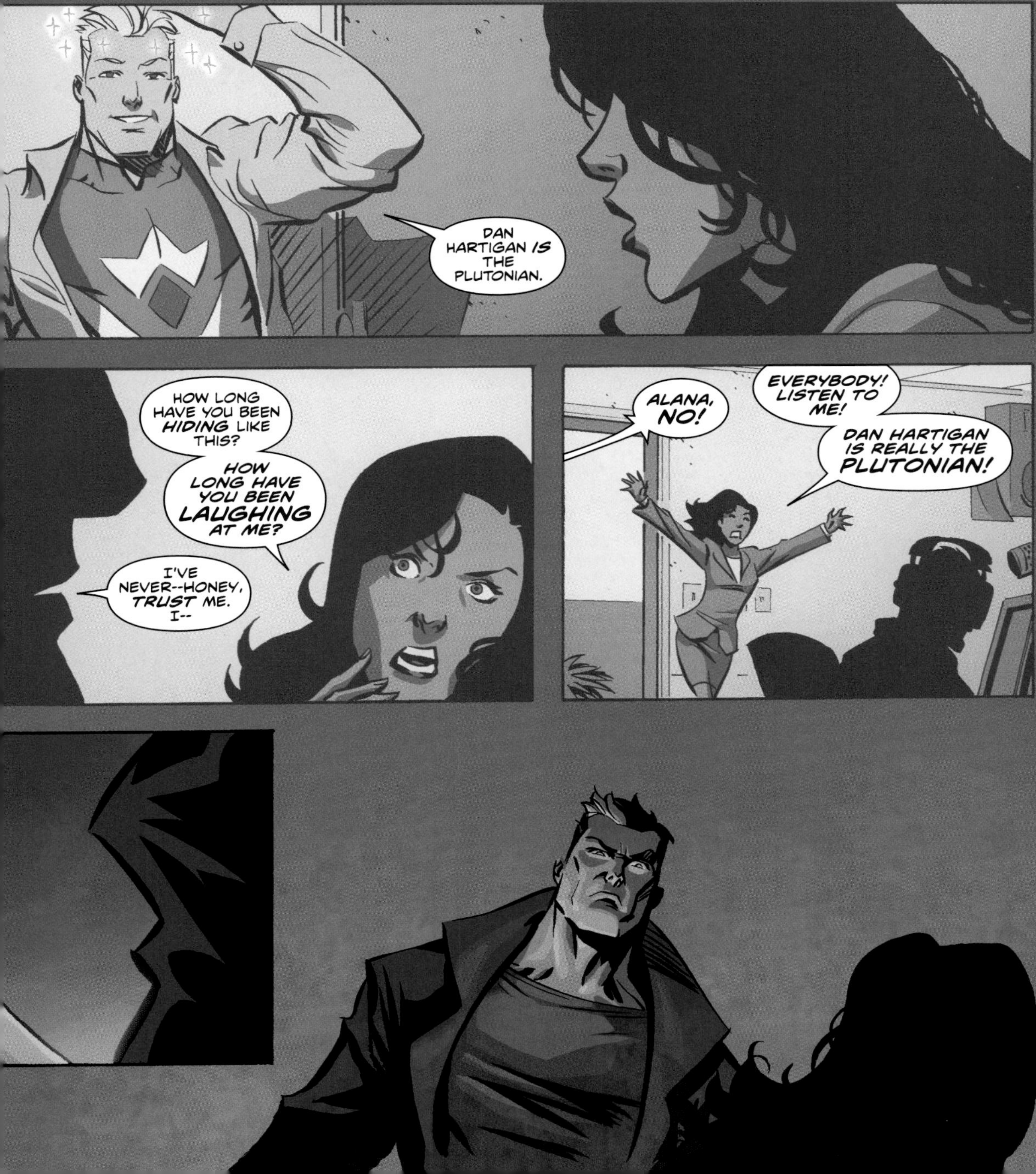
DAN HARTIGAN *IS* THE PLUTONIAN.
HOW LONG HAVE YOU BEEN *HIDING* LIKE THIS?
HOW LONG HAVE YOU BEEN LAUGHING AT ME?
I'VE NEVER--HONEY, *TRUST* ME. I--
EVERYBODY! LISTEN TO ME!
ALANA, NO!
*DAN HARTIGAN IS REALLY THE **PLUTONIAN!***

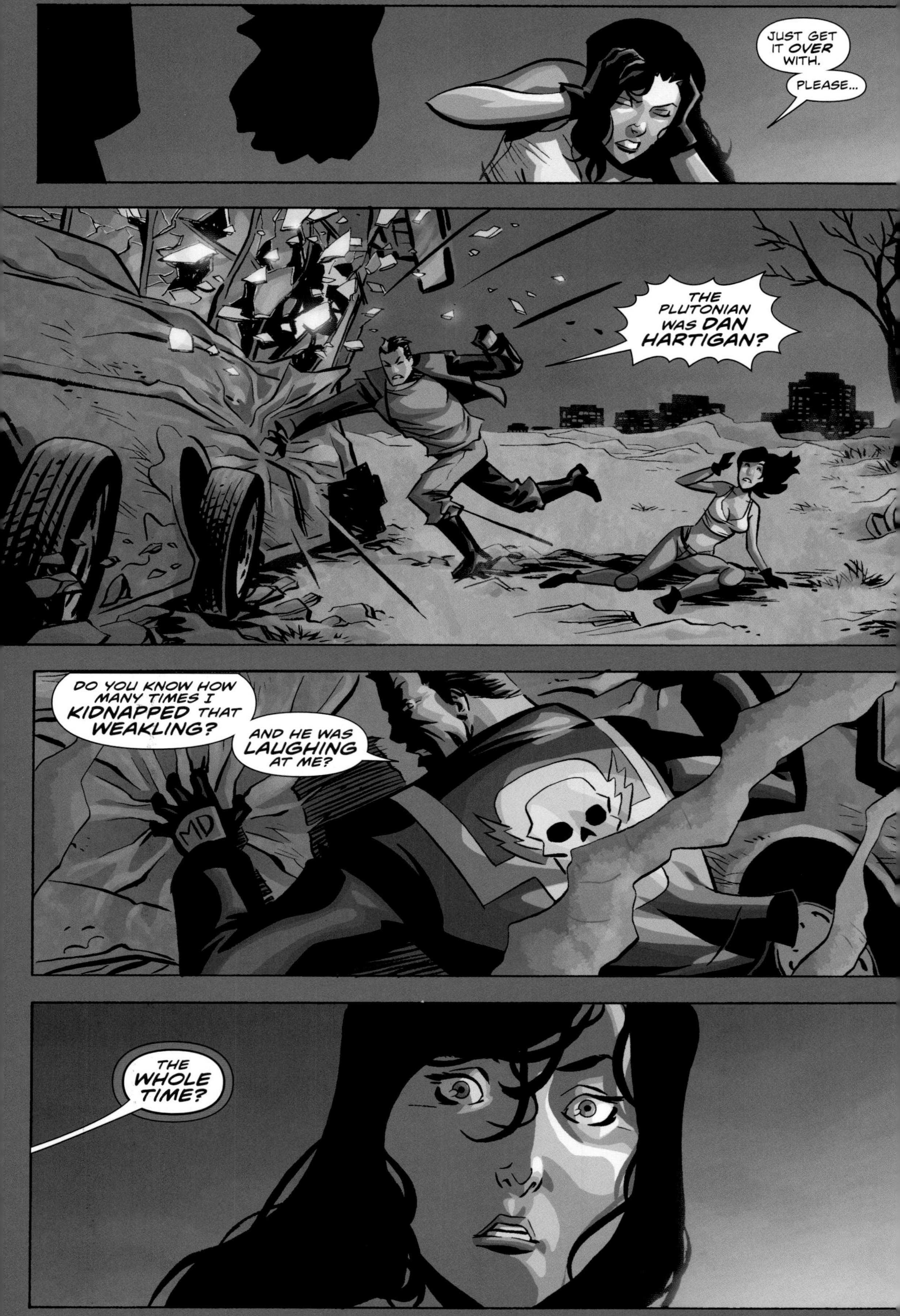
JUST GET IT OVER WITH.
PLEASE...
THE PLUTONIAN WAS DAN HARTIGAN?
DO YOU KNOW HOW MANY TIMES I KIDNAPPED THAT WEAKLING?
AND HE WAS LAUGHING AT ME?
MD
THE WHOLE TIME?

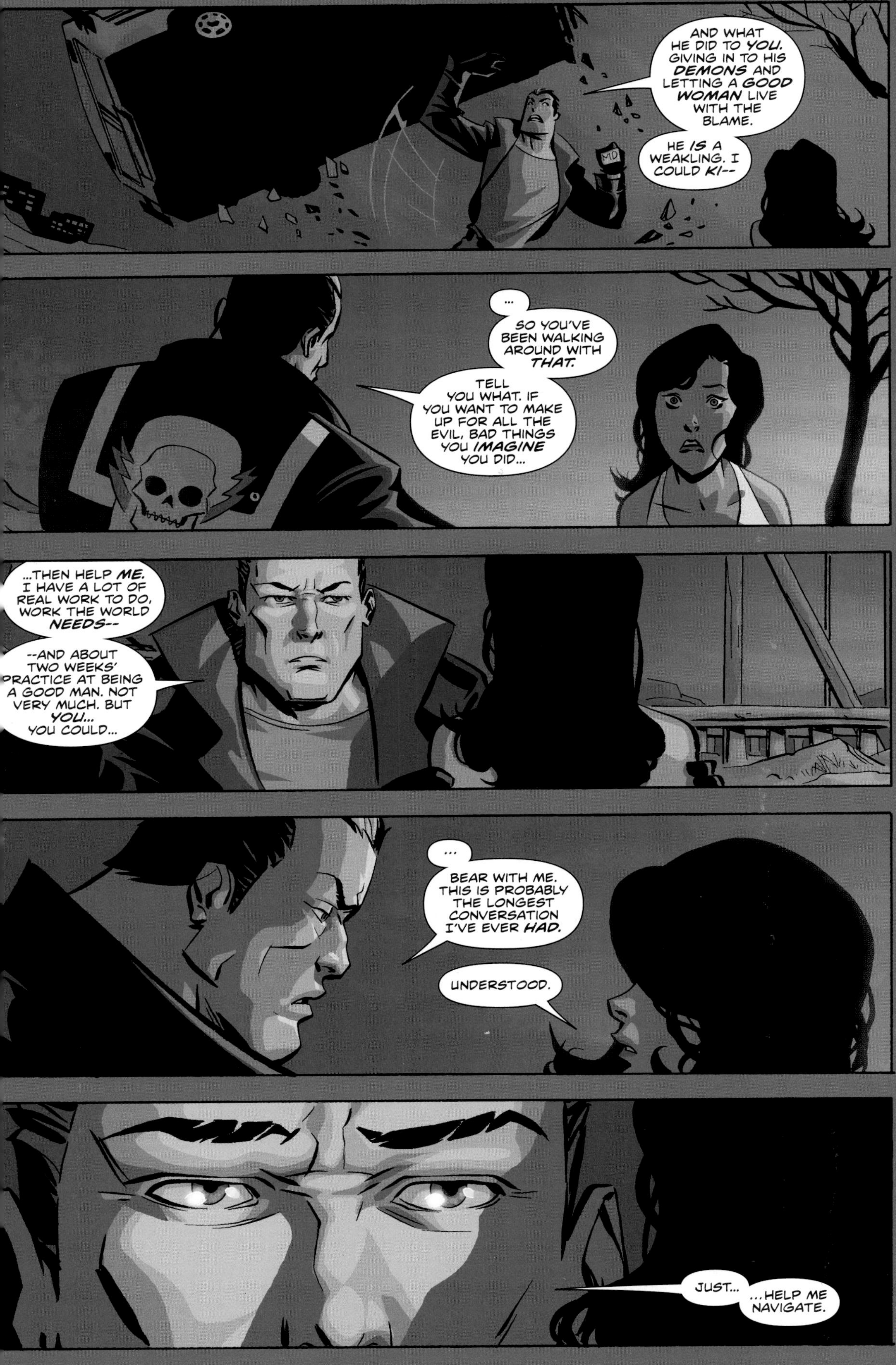
AND WHAT HE DID TO *YOU.* GIVING IN TO HIS *DEMONS* AND LETTING A *GOOD WOMAN* LIVE WITH THE BLAME.
HE *IS* A WEAKLING. I COULD *KI--*
...
SO YOU'VE BEEN WALKING AROUND WITH *THAT.*
TELL YOU WHAT. IF YOU WANT TO MAKE UP FOR ALL THE EVIL, BAD THINGS YOU *IMAGINE* YOU DID...
...THEN HELP *ME.* I HAVE A LOT OF REAL WORK TO DO, WORK THE WORLD *NEEDS--*
--AND ABOUT TWO WEEKS' PRACTICE AT BEING A GOOD MAN. NOT VERY MUCH. BUT *YOU...* YOU COULD...
...
BEAR WITH ME. THIS IS PROBABLY THE LONGEST CONVERSATION I'VE EVER *HAD.*
UNDERSTOOD.
JUST...
...HELP ME NAVIGATE.

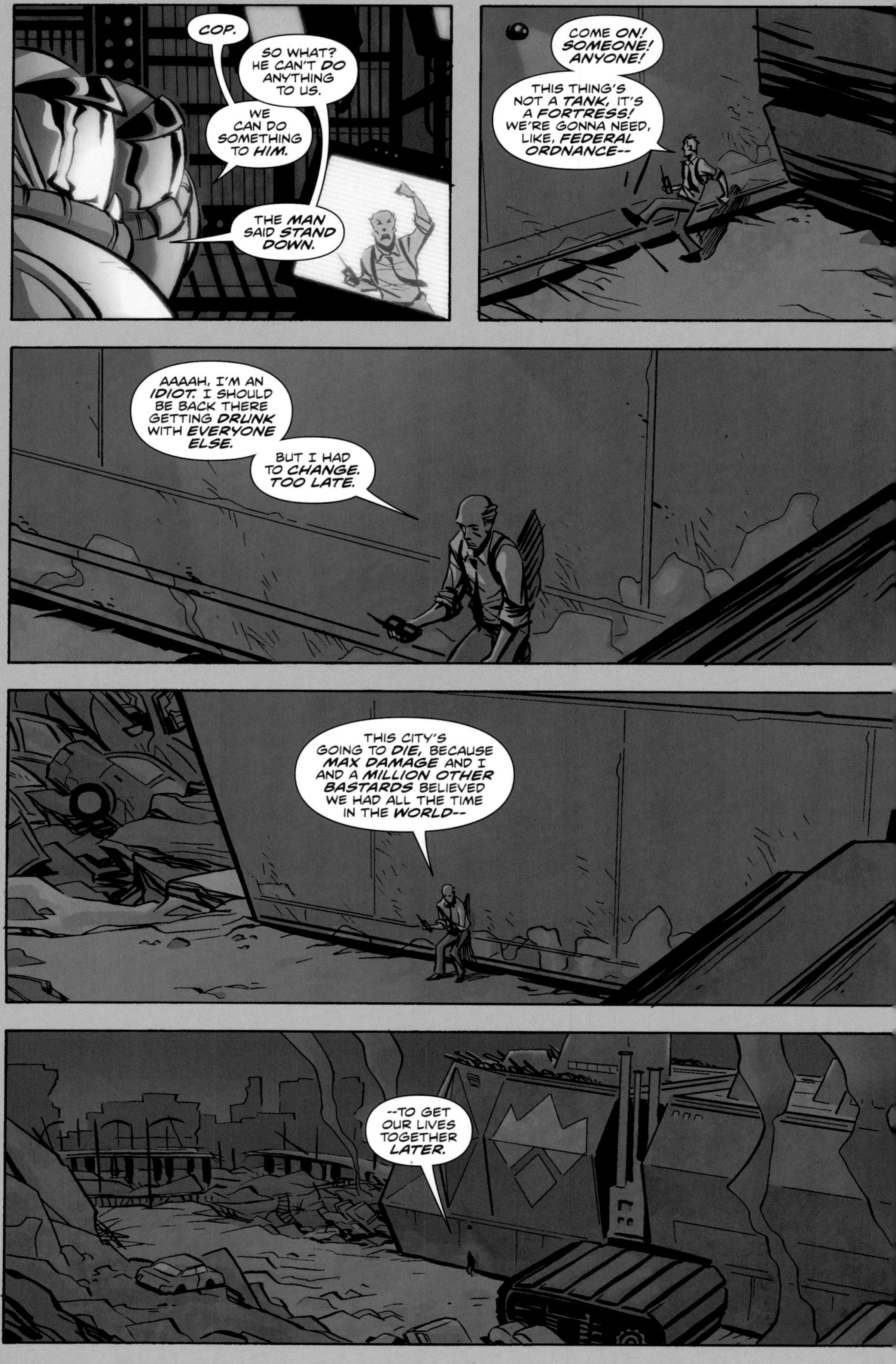
COP.
SO WHAT? HE CAN'T DO ANYTHING TO US.
WE CAN DO SOMETHING TO HIM.
THE MAN SAID STAND DOWN.
COME ON! SOMEONE! ANYONE!
THIS THING'S NOT A TANK, IT'S A FORTRESS! WE'RE GONNA NEED, LIKE, FEDERAL ORDNANCE--
AAAAH, I'M AN IDIOT. I SHOULD BE BACK THERE GETTING DRUNK WITH EVERYONE ELSE.
BUT I HAD TO CHANGE. TOO LATE.
THIS CITY'S GOING TO DIE, BECAUSE MAX DAMAGE AND I AND A MILLION OTHER BASTARDS BELIEVED WE HAD ALL THE TIME IN THE WORLD--
--TO GET OUR LIVES TOGETHER LATER.

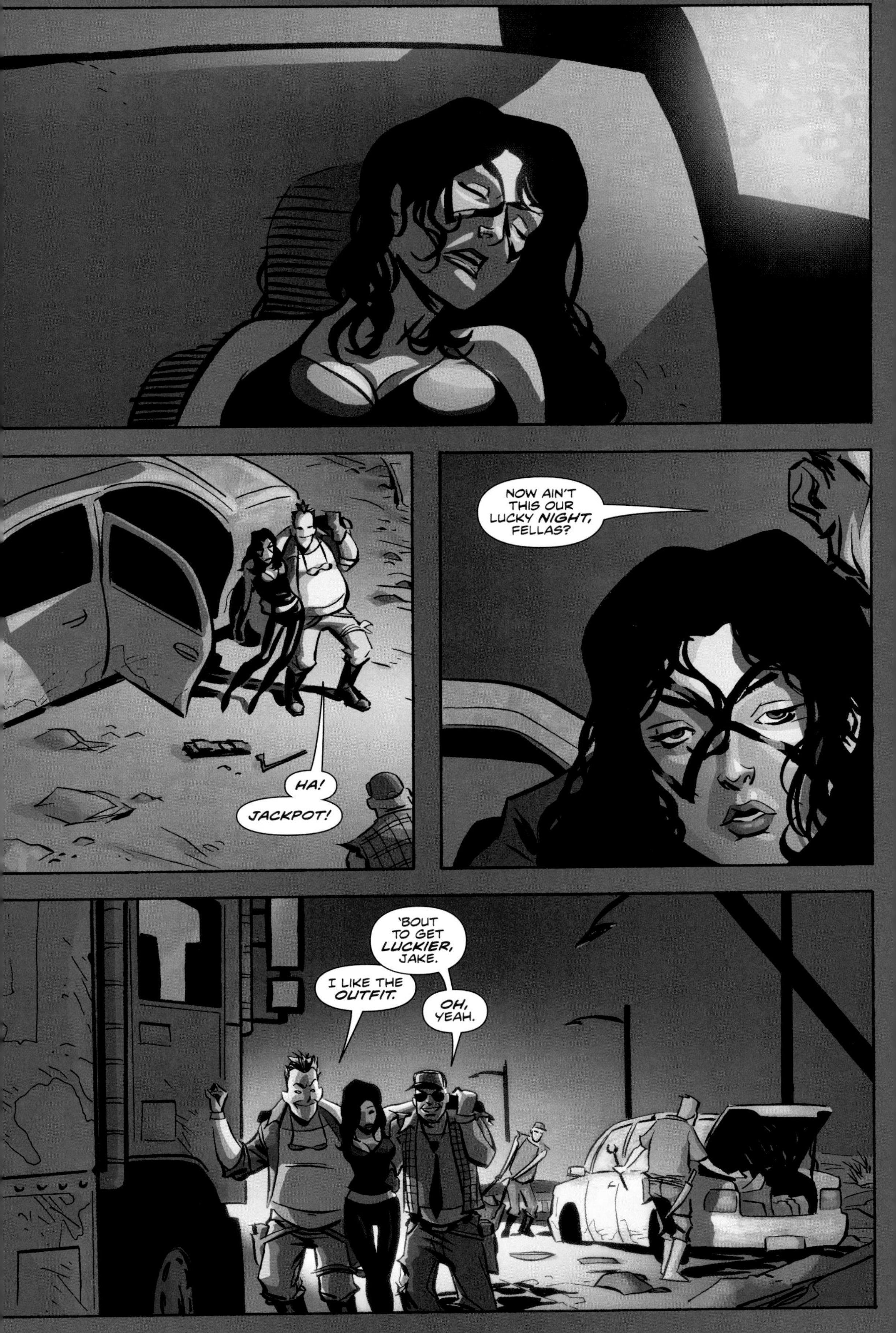
HA!
JACKPOT!
NOW AIN'T THIS OUR LUCKY NIGHT, FELLAS?
I LIKE THE OUTFIT.
'BOUT TO GET LUCKIER, JAKE.
OH, YEAH.

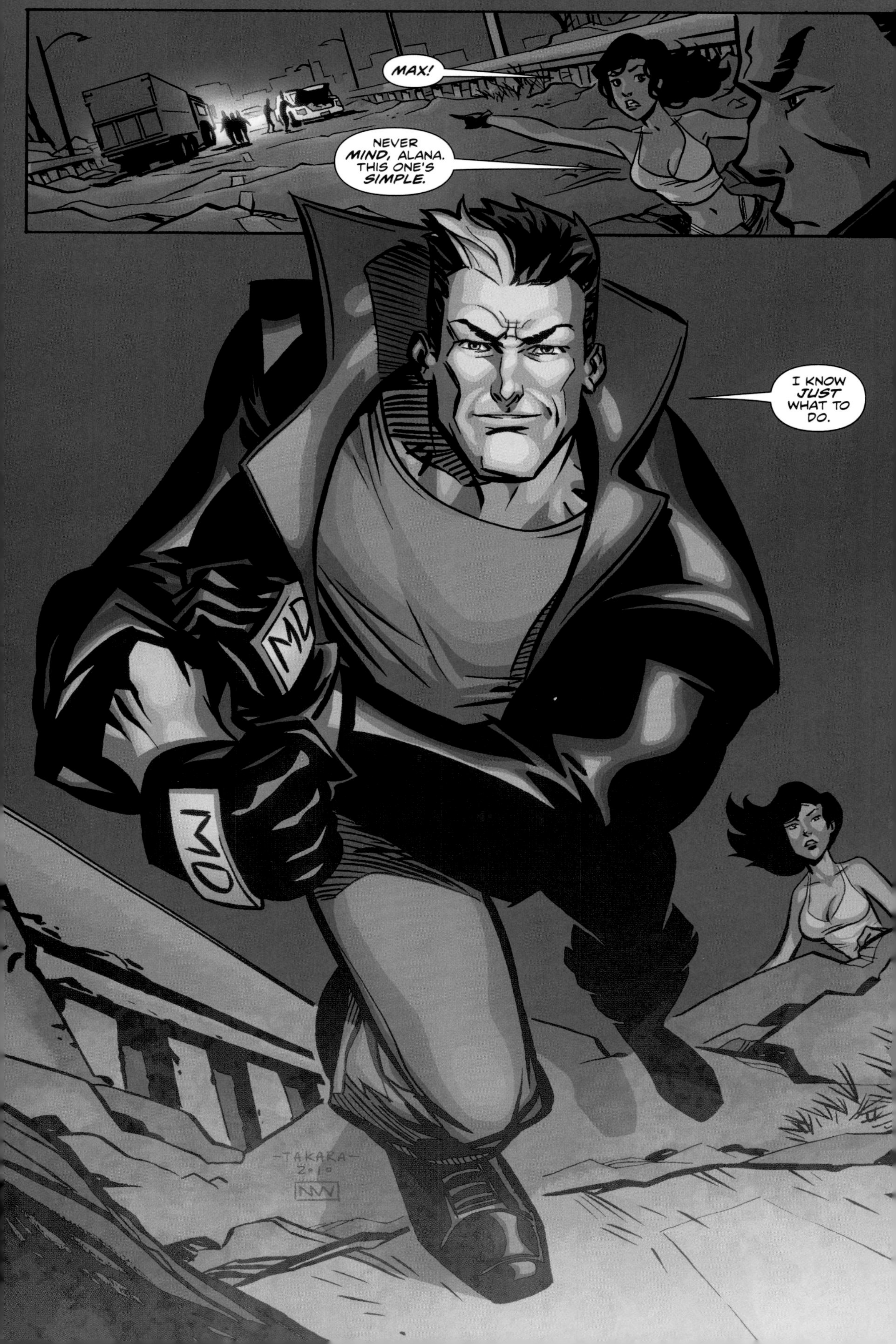
MAX!
NEVER MIND, ALANA. THIS ONE'S SIMPLE.
I KNOW JUST WHAT TO DO.
-TAKARA- 2010
NVV

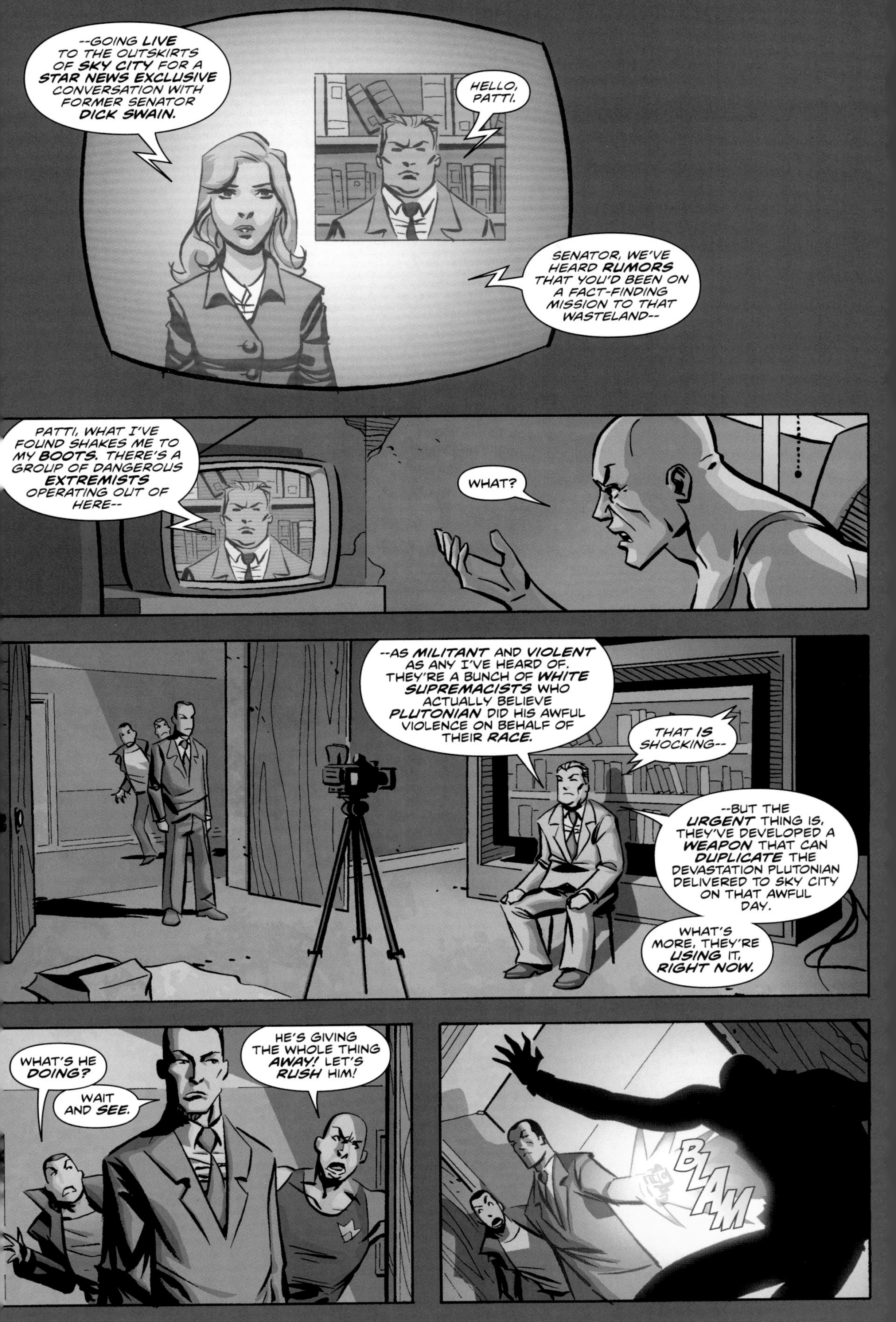
--GOING LIVE TO THE OUTSKIRTS OF SKY CITY FOR A STAR NEWS EXCLUSIVE CONVERSATION WITH FORMER SENATOR DICK SWAIN.
HELLO, PATTI.
SENATOR, WE'VE HEARD RUMORS THAT YOU'D BEEN ON A FACT-FINDING MISSION TO THAT WASTELAND--
PATTI, WHAT I'VE FOUND SHAKES ME TO MY BOOTS. THERE'S A GROUP OF DANGEROUS EXTREMISTS OPERATING OUT OF HERE--
WHAT?
--AS MILITANT AND VIOLENT AS ANY I'VE HEARD OF. THEY'RE A BUNCH OF WHITE SUPREMACISTS WHO ACTUALLY BELIEVE PLUTONIAN DID HIS AWFUL VIOLENCE ON BEHALF OF THEIR RACE.
THAT IS SHOCKING--
--BUT THE URGENT THING IS, THEY'VE DEVELOPED A WEAPON THAT CAN DUPLICATE THE DEVASTATION PLUTONIAN DELIVERED TO SKY CITY ON THAT AWFUL DAY.
WHAT'S MORE, THEY'RE USING IT, RIGHT NOW.
WHAT'S HE DOING?
WAIT AND SEE.
HE'S GIVING THE WHOLE THING AWAY! LET'S RUSH HIM!
BLAM

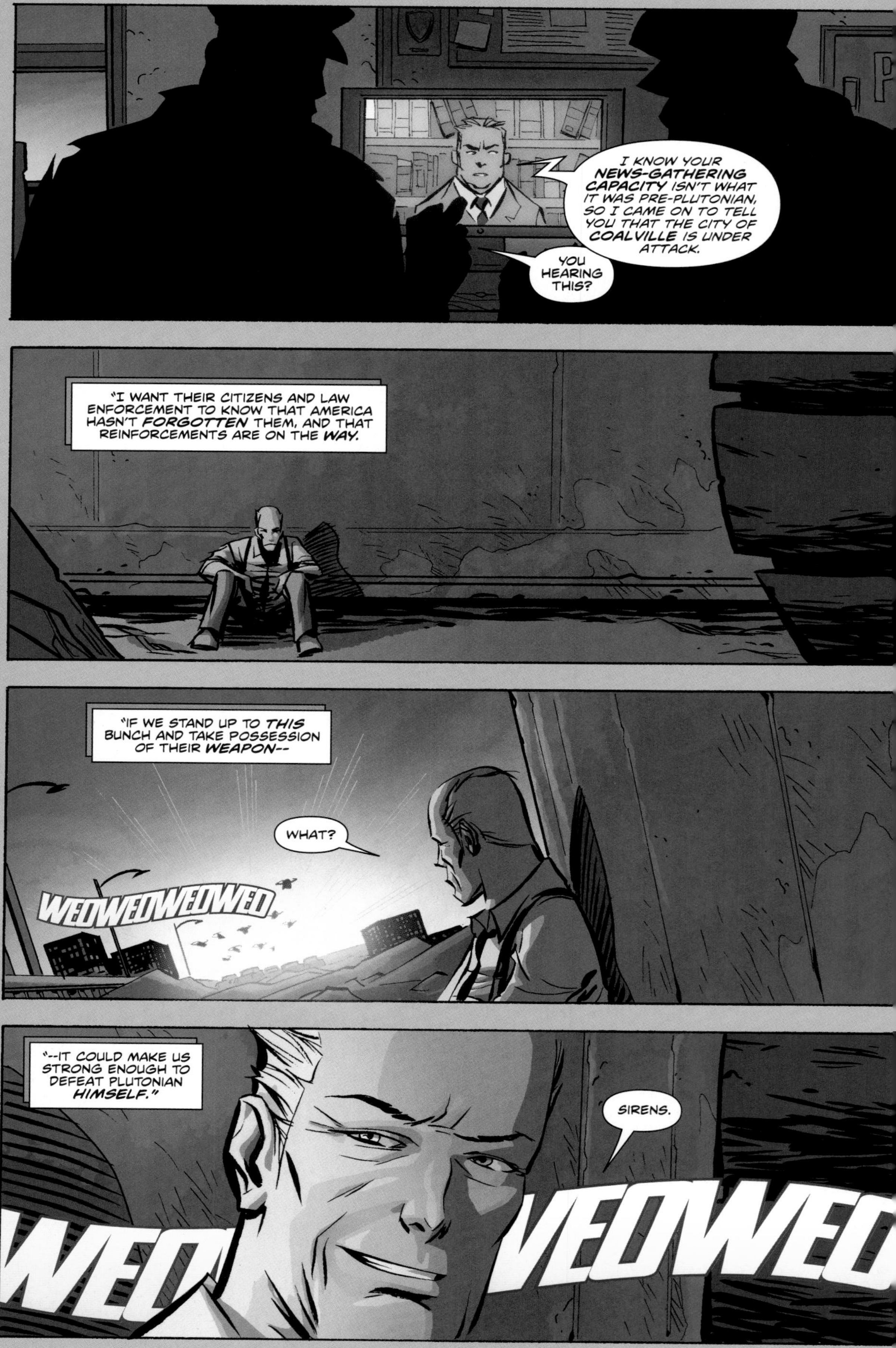
I KNOW YOUR NEWS-GATHERING CAPACITY ISN'T WHAT IT WAS PRE-PLUTONIAN, SO I CAME ON TO TELL YOU THAT THE CITY OF COALVILLE IS UNDER ATTACK.
YOU HEARING THIS?
"I WANT THEIR CITIZENS AND LAW ENFORCEMENT TO KNOW THAT AMERICA HASN'T FORGOTTEN THEM, AND THAT REINFORCEMENTS ARE ON THE WAY.
"IF WE STAND UP TO THIS BUNCH AND TAKE POSSESSION OF THEIR WEAPON--
WHAT?
WEOWEOWEOWEO
"--IT COULD MAKE US STRONG ENOUGH TO DEFEAT PLUTONIAN HIMSELF."
SIRENS.
WEO
WEOWEO

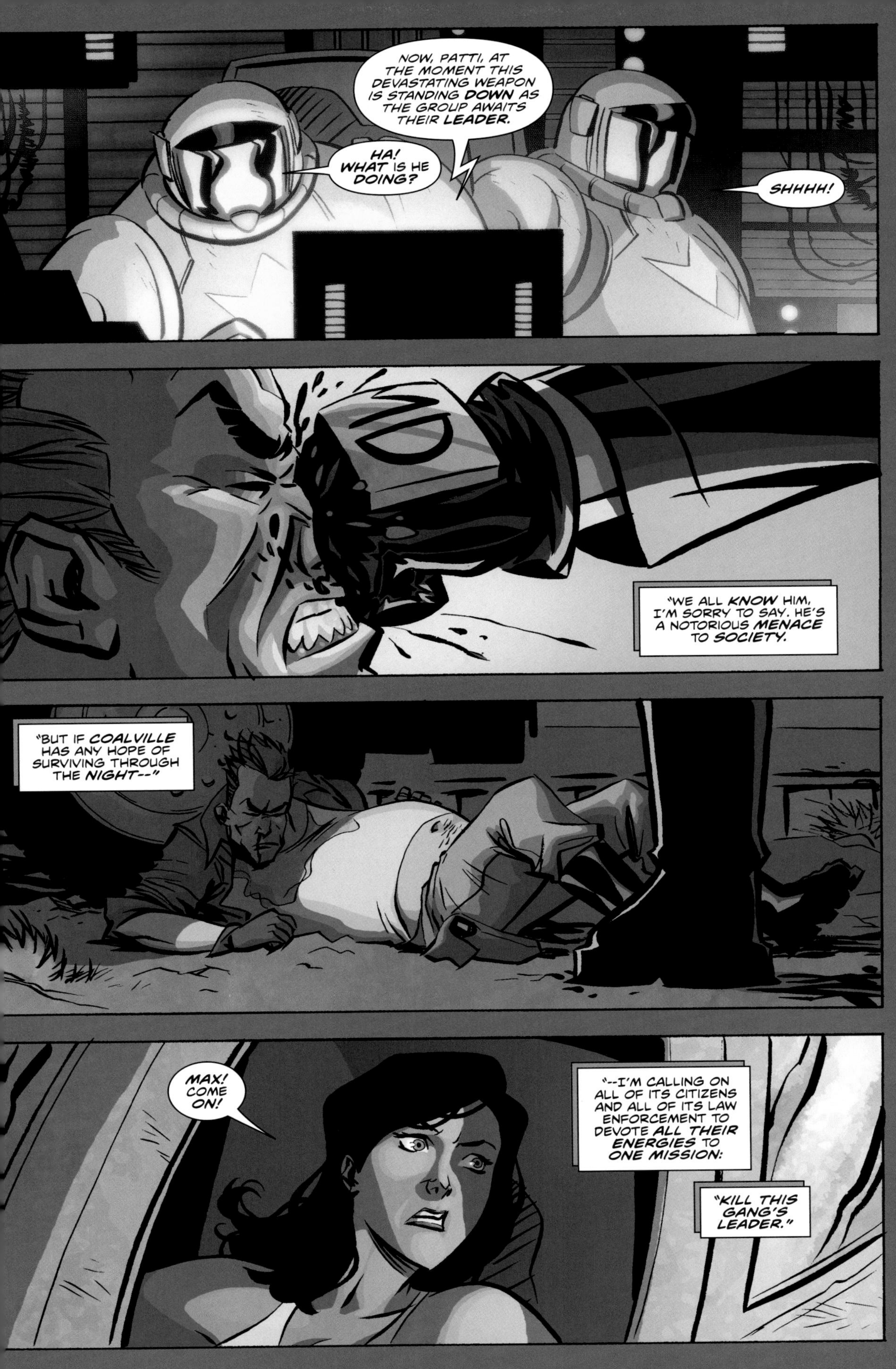
NOW, PATTI, AT THE MOMENT THIS DEVASTATING WEAPON IS STANDING DOWN AS THE GROUP AWAITS THEIR LEADER.
HA! WHAT IS HE DOING?
SHHHH!
"WE ALL KNOW HIM, I'M SORRY TO SAY. HE'S A NOTORIOUS MENACE TO SOCIETY.
"BUT IF COALVILLE HAS ANY HOPE OF SURVIVING THROUGH THE NIGHT--"
MAX! COME ON!
"--I'M CALLING ON ALL OF ITS CITIZENS AND ALL OF ITS LAW ENFORCEMENT TO DEVOTE ALL THEIR ENERGIES TO ONE MISSION:
"KILL THIS GANG'S LEADER."

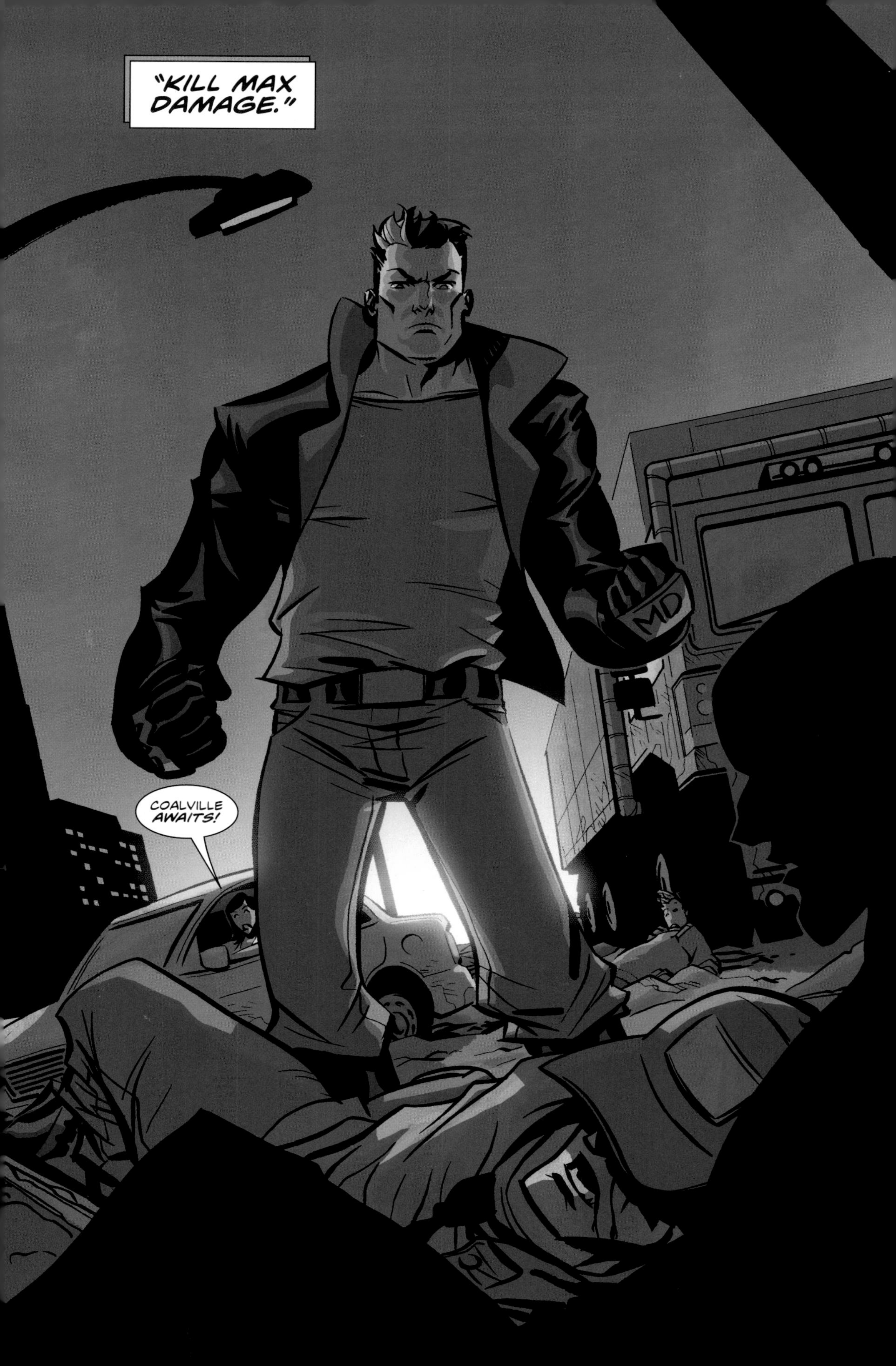
"KILL MAX DAMAGE."
COALVILLE AWAITS!
MD

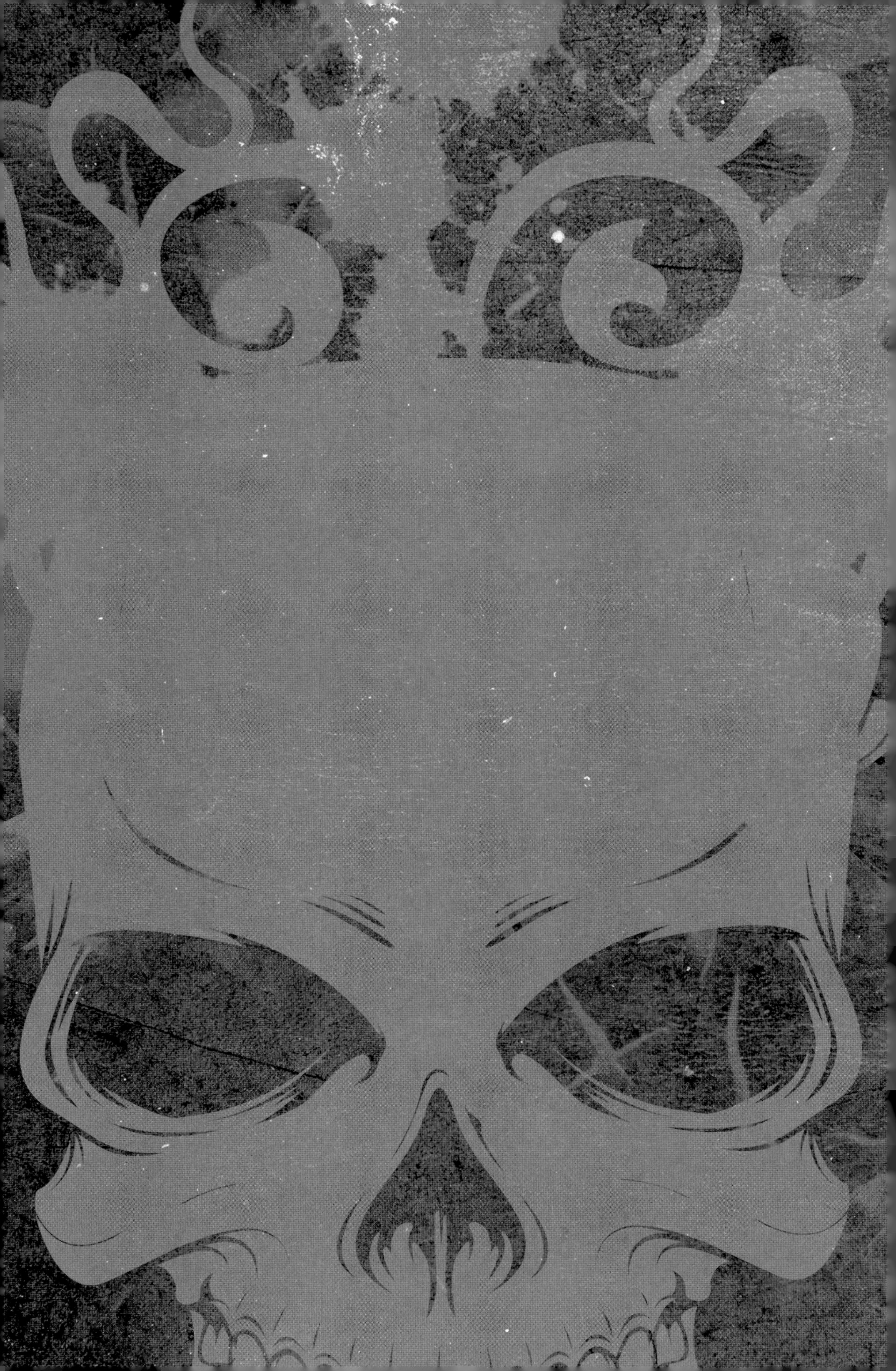

CHAPTER 12

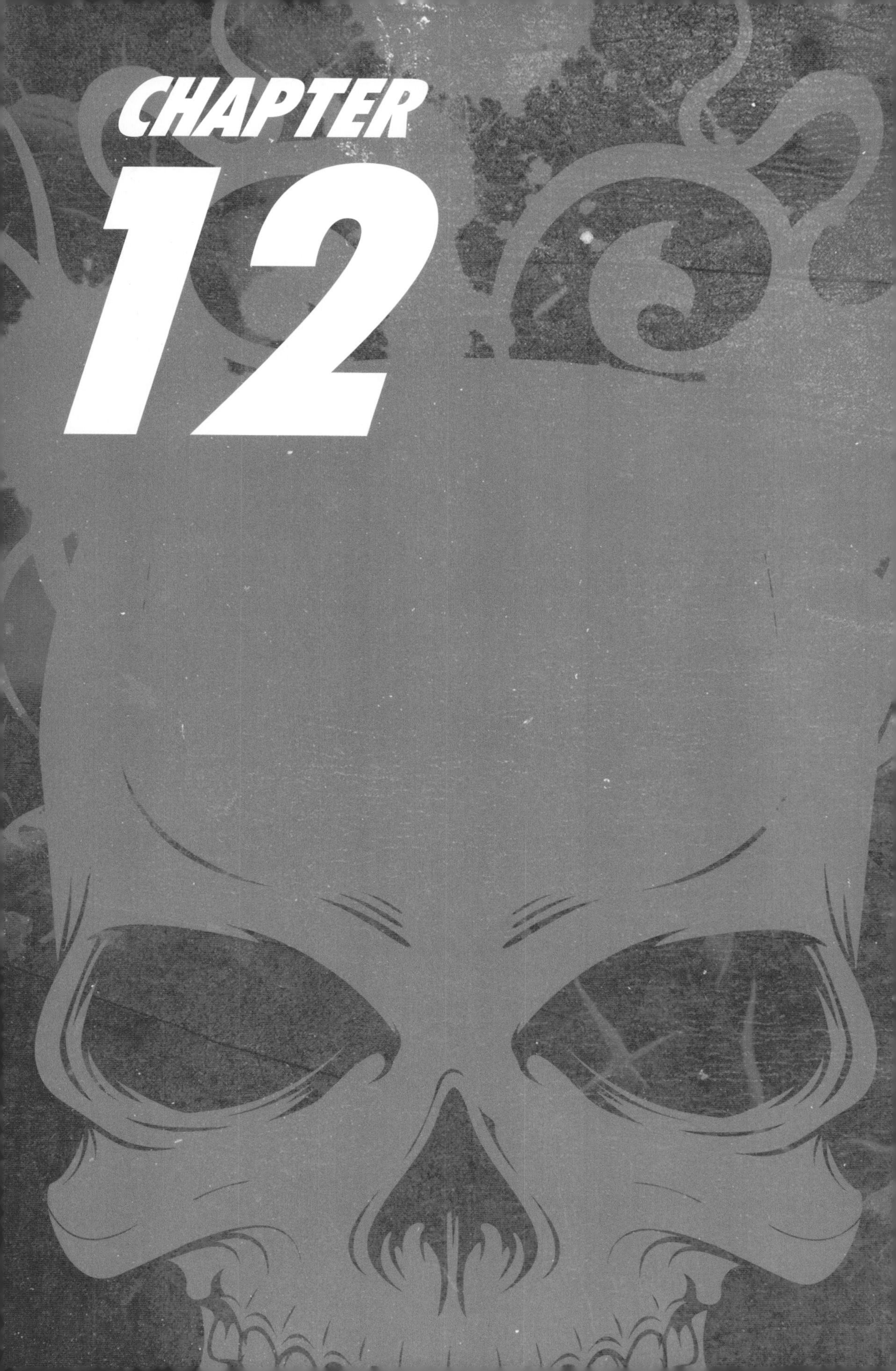

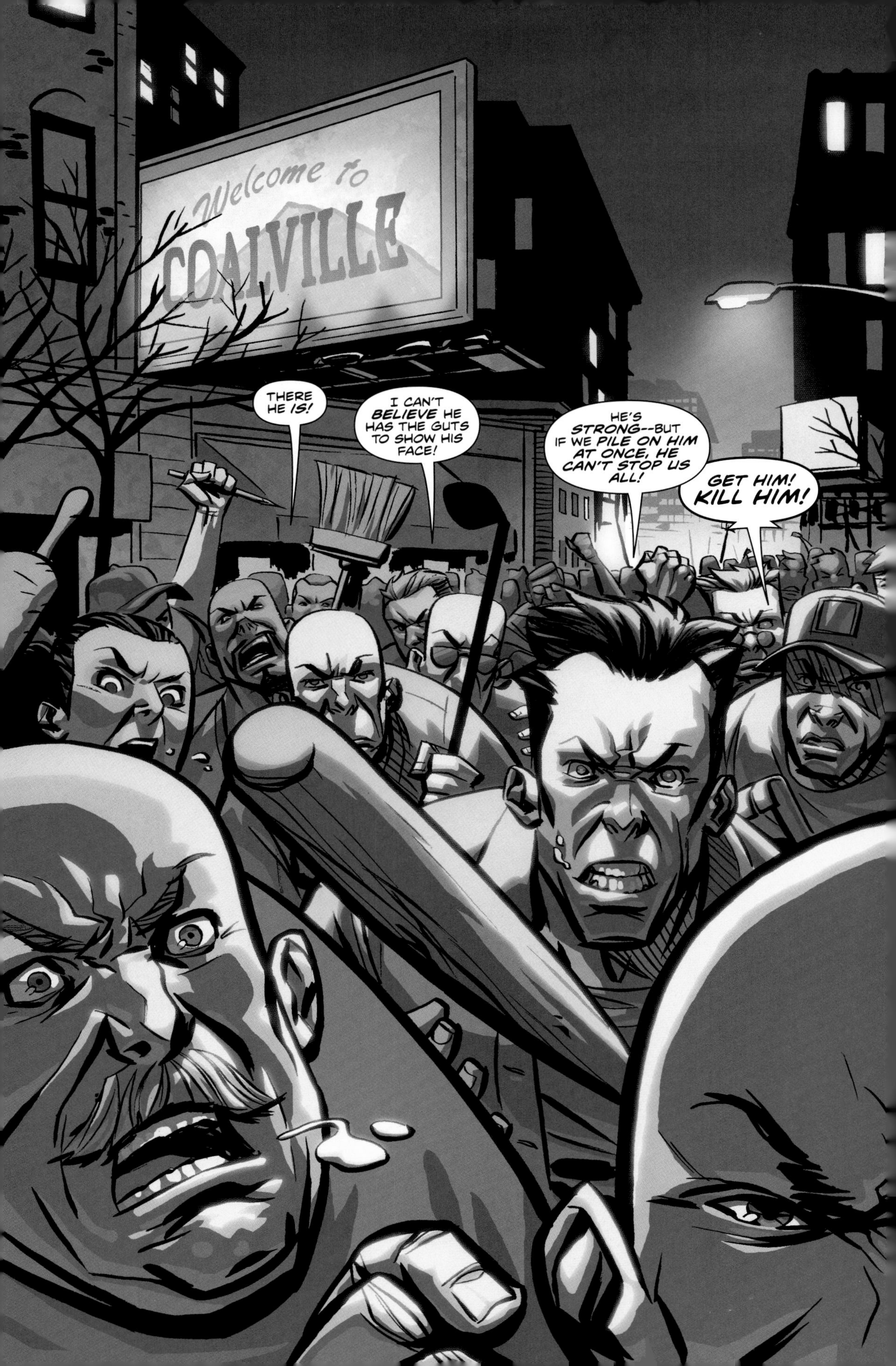
Welcome to
COALVILLE
THERE HE IS!
I CAN'T BELIEVE HE HAS THE GUTS TO SHOW HIS FACE!
HE'S STRONG--BUT IF WE PILE ON HIM AT ONCE, HE CAN'T STOP US ALL!
GET HIM! KILL HIM!

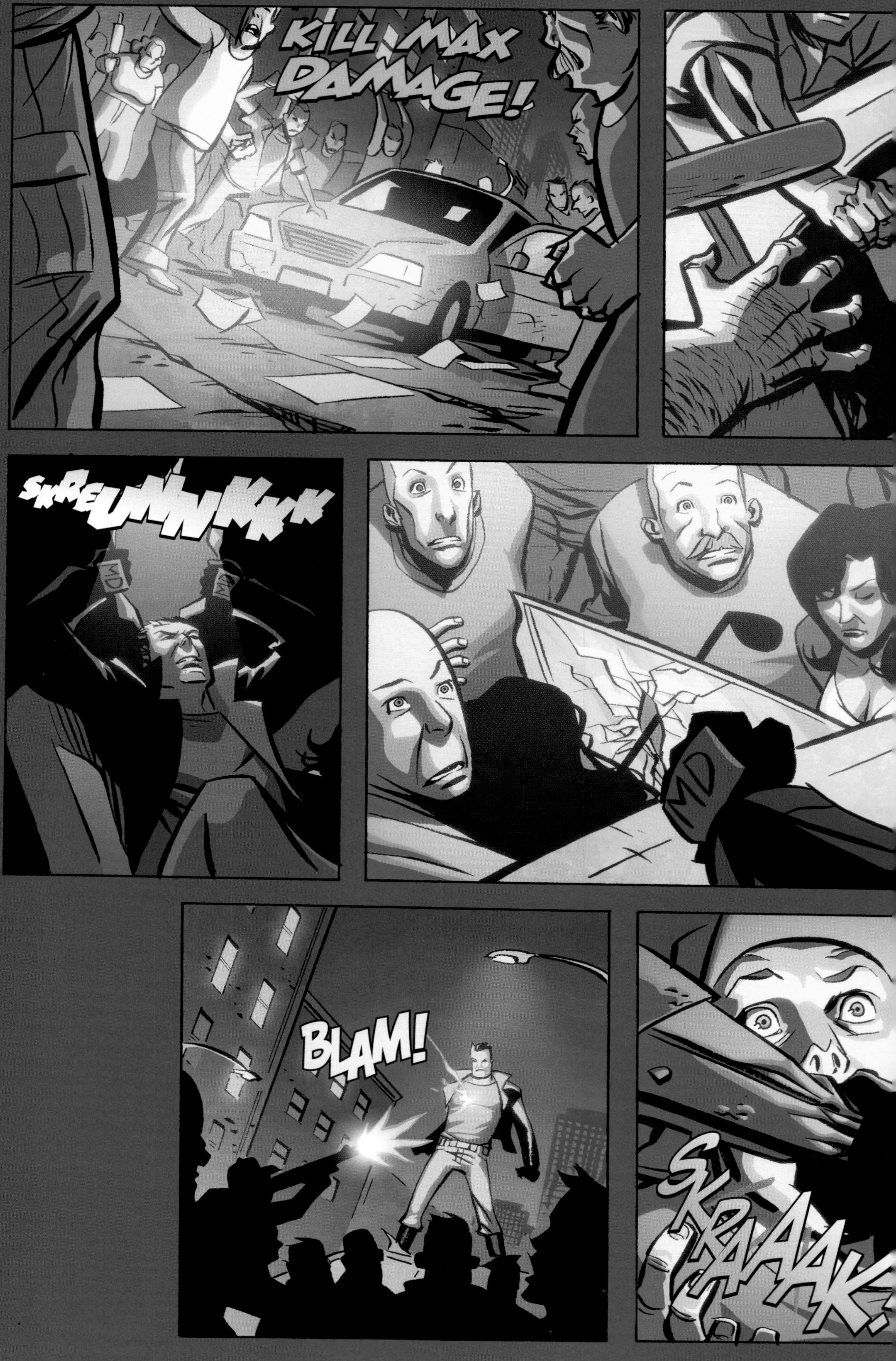
KILL MAX DAMAGE!
SKREUNNKKK
BLAM!
SKRAAAK!

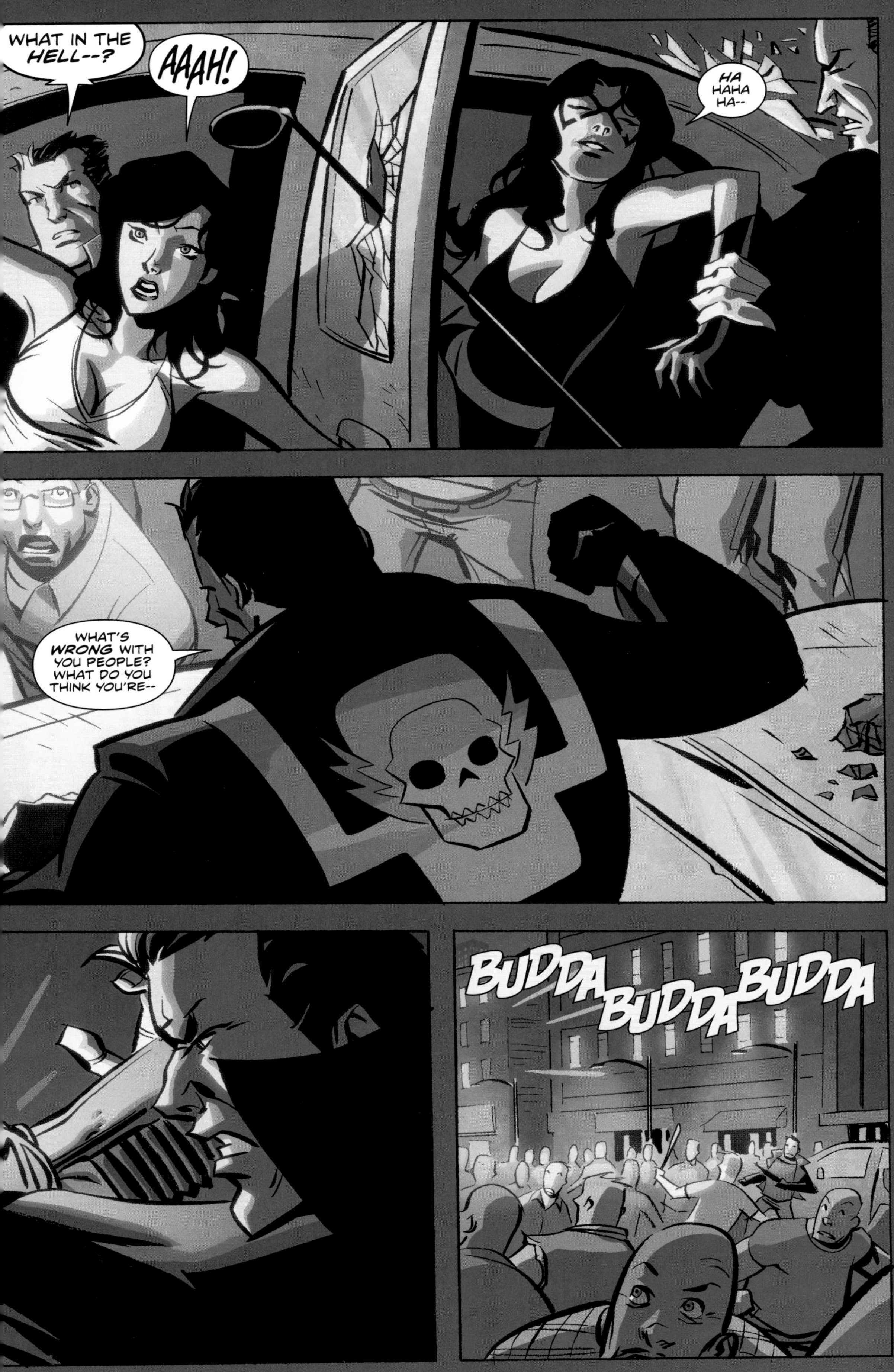
WHAT IN THE HELL--?
AAAH!
HA HAHA HA--
WHAT'S WRONG WITH YOU PEOPLE? WHAT DO YOU THINK YOU'RE--
BUDDA BUDDA BUDDA

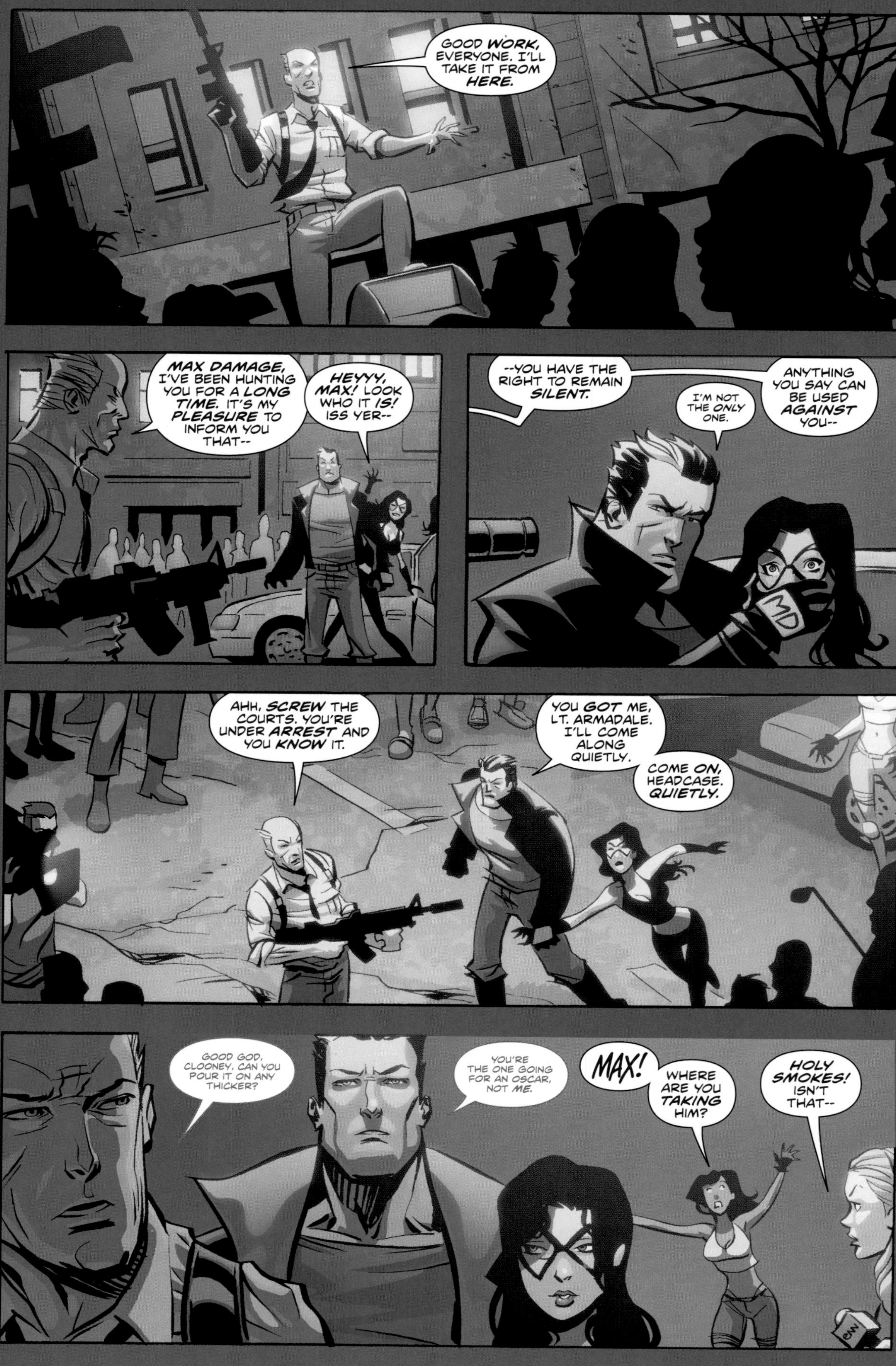
GOOD WORK, EVERYONE. I'LL TAKE IT FROM HERE.
MAX DAMAGE, I'VE BEEN HUNTING YOU FOR A LONG TIME. IT'S MY PLEASURE TO INFORM YOU THAT--
HEYYY, MAX! LOOK WHO IT IS! ISS YER--
--YOU HAVE THE RIGHT TO REMAIN SILENT.
I'M NOT THE ONLY ONE.
ANYTHING YOU SAY CAN BE USED AGAINST YOU--
AHH, SCREW THE COURTS. YOU'RE UNDER ARREST AND YOU KNOW IT.
YOU GOT ME, LT. ARMADALE. I'LL COME ALONG QUIETLY.
COME ON, HEADCASE. QUIETLY.
GOOD GOD, CLOONEY, CAN YOU POUR IT ON ANY THICKER?
YOU'RE THE ONE GOING FOR AN OSCAR, NOT ME.
MAX!
WHERE ARE YOU TAKING HIM?
HOLY SMOKES! ISN'T THAT--

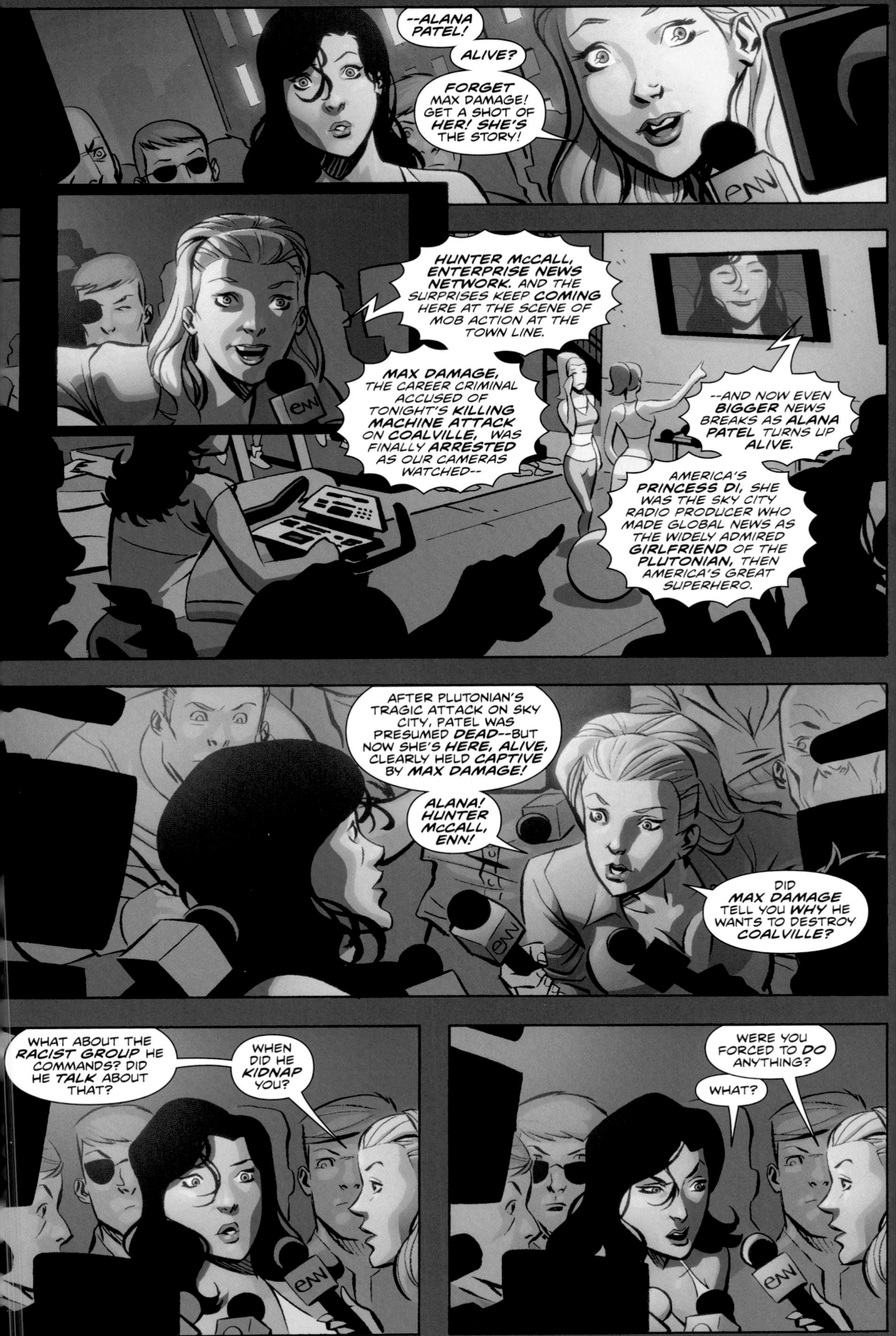
--ALANA PATEL!
ALIVE?
FORGET MAX DAMAGE! GET A SHOT OF HER! SHE'S THE STORY!
HUNTER McCALL, ENTERPRISE NEWS NETWORK. AND THE SURPRISES KEEP COMING HERE AT THE SCENE OF MOB ACTION AT THE TOWN LINE.
MAX DAMAGE, THE CAREER CRIMINAL ACCUSED OF TONIGHT'S KILLING MACHINE ATTACK ON COALVILLE, WAS FINALLY ARRESTED AS OUR CAMERAS WATCHED--
--AND NOW EVEN BIGGER NEWS BREAKS AS ALANA PATEL TURNS UP ALIVE.
AMERICA'S PRINCESS DI, SHE WAS THE SKY CITY RADIO PRODUCER WHO MADE GLOBAL NEWS AS THE WIDELY ADMIRED GIRLFRIEND OF THE PLUTONIAN, THEN AMERICA'S GREAT SUPERHERO.
AFTER PLUTONIAN'S TRAGIC ATTACK ON SKY CITY, PATEL WAS PRESUMED DEAD--BUT NOW SHE'S HERE, ALIVE, CLEARLY HELD CAPTIVE BY MAX DAMAGE!
ALANA! HUNTER McCALL, ENN!
DID MAX DAMAGE TELL YOU WHY HE WANTS TO DESTROY COALVILLE?
WHAT ABOUT THE RACIST GROUP HE COMMANDS? DID HE TALK ABOUT THAT?
WHEN DID HE KIDNAP YOU?
WERE YOU FORCED TO DO ANYTHING?
WHAT?

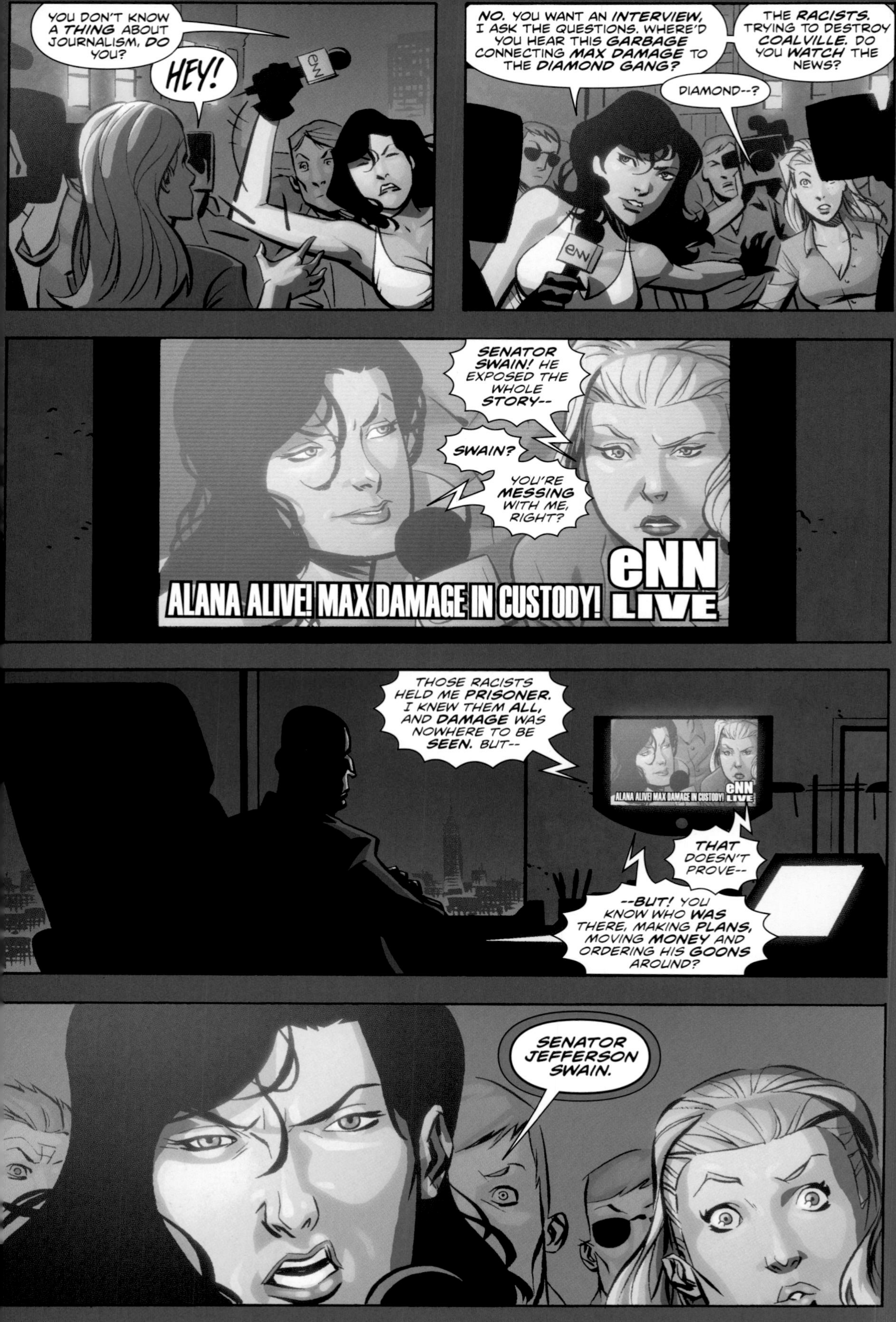
YOU DON'T KNOW A THING ABOUT JOURNALISM, DO YOU?
HEY!
eNN
NO. YOU WANT AN INTERVIEW, I ASK THE QUESTIONS. WHERE'D YOU HEAR THIS GARBAGE CONNECTING MAX DAMAGE TO THE DIAMOND GANG?
THE RACISTS. TRYING TO DESTROY COALVILLE. DO YOU WATCH THE NEWS?
DIAMOND--?
eNN
SENATOR SWAIN! HE EXPOSED THE WHOLE STORY--
SWAIN?
YOU'RE MESSING WITH ME, RIGHT?
ALANA ALIVE! MAX DAMAGE IN CUSTODY!
eNN LIVE
THOSE RACISTS HELD ME PRISONER. I KNEW THEM ALL, AND DAMAGE WAS NOWHERE TO BE SEEN. BUT--
ALANA ALIVE! MAX DAMAGE IN CUSTODY!
eNN LIVE
THAT DOESN'T PROVE--
--BUT! YOU KNOW WHO WAS THERE, MAKING PLANS, MOVING MONEY AND ORDERING HIS GOONS AROUND?
SENATOR JEFFERSON SWAIN.

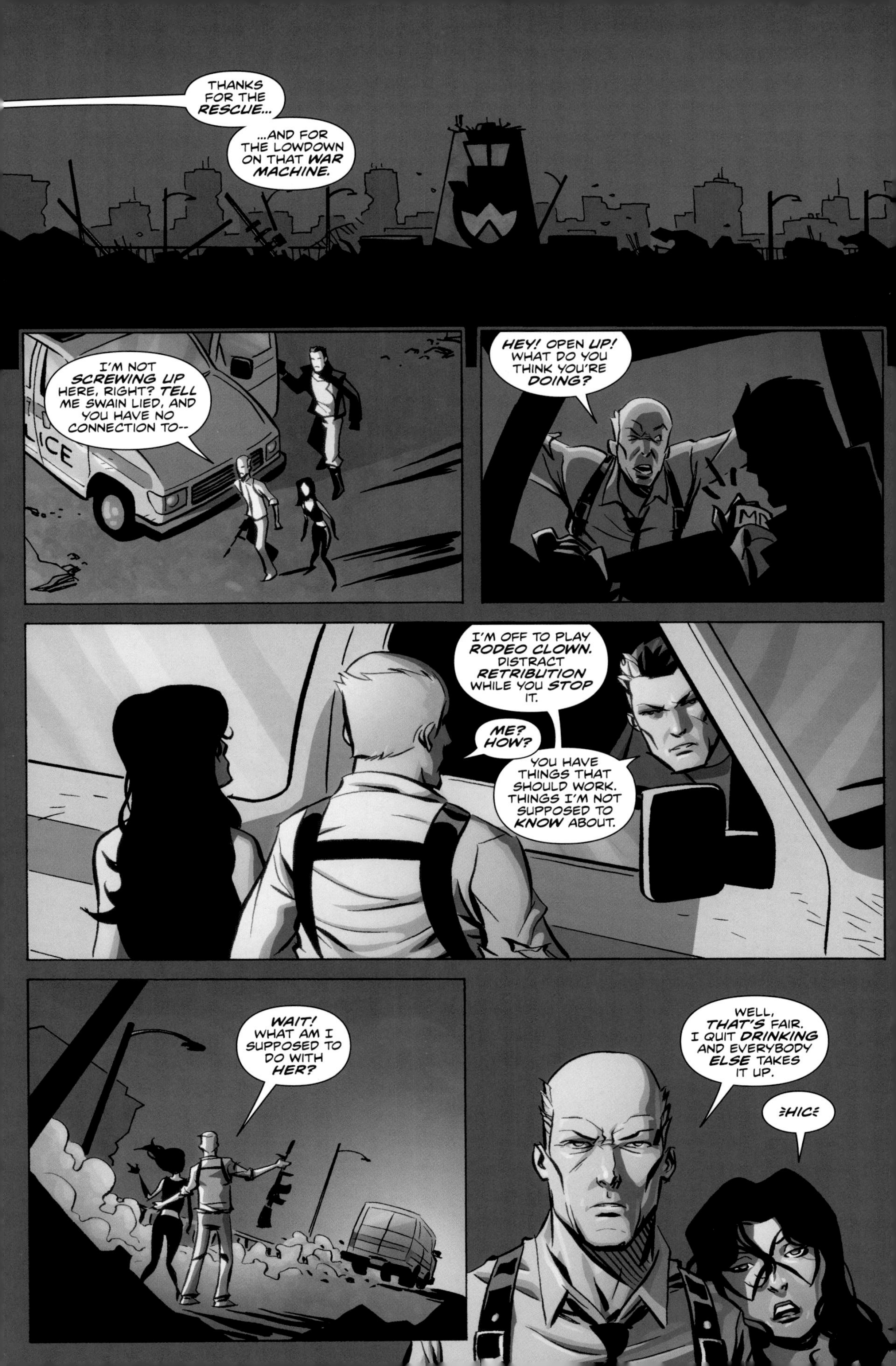

THANKS FOR THE RESCUE...
...AND FOR THE LOWDOWN ON THAT WAR MACHINE.
I'M NOT SCREWING UP HERE, RIGHT? TELL ME SWAIN LIED, AND YOU HAVE NO CONNECTION TO--
ICE
HEY! OPEN UP! WHAT DO YOU THINK YOU'RE DOING?
I'M OFF TO PLAY RODEO CLOWN. DISTRACT RETRIBUTION WHILE YOU STOP IT.
ME? HOW?
YOU HAVE THINGS THAT SHOULD WORK. THINGS I'M NOT SUPPOSED TO KNOW ABOUT.
WAIT! WHAT AM I SUPPOSED TO DO WITH HER?
WELL, THAT'S FAIR. I QUIT DRINKING AND EVERYBODY ELSE TAKES IT UP.
HIC

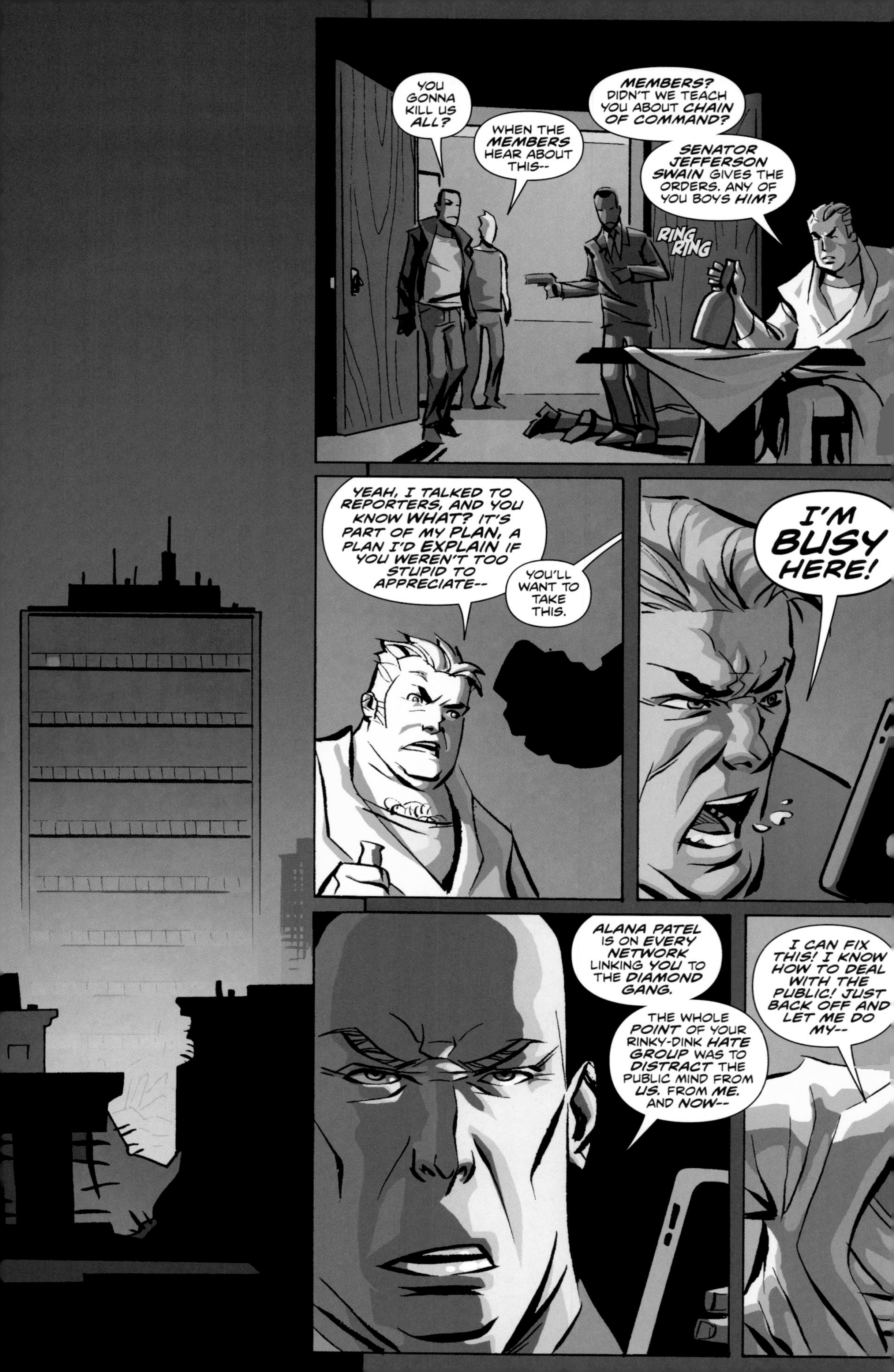
YOU GONNA KILL US ALL?
WHEN THE MEMBERS HEAR ABOUT THIS--
MEMBERS? DIDN'T WE TEACH YOU ABOUT CHAIN OF COMMAND?
SENATOR JEFFERSON SWAIN GIVES THE ORDERS. ANY OF YOU BOYS HIM?
RING RING
YEAH, I TALKED TO REPORTERS, AND YOU KNOW WHAT? IT'S PART OF MY PLAN, A PLAN I'D EXPLAIN IF YOU WEREN'T TOO STUPID TO APPRECIATE--
YOU'LL WANT TO TAKE THIS.
I'M BUSY HERE!
ALANA PATEL IS ON EVERY NETWORK LINKING YOU TO THE DIAMOND GANG.
THE WHOLE POINT OF YOUR RINKY-DINK HATE GROUP WAS TO DISTRACT THE PUBLIC MIND FROM US. FROM ME. AND NOW--
I CAN FIX THIS! I KNOW HOW TO DEAL WITH THE PUBLIC! JUST BACK OFF AND LET ME DO MY--

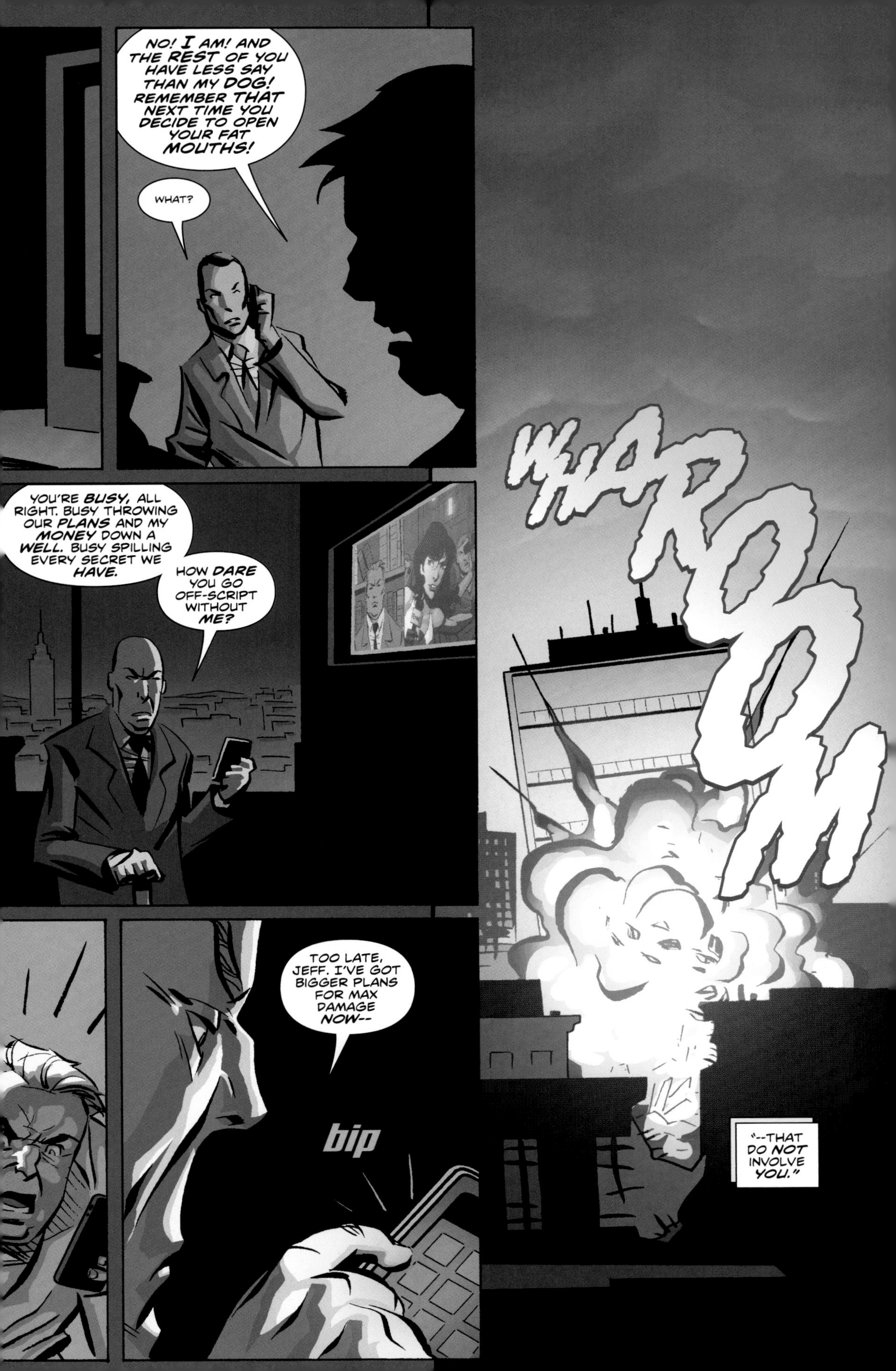

NO! I AM! AND THE REST OF YOU HAVE LESS SAY THAN MY DOG! REMEMBER THAT NEXT TIME YOU DECIDE TO OPEN YOUR FAT MOUTHS!
WHAT?
YOU'RE BUSY, ALL RIGHT. BUSY THROWING OUR PLANS AND MY MONEY DOWN A WELL. BUSY SPILLING EVERY SECRET WE HAVE.
HOW DARE YOU GO OFF-SCRIPT WITHOUT ME?
TOO LATE, JEFF. I'VE GOT BIGGER PLANS FOR MAX DAMAGE NOW--
bip
WHAROOM
"--THAT DO NOT INVOLVE YOU."

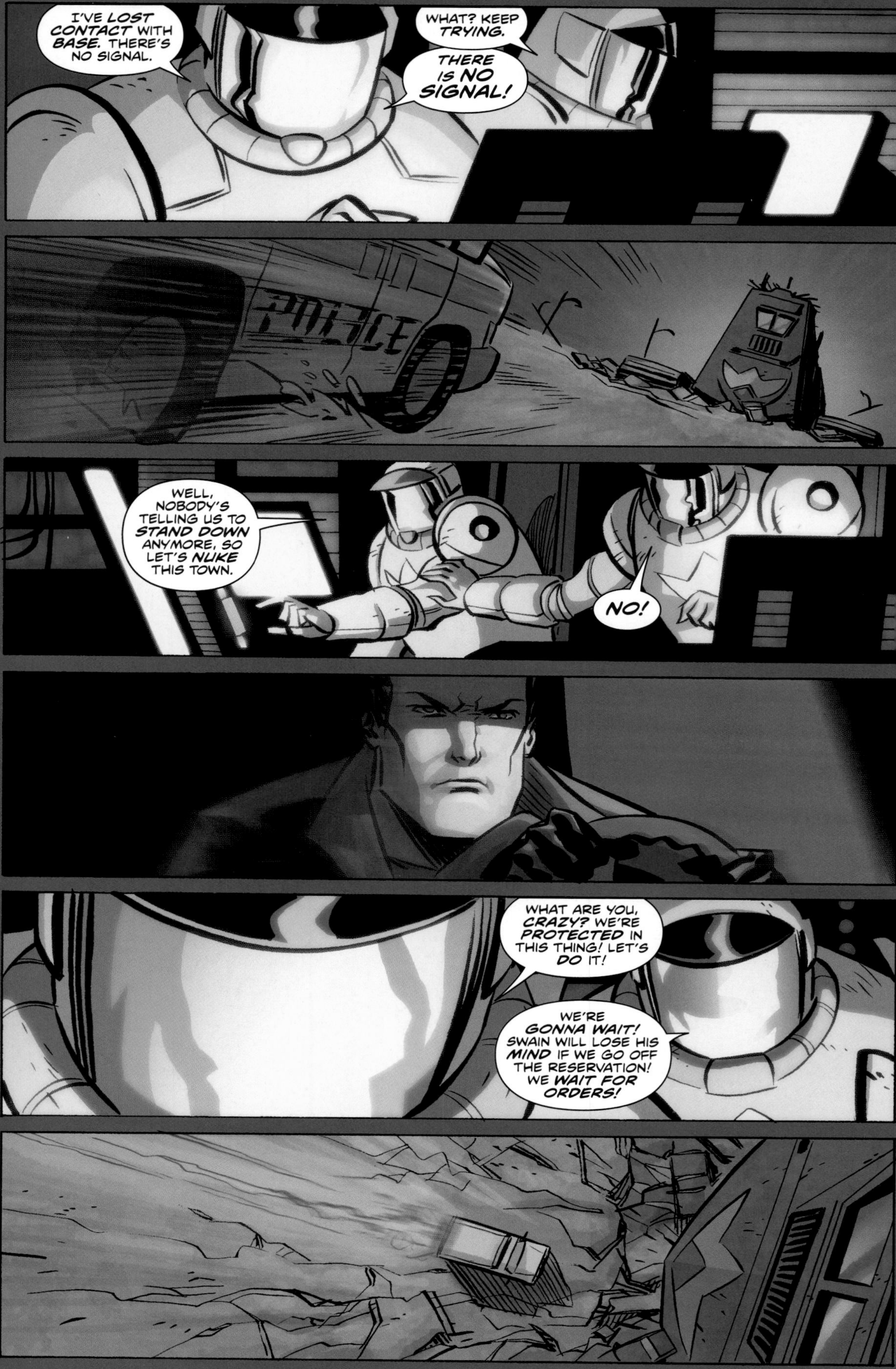
I'VE LOST CONTACT WITH BASE. THERE'S NO SIGNAL.
WHAT? KEEP TRYING.
THERE IS NO SIGNAL!
POLICE
WELL, NOBODY'S TELLING US TO STAND DOWN ANYMORE, SO LET'S NUKE THIS TOWN.
NO!
WHAT ARE YOU, CRAZY? WE'RE PROTECTED IN THIS THING! LET'S DO IT!
WE'RE GONNA WAIT! SWAIN WILL LOSE HIS MIND IF WE GO OFF THE RESERVATION! WE WAIT FOR ORDERS!

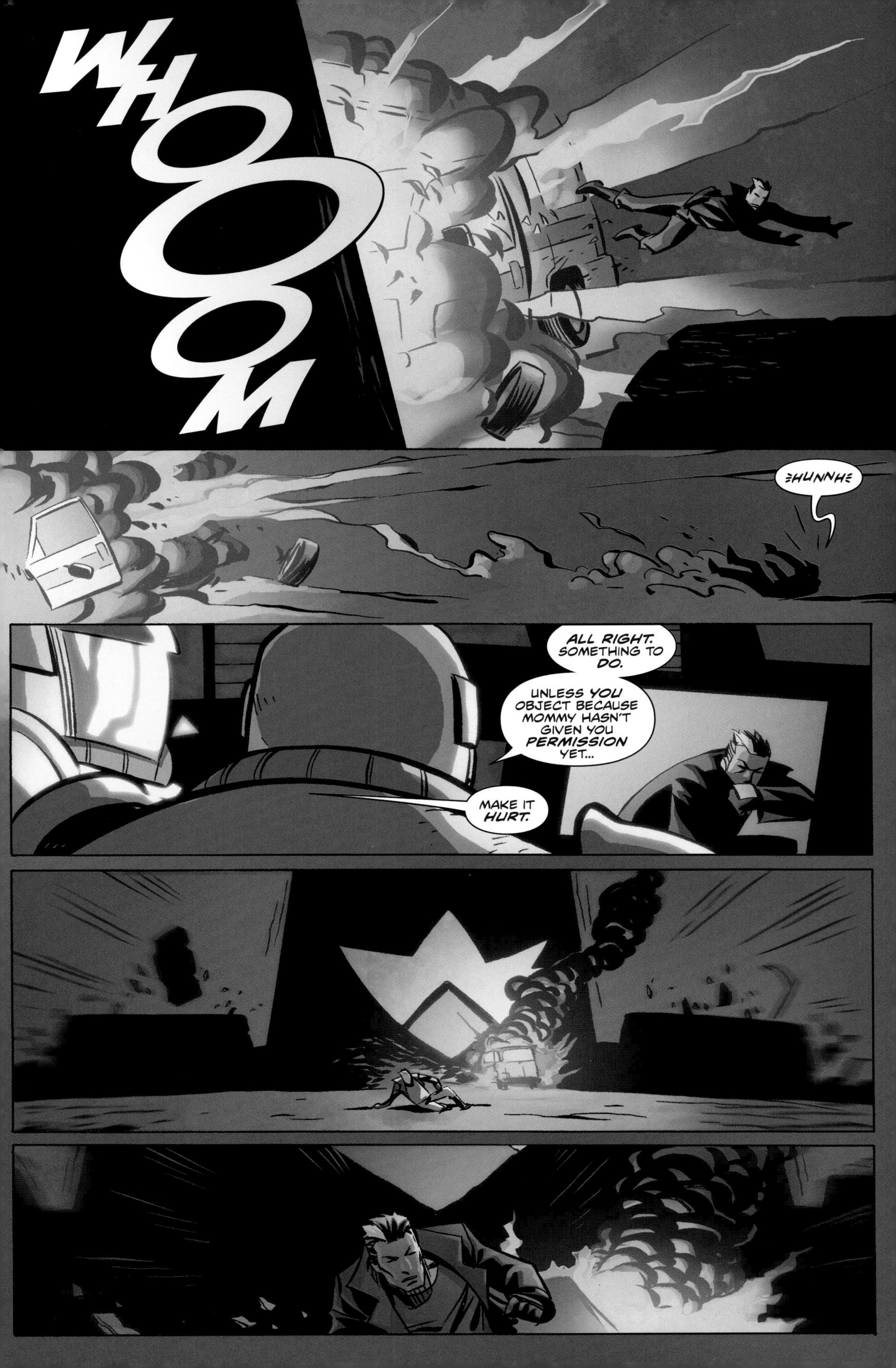
WHOOOM
HUNNH
ALL RIGHT. SOMETHING TO DO.
UNLESS YOU OBJECT BECAUSE MOMMY HASN'T GIVEN YOU PERMISSION YET...
MAKE IT HURT.

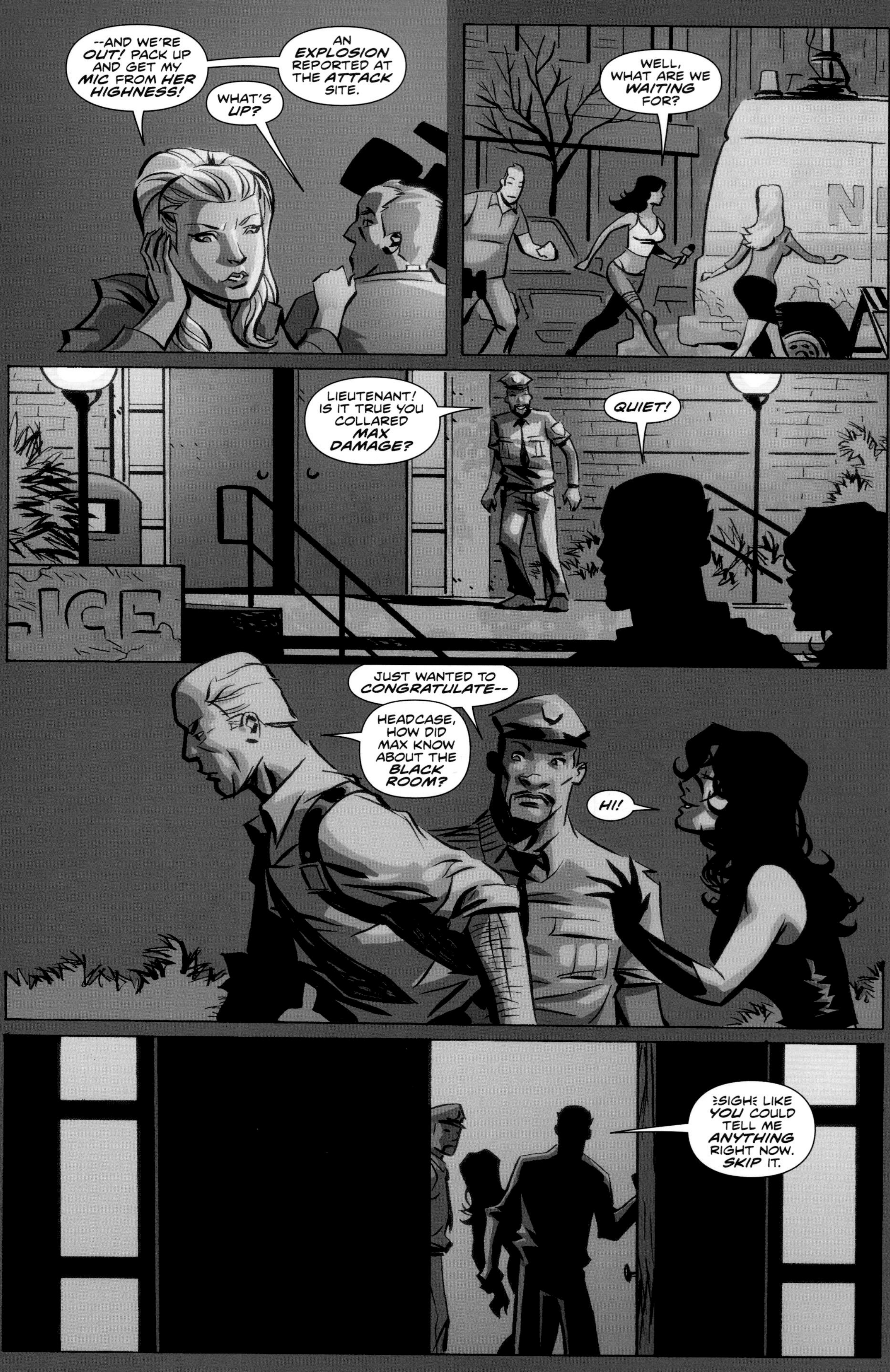
--AND WE'RE OUT! PACK UP AND GET MY MIC FROM HER HIGHNESS!
WHAT'S UP?
AN EXPLOSION REPORTED AT THE ATTACK SITE.
WELL, WHAT ARE WE WAITING FOR?
LIEUTENANT! IS IT TRUE YOU COLLARED MAX DAMAGE?
QUIET!
JUST WANTED TO CONGRATULATE--
HEADCASE, HOW DID MAX KNOW ABOUT THE BLACK ROOM?
HI!
ƸSIGHƷ LIKE YOU COULD TELL ME ANYTHING RIGHT NOW. SKIP IT.

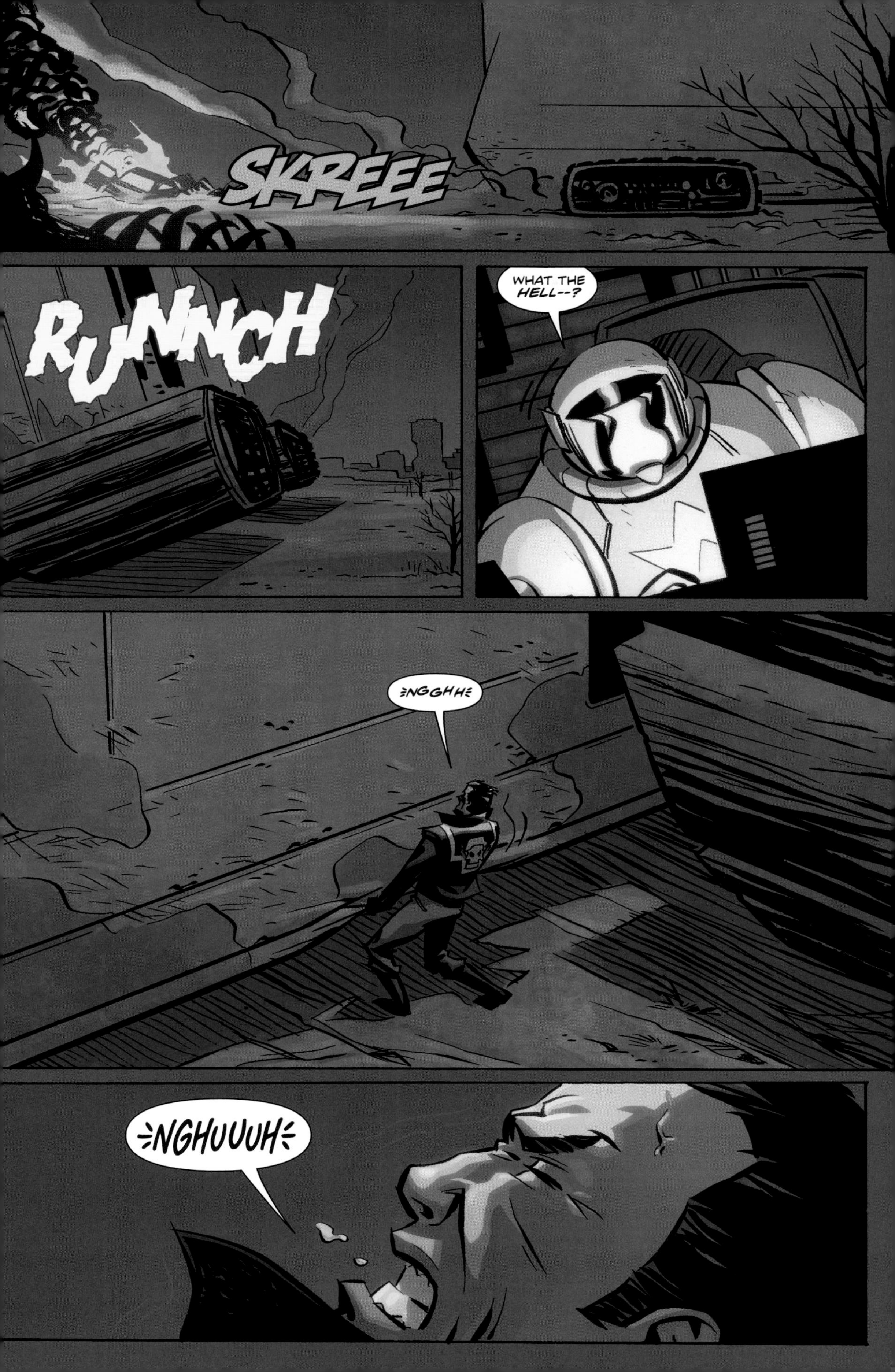
SKREEE
RUNNCH
WHAT THE HELL--?
NGGHH
NGHUUUH

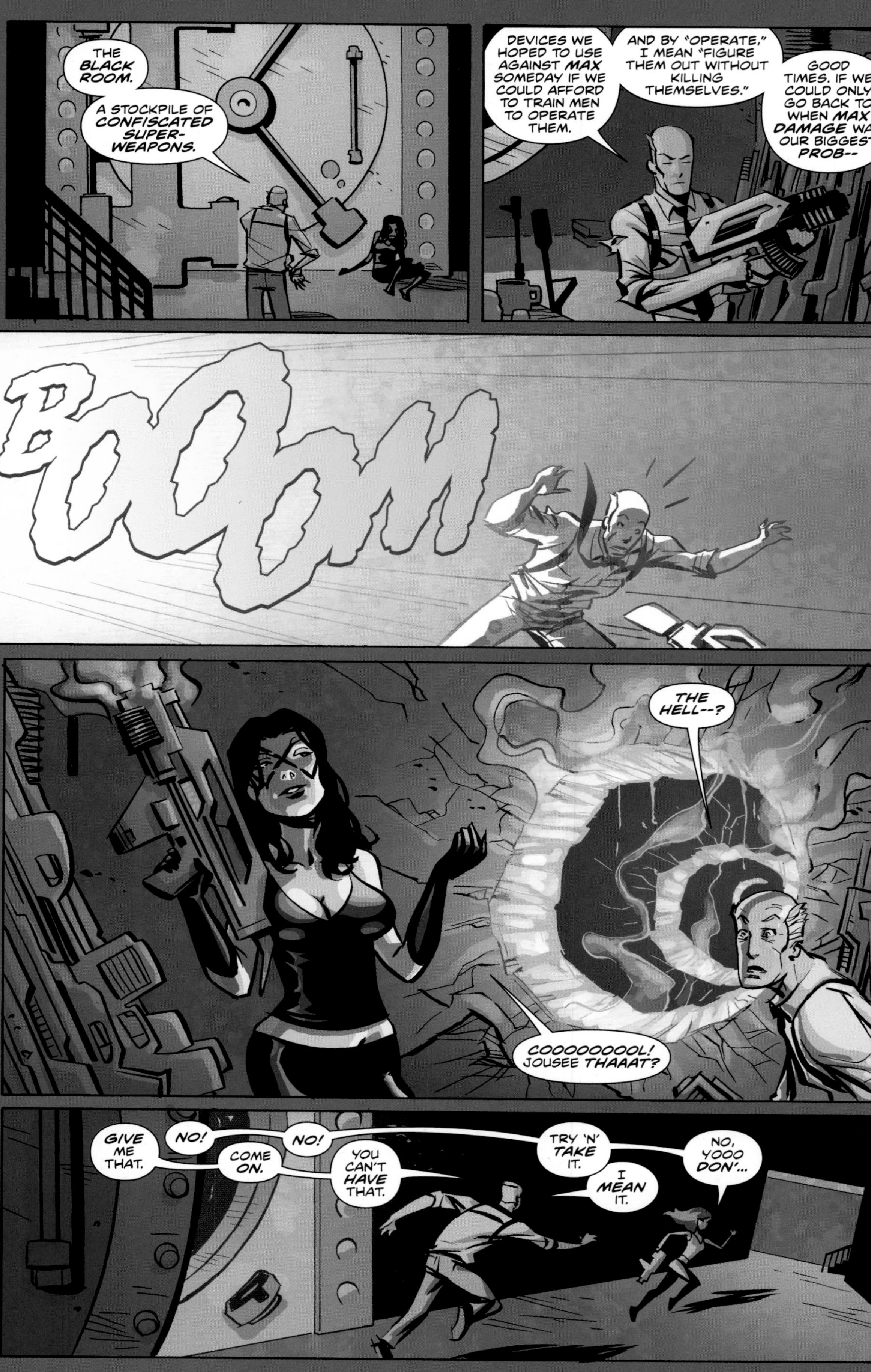
THE BLACK ROOM.
A STOCKPILE OF CONFISCATED SUPER-WEAPONS.
DEVICES WE HOPED TO USE AGAINST MAX SOMEDAY IF WE COULD AFFORD TO TRAIN MEN TO OPERATE THEM.
AND BY "OPERATE," I MEAN "FIGURE THEM OUT WITHOUT KILLING THEMSELVES."
GOOD TIMES. IF WE COULD ONLY GO BACK TO WHEN MAX DAMAGE WAS OUR BIGGEST PROB--
BOOOM
THE HELL--?
COOOOOOOOL! JOUSEE THAAAT?
GIVE ME THAT.
NO!
COME ON.
NO!
YOU CAN'T HAVE THAT.
TRY 'N' TAKE IT.
I MEAN IT.
NO, YOOO DON'...

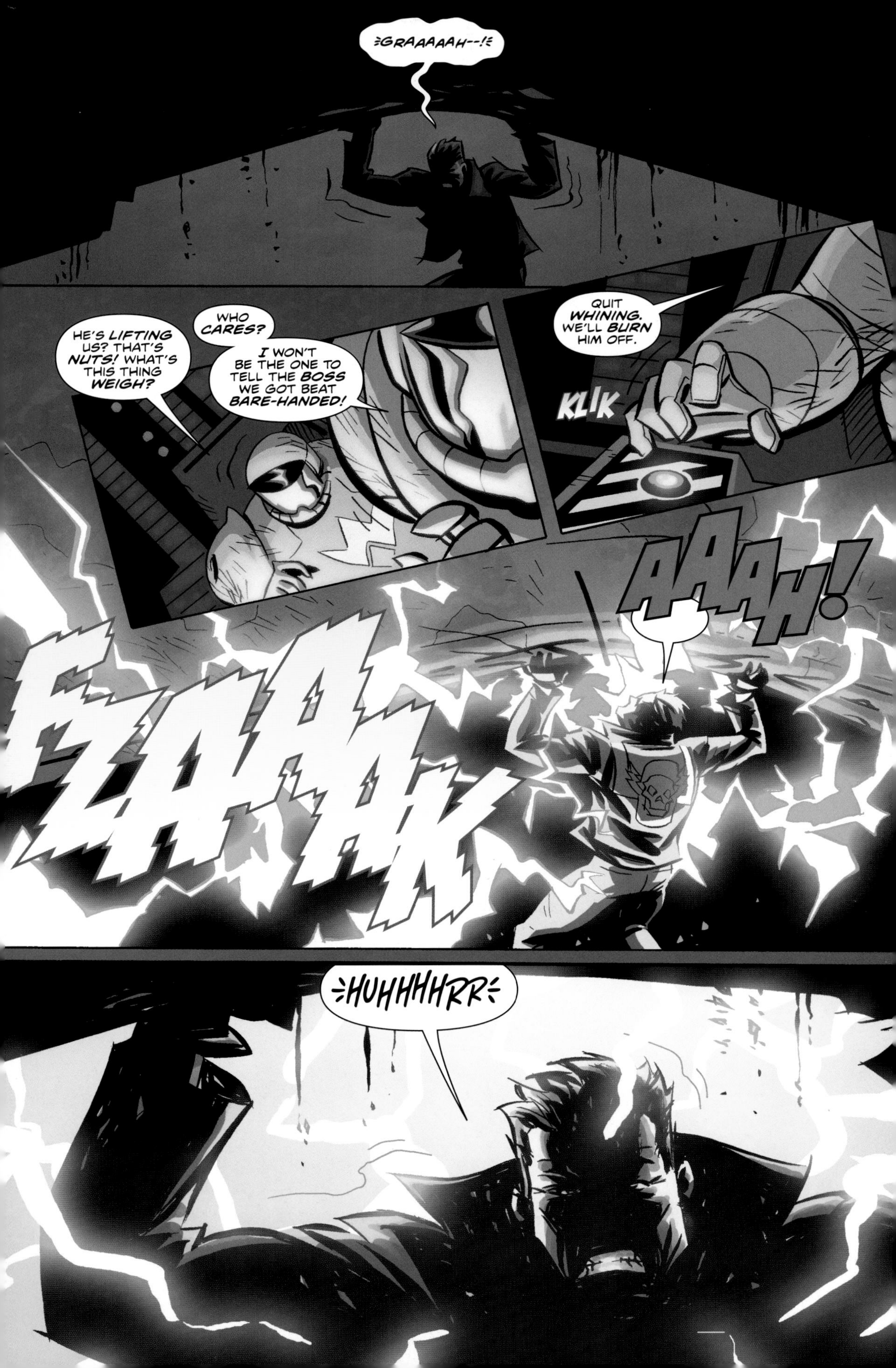

GRAAAAAH--!
HE'S LIFTING US? THAT'S NUTS! WHAT'S THIS THING WEIGH?
WHO CARES?
I WON'T BE THE ONE TO TELL THE BOSS WE GOT BEAT BARE-HANDED!
QUIT WHINING. WE'LL BURN HIM OFF.
KLIK
AAAH!
ZAAK
HUHHHHRR

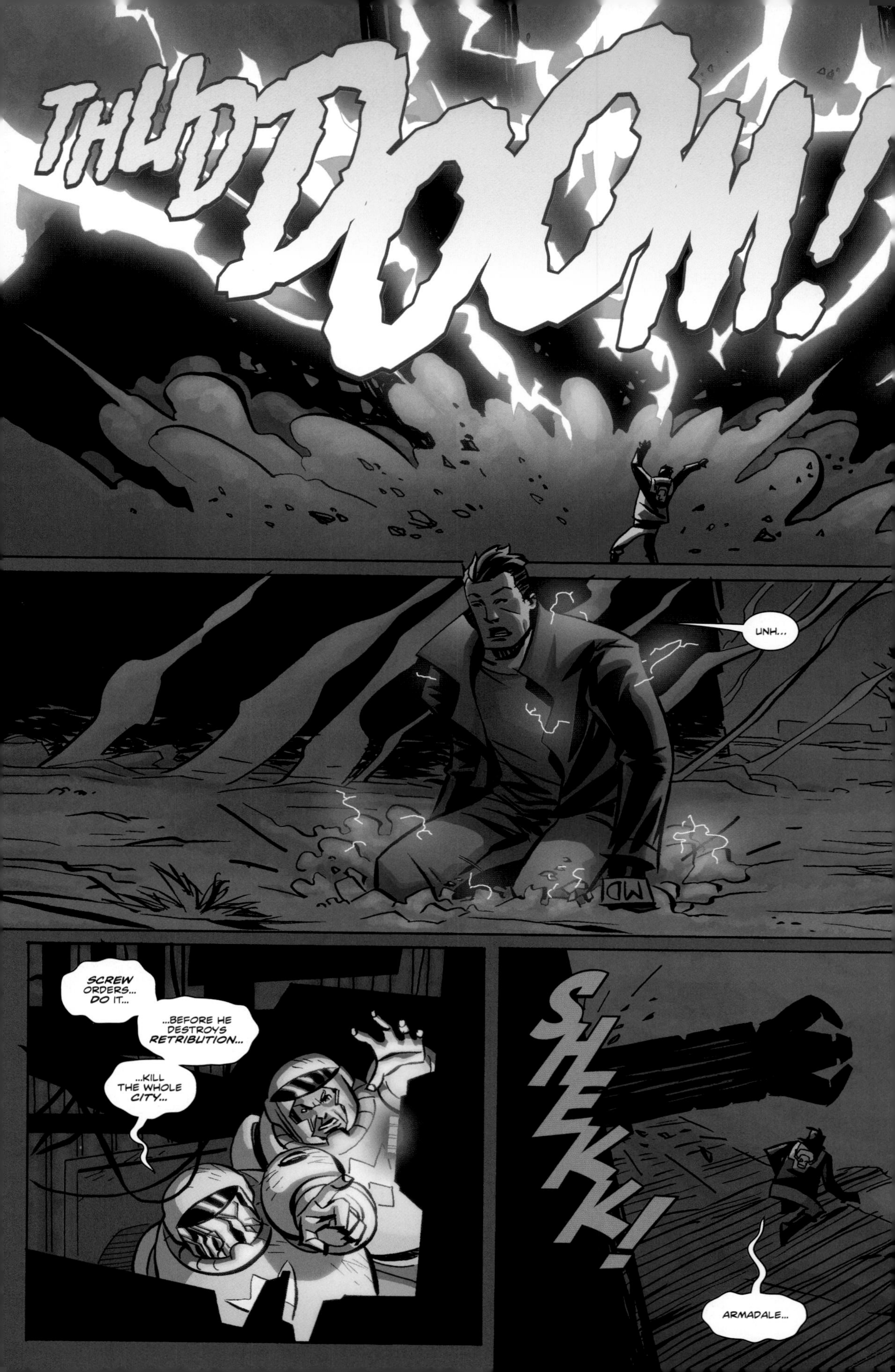
THUDDOOM!
UNH...
SCREW ORDERS... DO IT...
...BEFORE HE DESTROYS RETRIBUTION...
...KILL THE WHOLE CITY...
SHEKK!
ARMADALE...

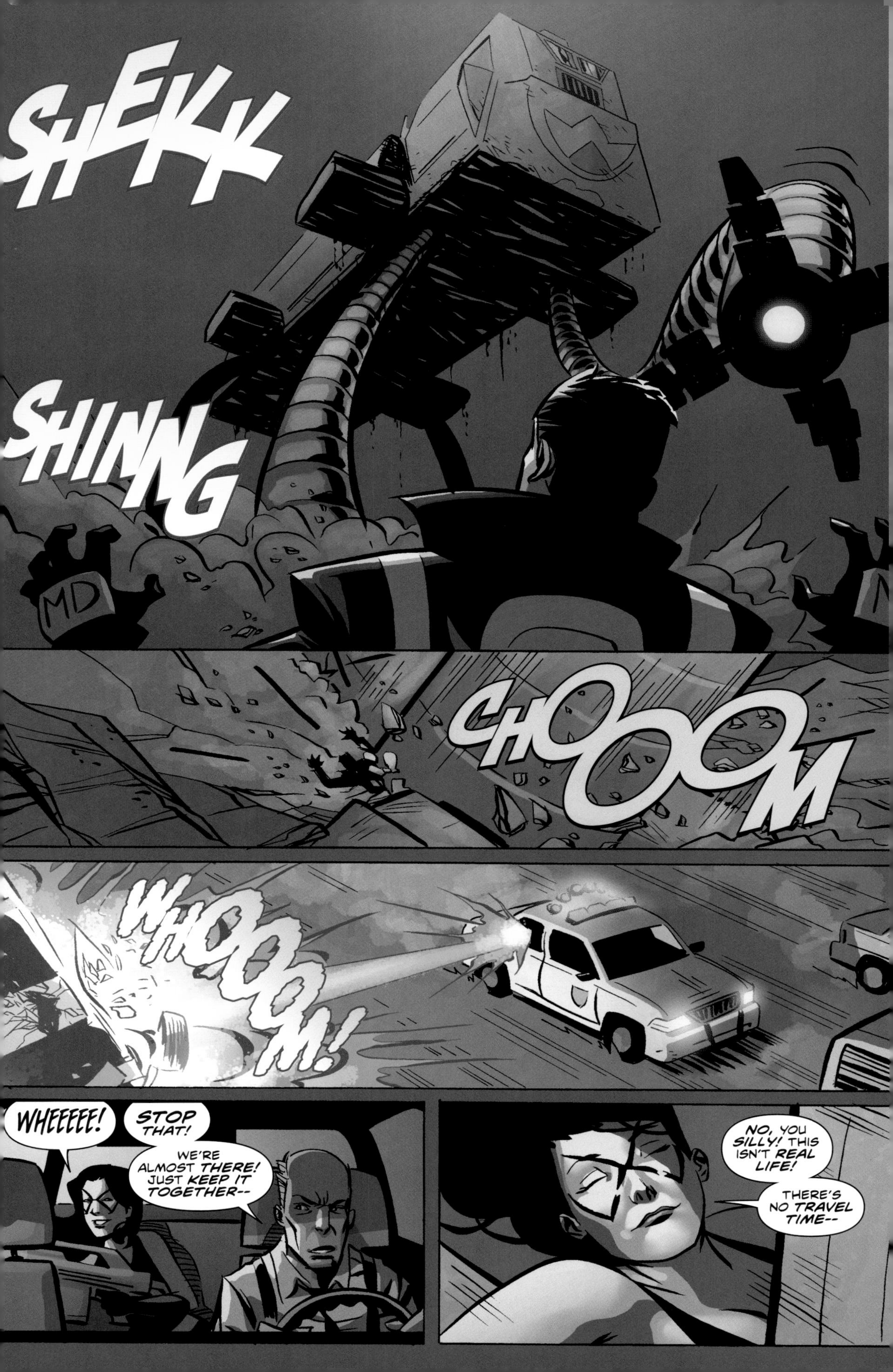
SHEKK
SHINNG
CHOOOM
WHOOOOM!
WHEEEEEE!
STOP THAT!
WE'RE ALMOST THERE! JUST KEEP IT TOGETHER--
NO, YOU SILLY! THIS ISN'T REAL LIFE!
THERE'S NO TRAVEL TIME--

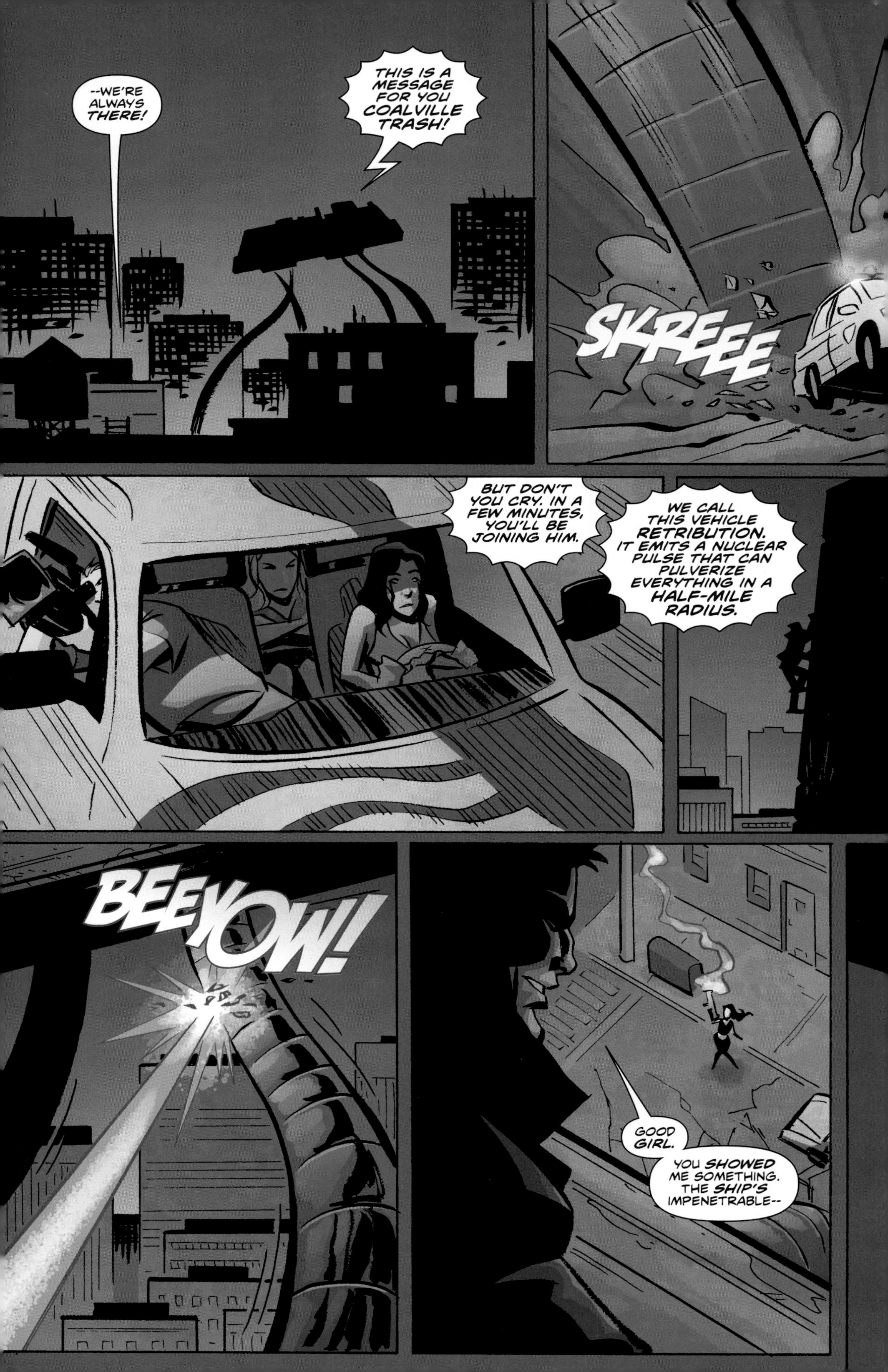
--WE'RE ALWAYS THERE!
THIS IS A MESSAGE FOR YOU COALVILLE TRASH!
SKREEE
BUT DON'T YOU CRY. IN A FEW MINUTES, YOU'LL BE JOINING HIM.
WE CALL THIS VEHICLE RETRIBUTION. IT EMITS A NUCLEAR PULSE THAT CAN PULVERIZE EVERYTHING IN A HALF-MILE RADIUS.
BEEYOW!
GOOD GIRL.
YOU SHOWED ME SOMETHING. THE SHIP'S IMPENETRABLE--

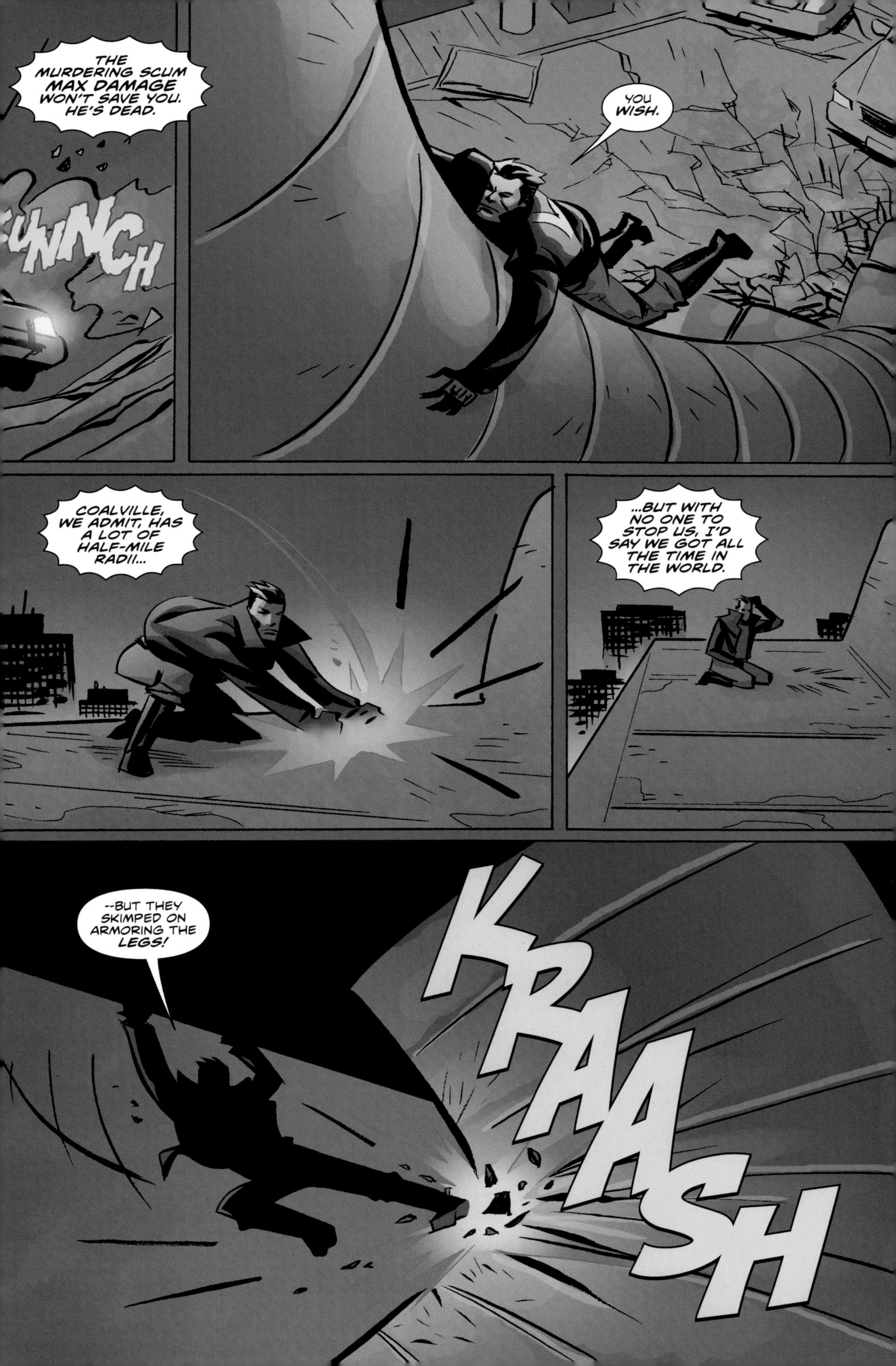
THE MURDERING SCUM MAX DAMAGE WON'T SAVE YOU. HE'S DEAD.
CUNNCH
YOU WISH.
COALVILLE, WE ADMIT, HAS A LOT OF HALF-MILE RADII...
...BUT WITH NO ONE TO STOP US, I'D SAY WE GOT ALL THE TIME IN THE WORLD.
--BUT THEY SKIMPED ON ARMORING THE LEGS!
KRAASH

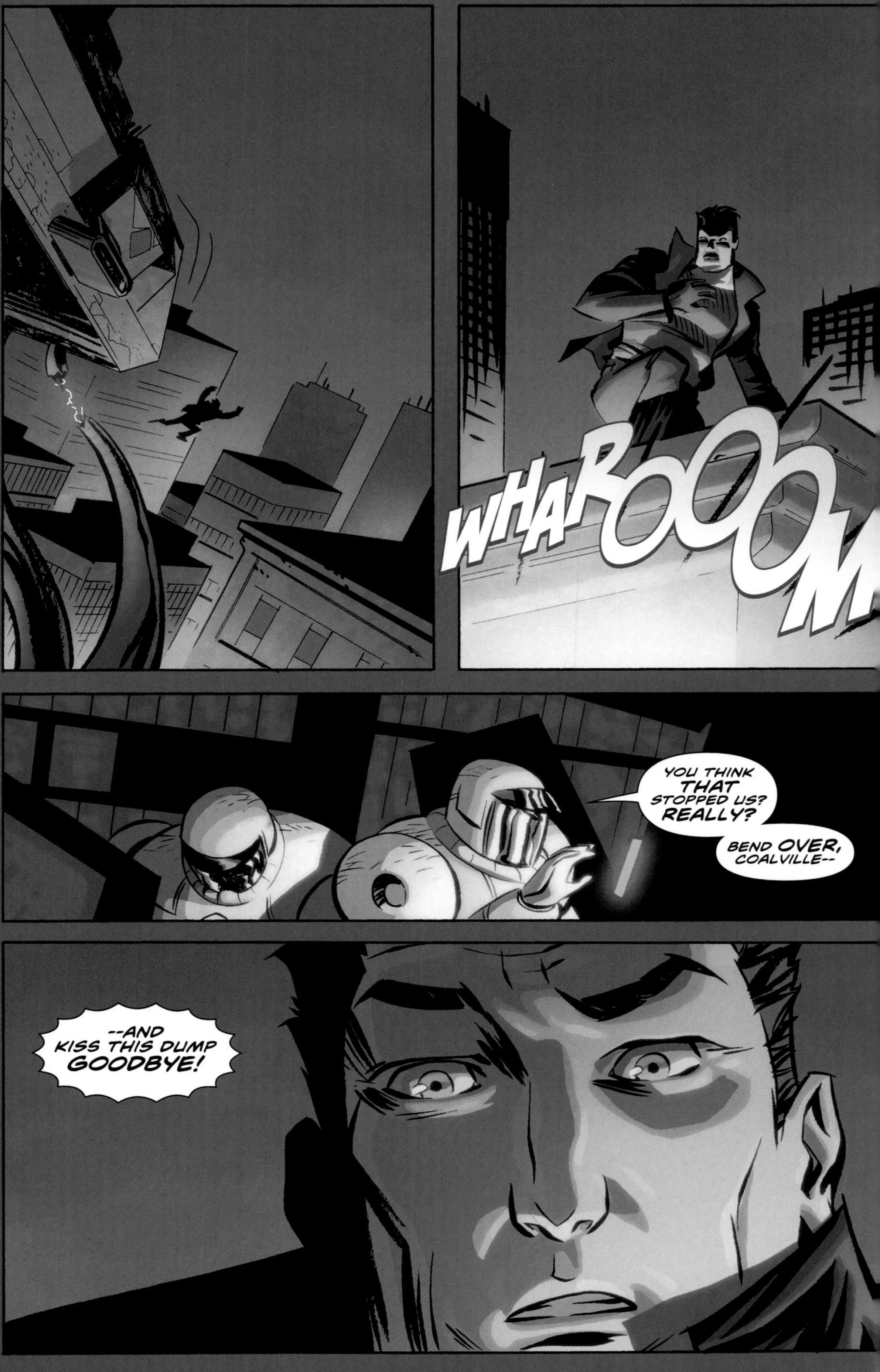
WHAROOOOM
YOU THINK THAT STOPPED US? REALLY?
BEND OVER, COALVILLE--
--AND KISS THIS DUMP GOODBYE!

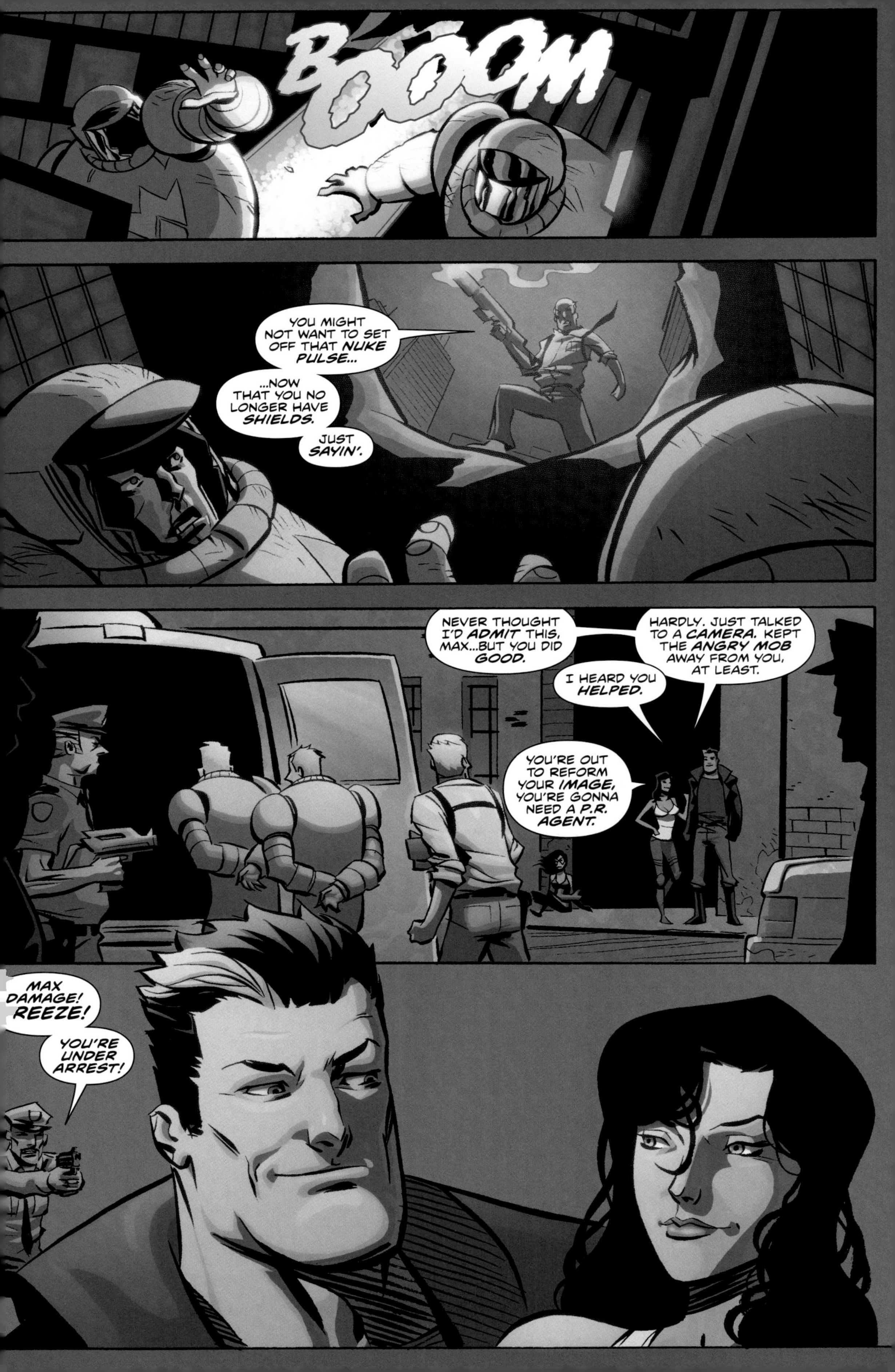
BOOOM
YOU MIGHT NOT WANT TO SET OFF THAT NUKE PULSE...
...NOW THAT YOU NO LONGER HAVE SHIELDS.
JUST SAYIN'.
NEVER THOUGHT I'D ADMIT THIS, MAX...BUT YOU DID GOOD.
HARDLY. JUST TALKED TO A CAMERA. KEPT THE ANGRY MOB AWAY FROM YOU, AT LEAST.
I HEARD YOU HELPED.
YOU'RE OUT TO REFORM YOUR IMAGE, YOU'RE GONNA NEED A P.R. AGENT.
MAX DAMAGE! REEZE!
YOU'RE UNDER ARREST!

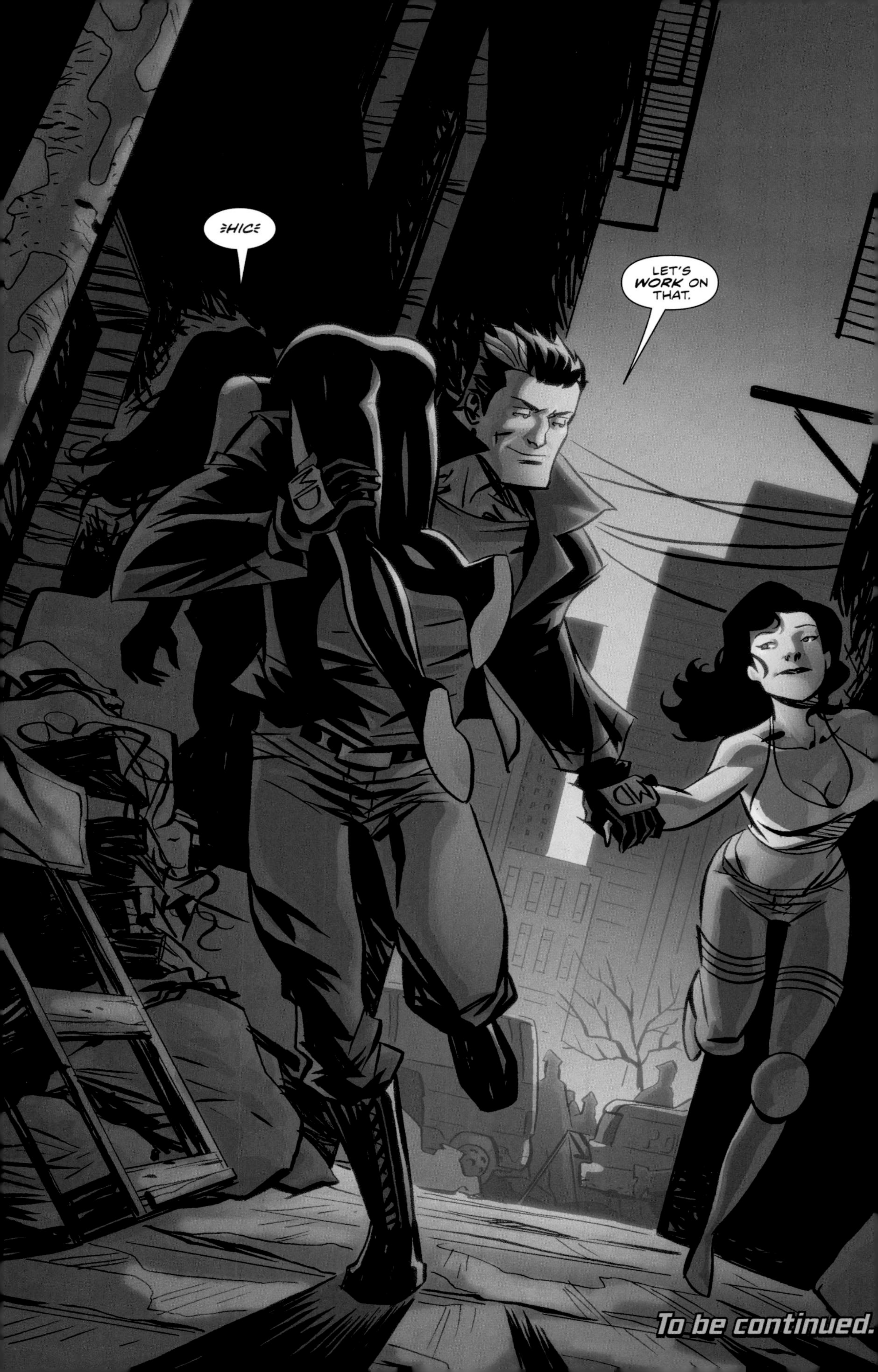
HIC
LET'S WORK ON THAT.
To be continued.

COVER
GALLERY

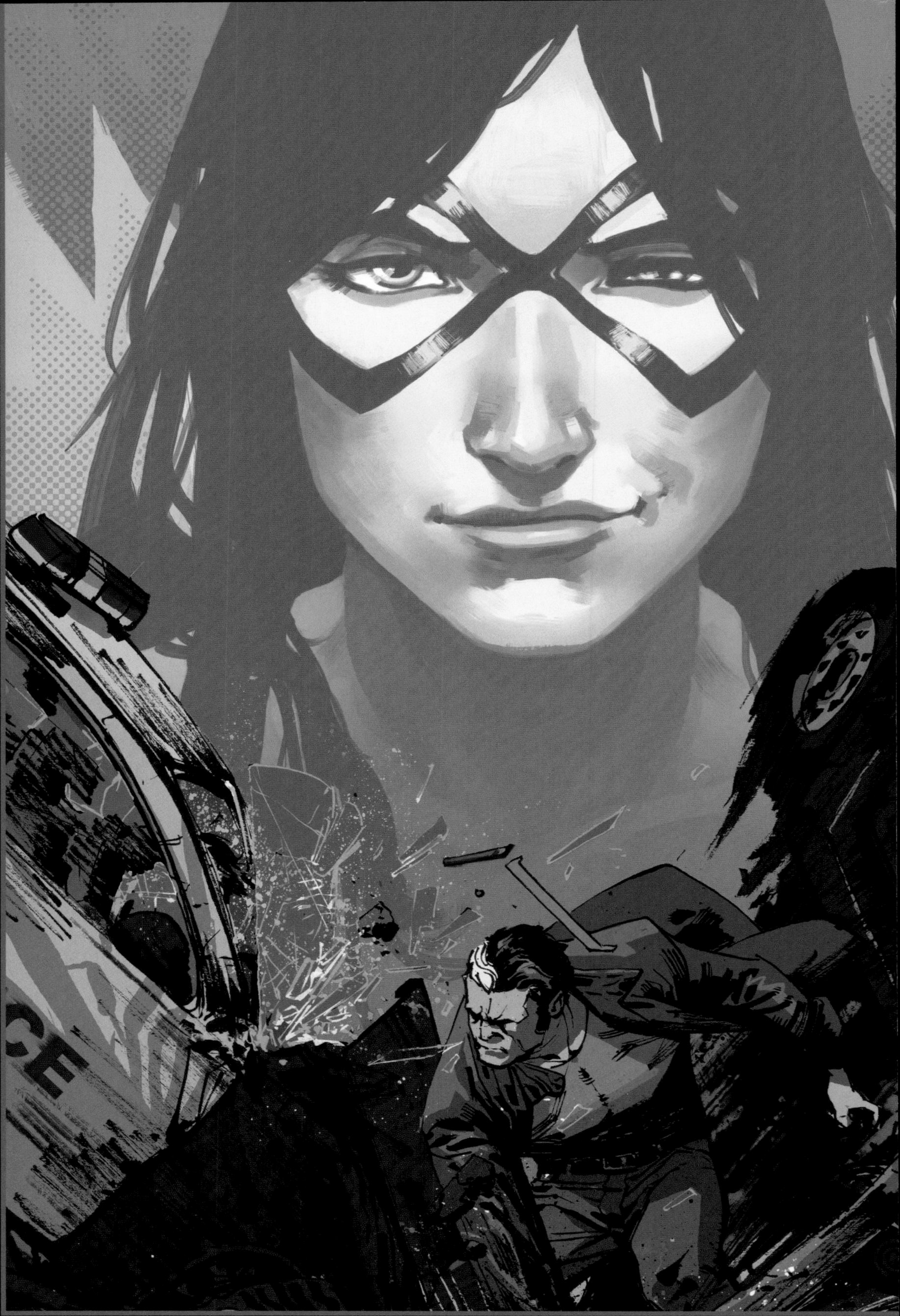

COVER 9A: CHRISTIAN NAUCK

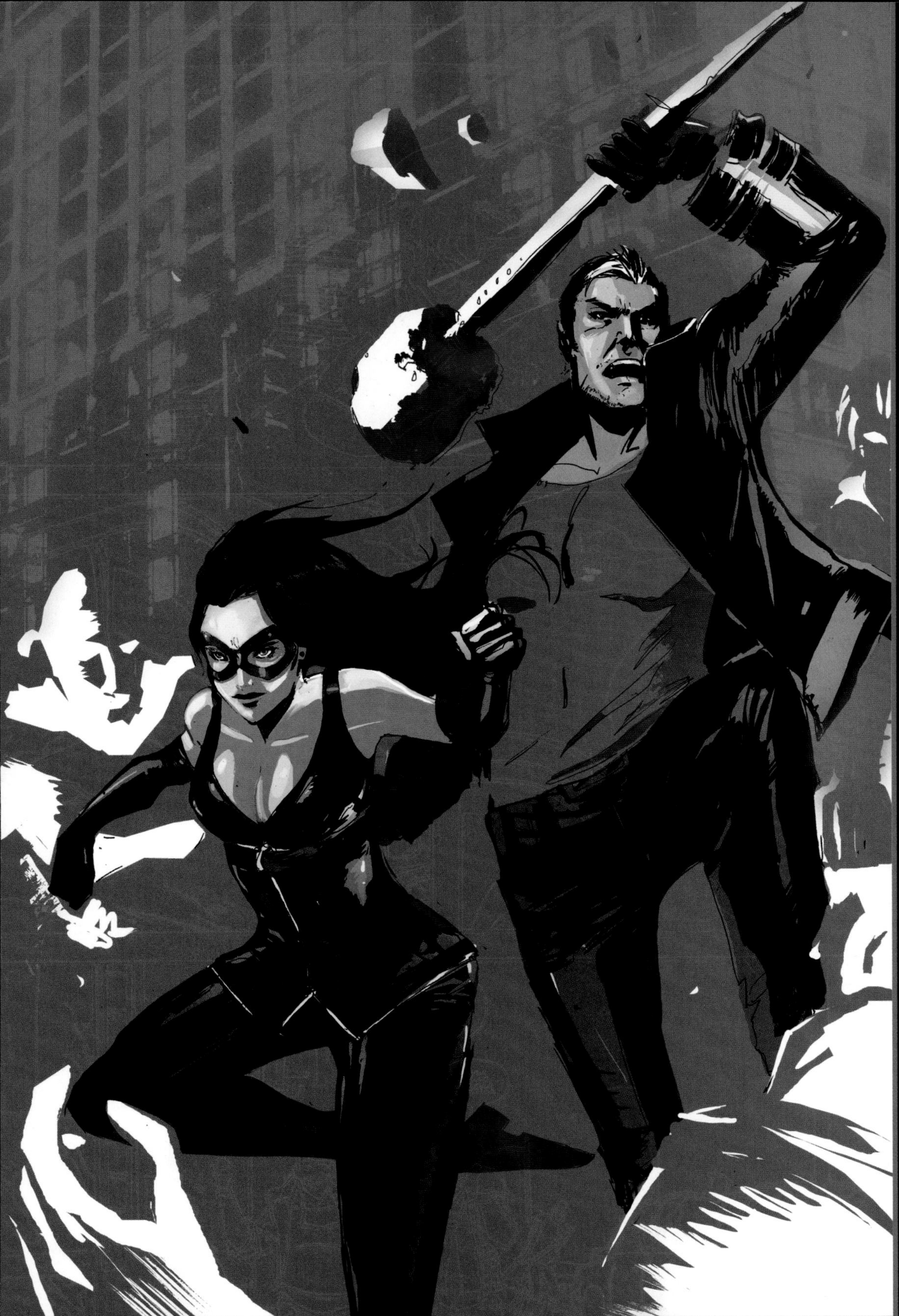

COVER 9B: **PETER NGUYEN**

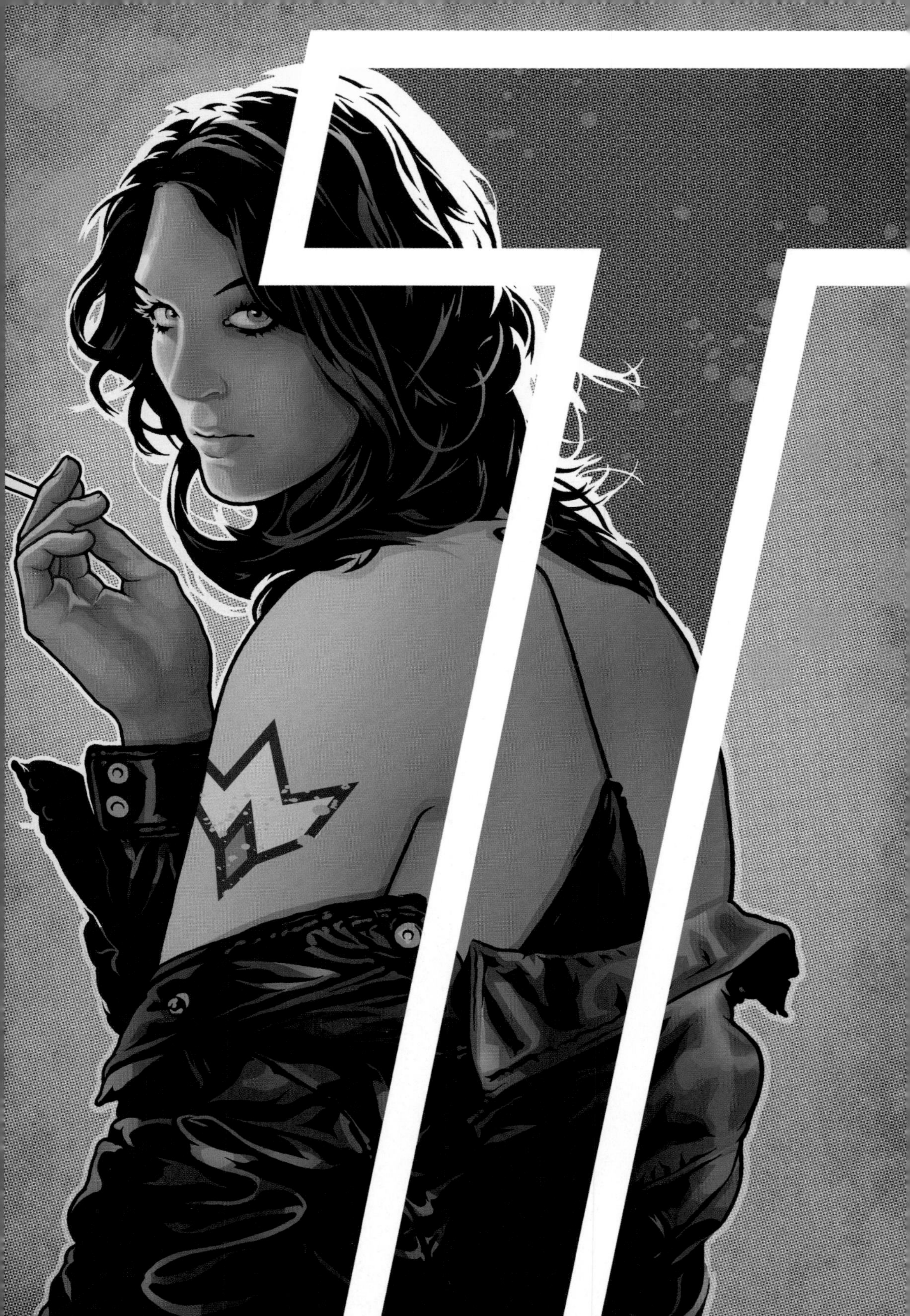

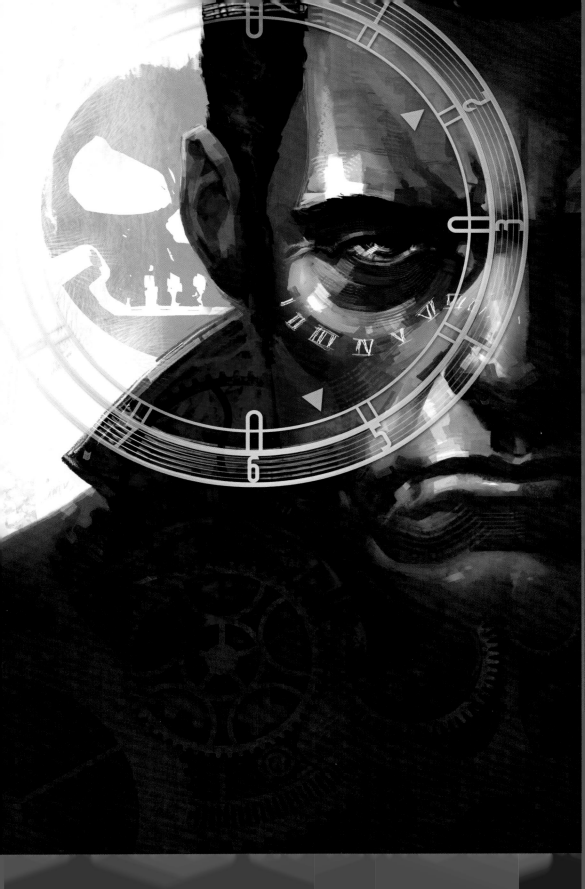

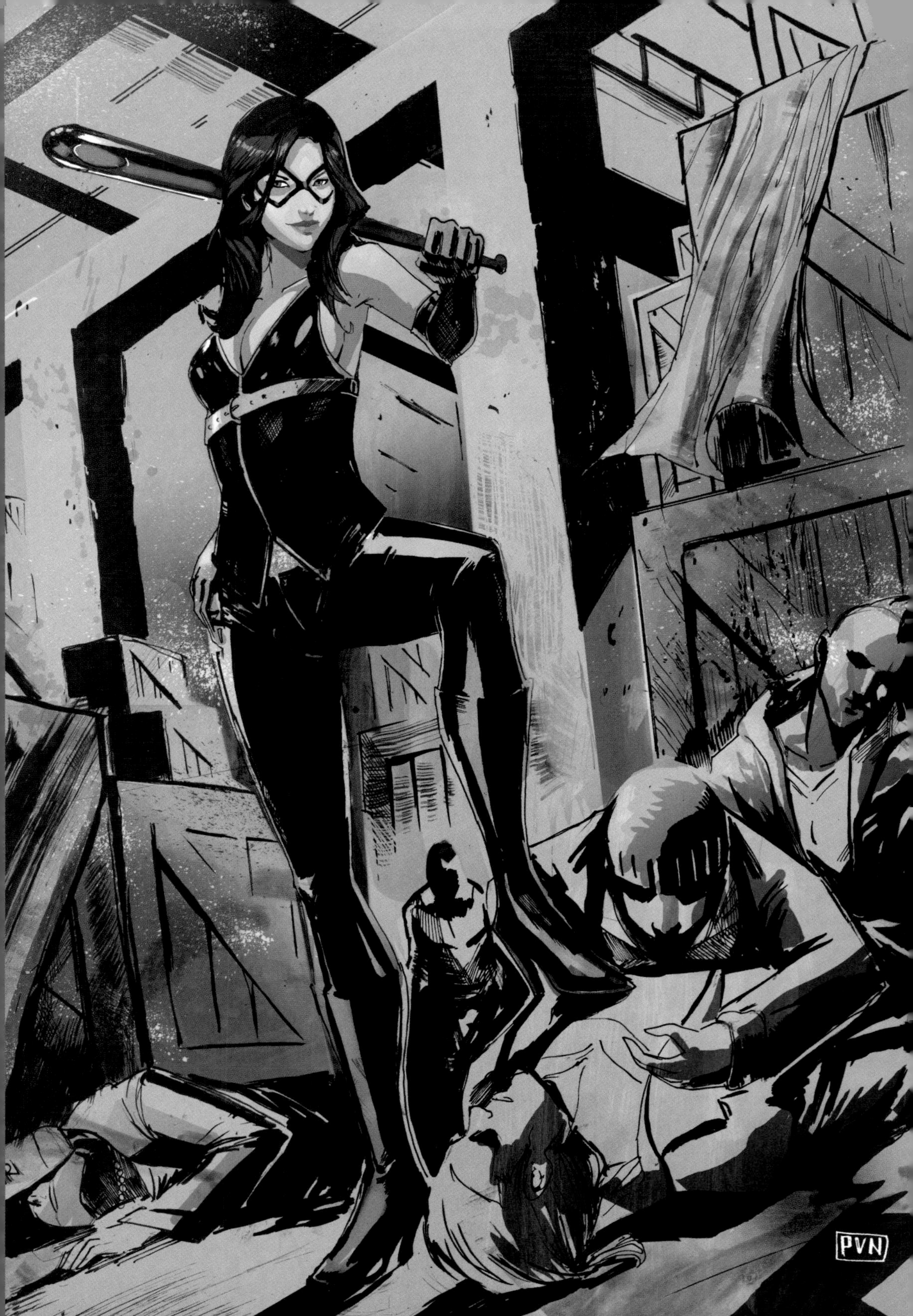
PVN

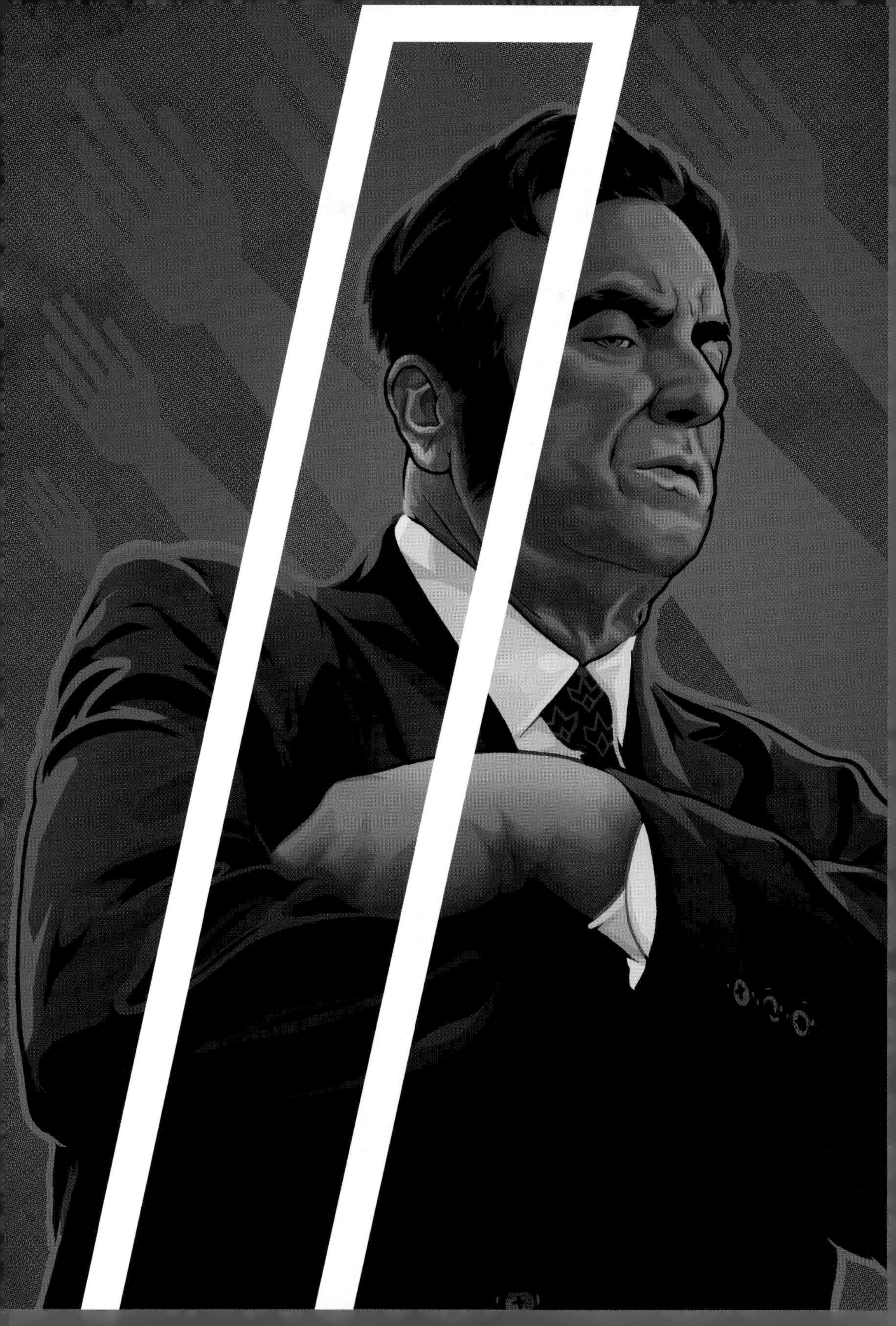

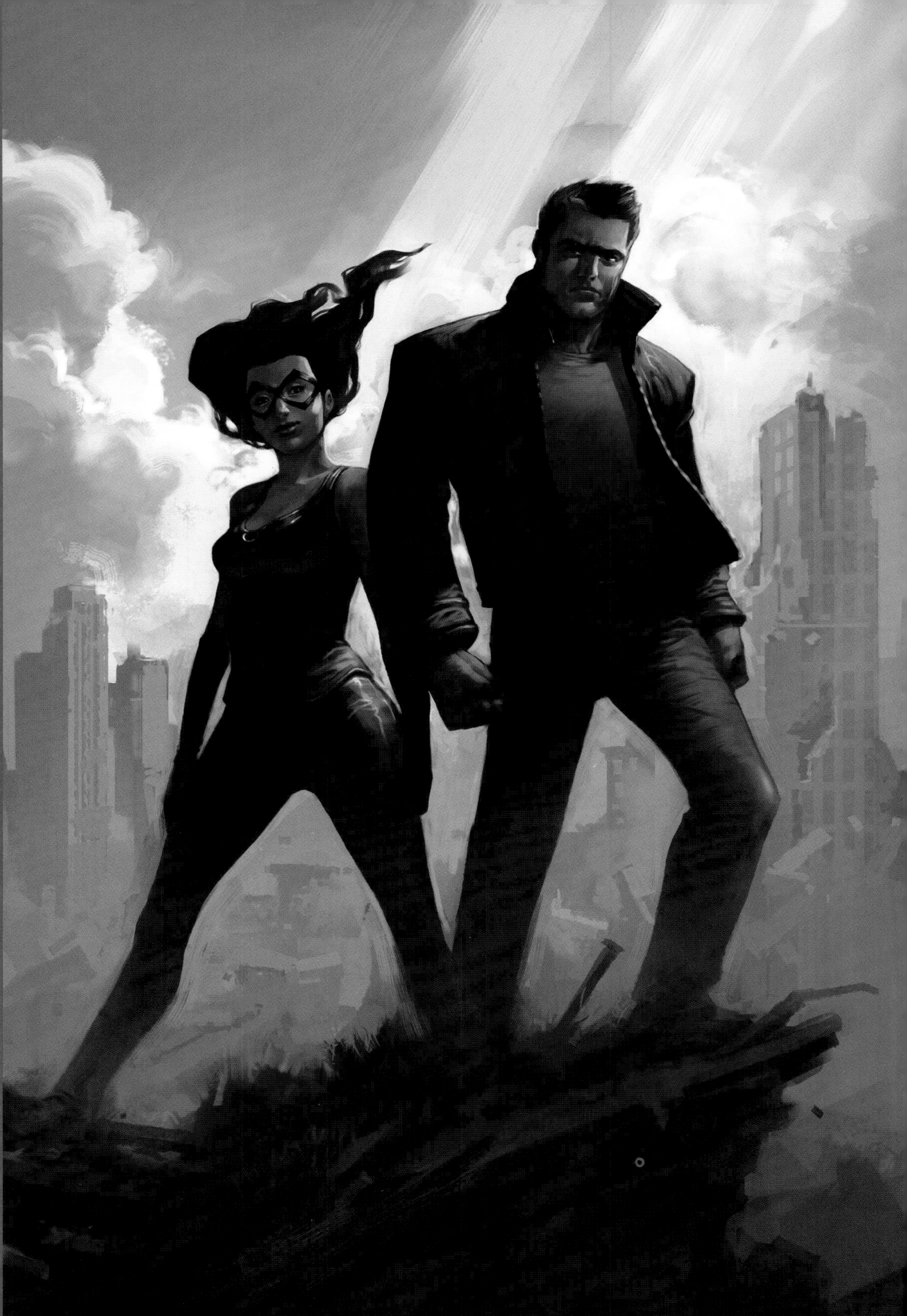

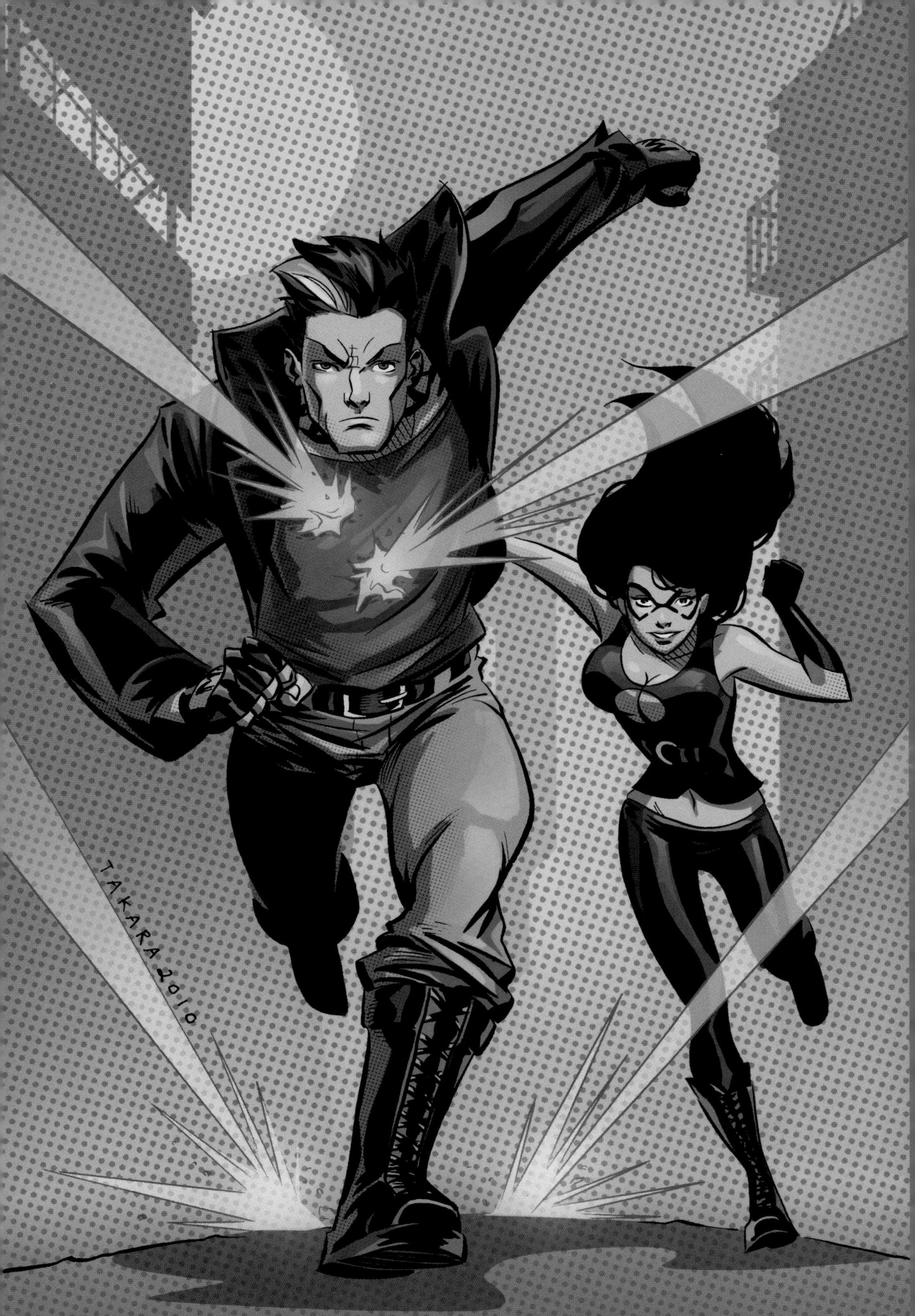
TAKARA 2010

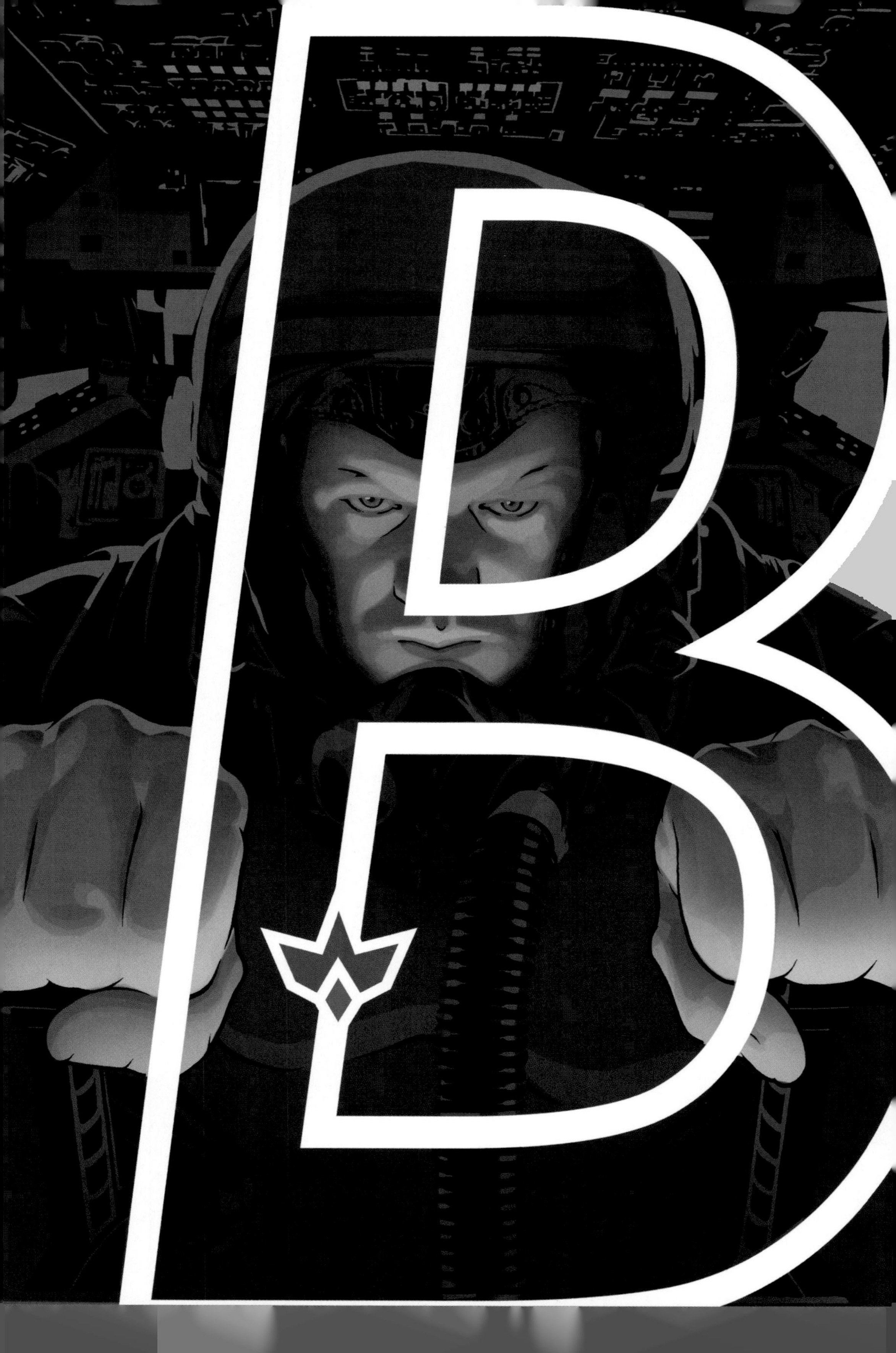

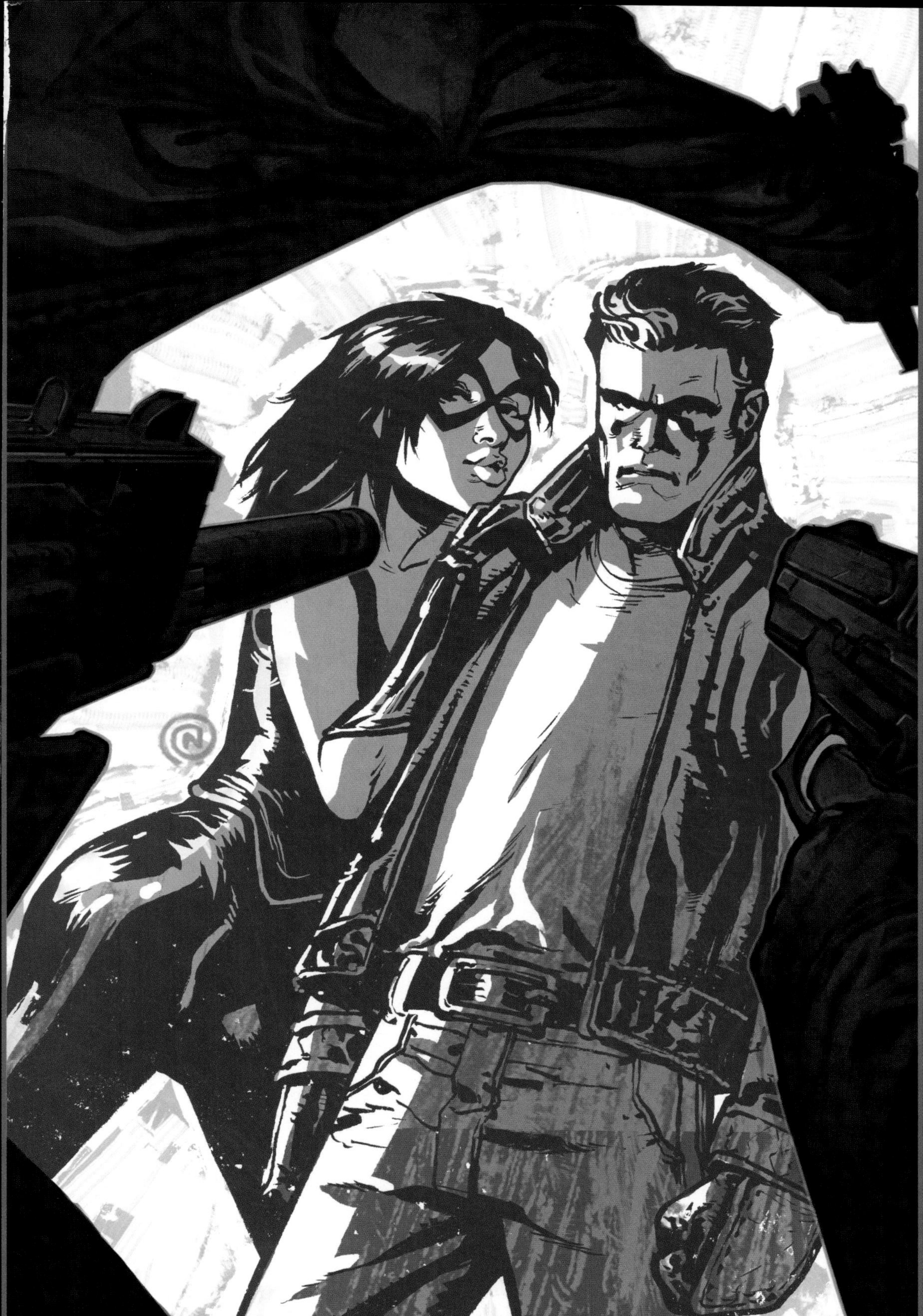

COVER 12A: CHRISTIAN NAUCK

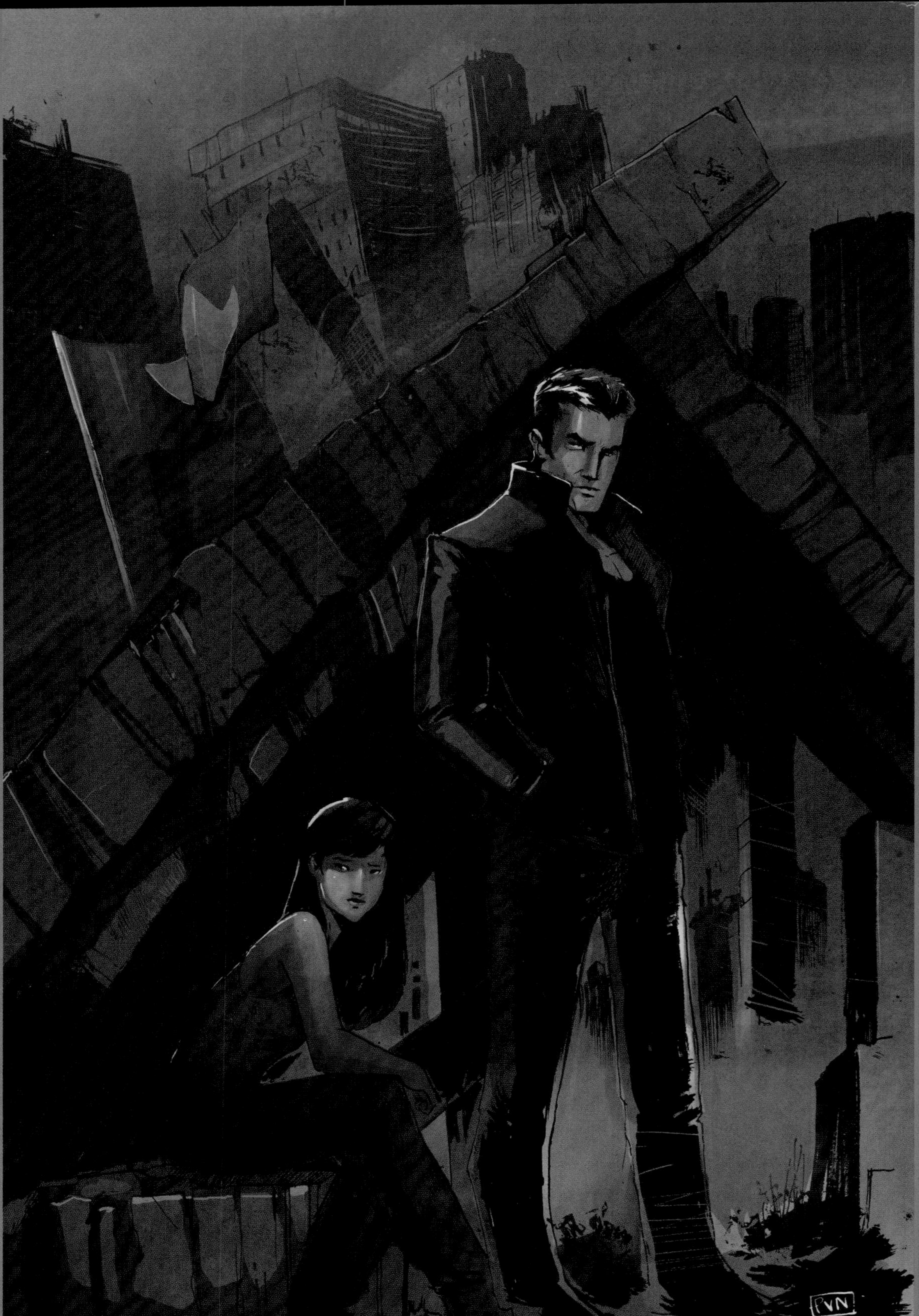
PVN

COVER 12B: PETER NGUYEN

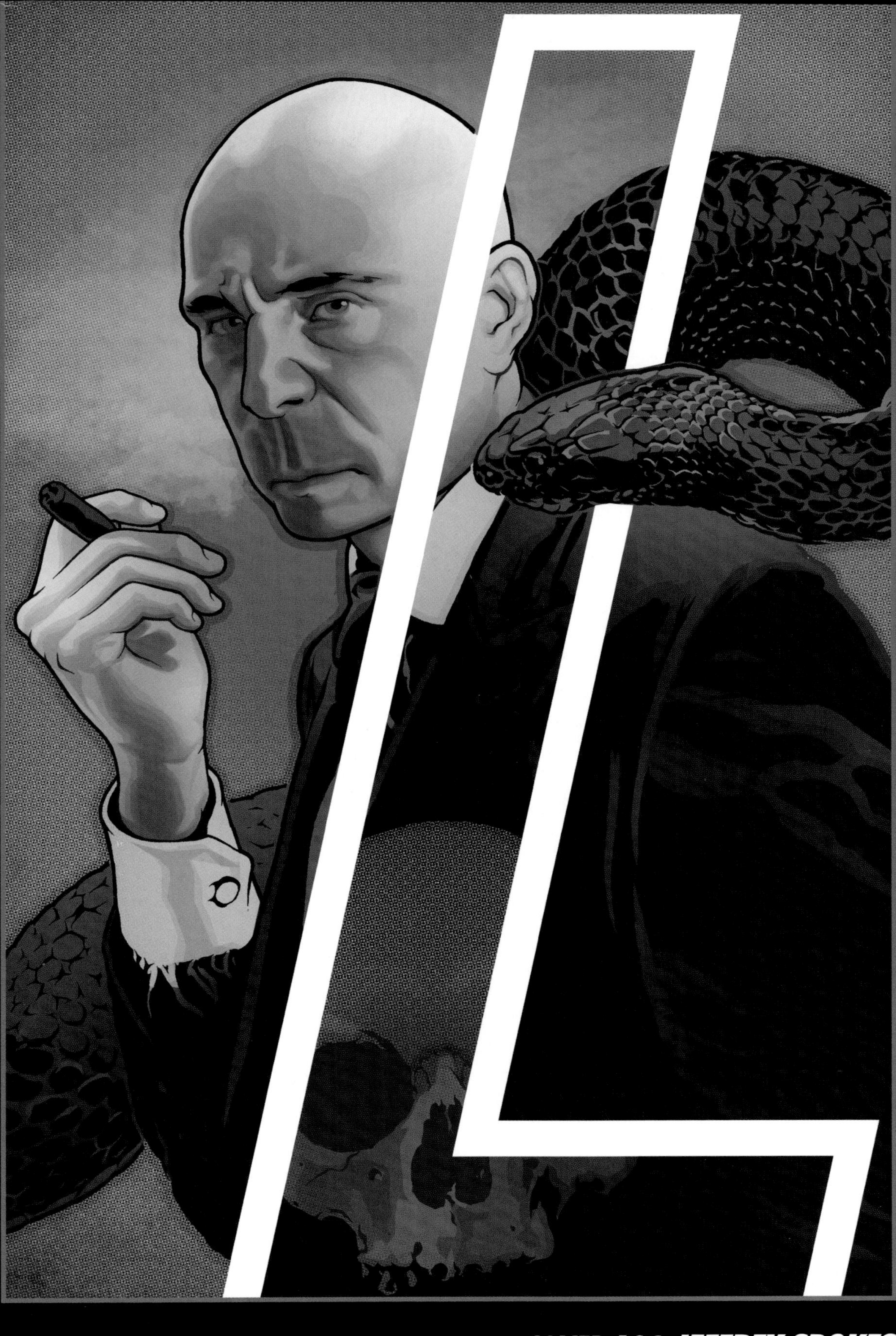

COVER 12C: JEFFREY SPOKES

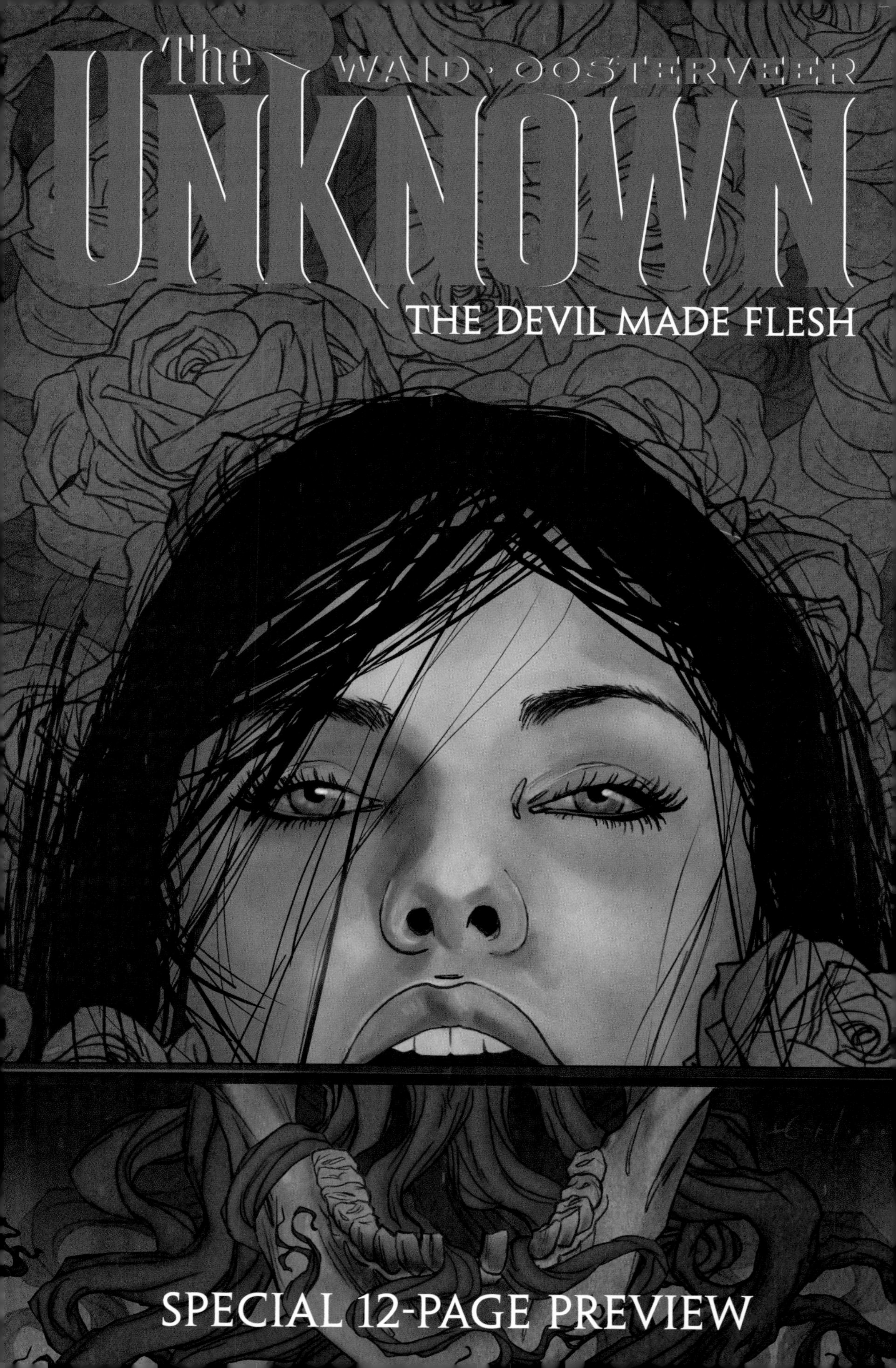

The Unknown
WAID · OOSTERVEER
THE DEVIL MADE FLESH
SPECIAL 12-PAGE PREVIEW

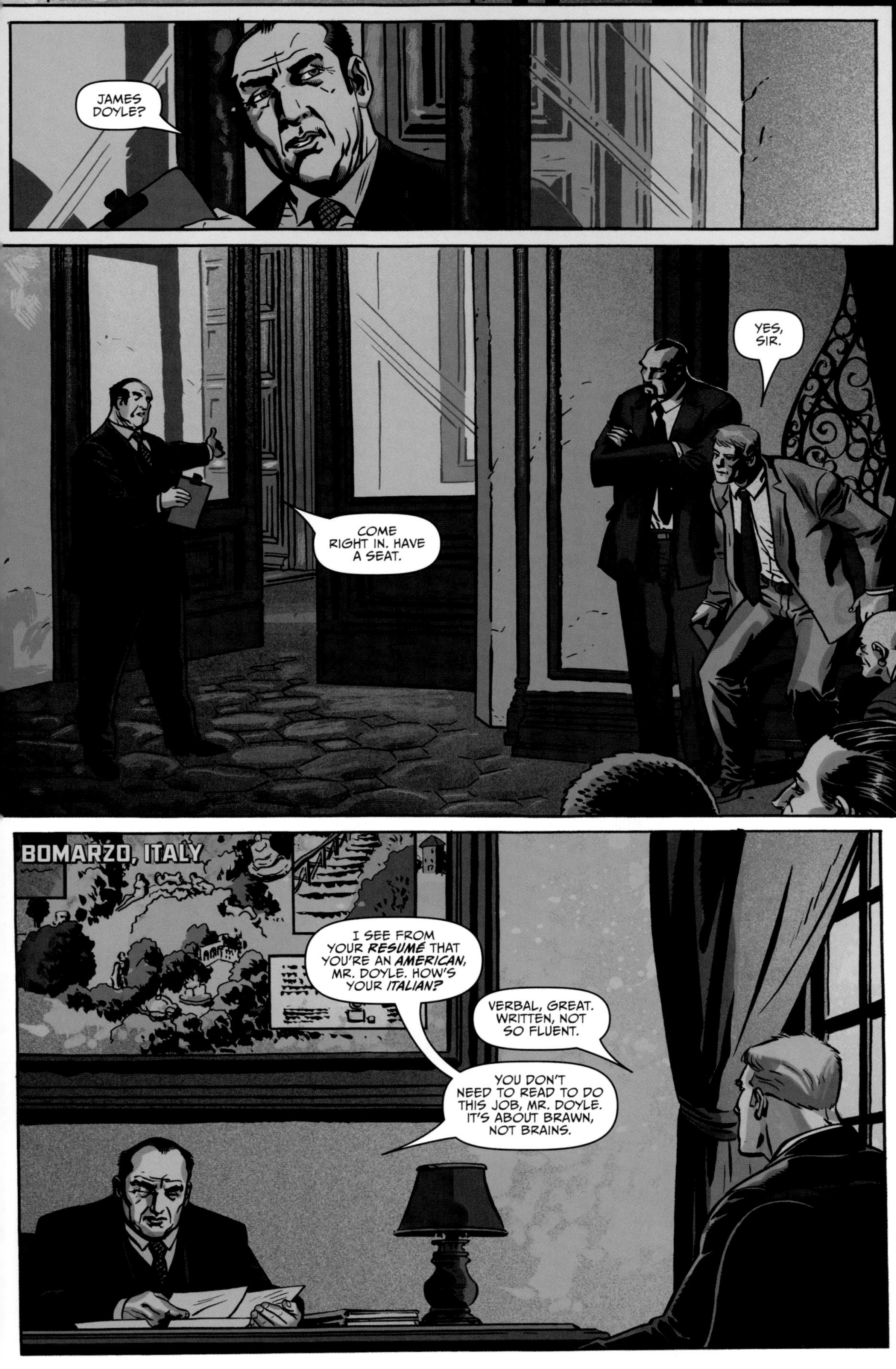
JAMES DOYLE?
YES, SIR.
COME RIGHT IN. HAVE A SEAT.
BOMARZO, ITALY
I SEE FROM YOUR **RESUMÉ** THAT YOU'RE AN ***AMERICAN***, MR. DOYLE. HOW'S YOUR ***ITALIAN?***
VERBAL, GREAT. WRITTEN, NOT SO FLUENT.
YOU DON'T NEED TO READ TO DO THIS JOB, MR. DOYLE. IT'S ABOUT BRAWN, NOT BRAINS.

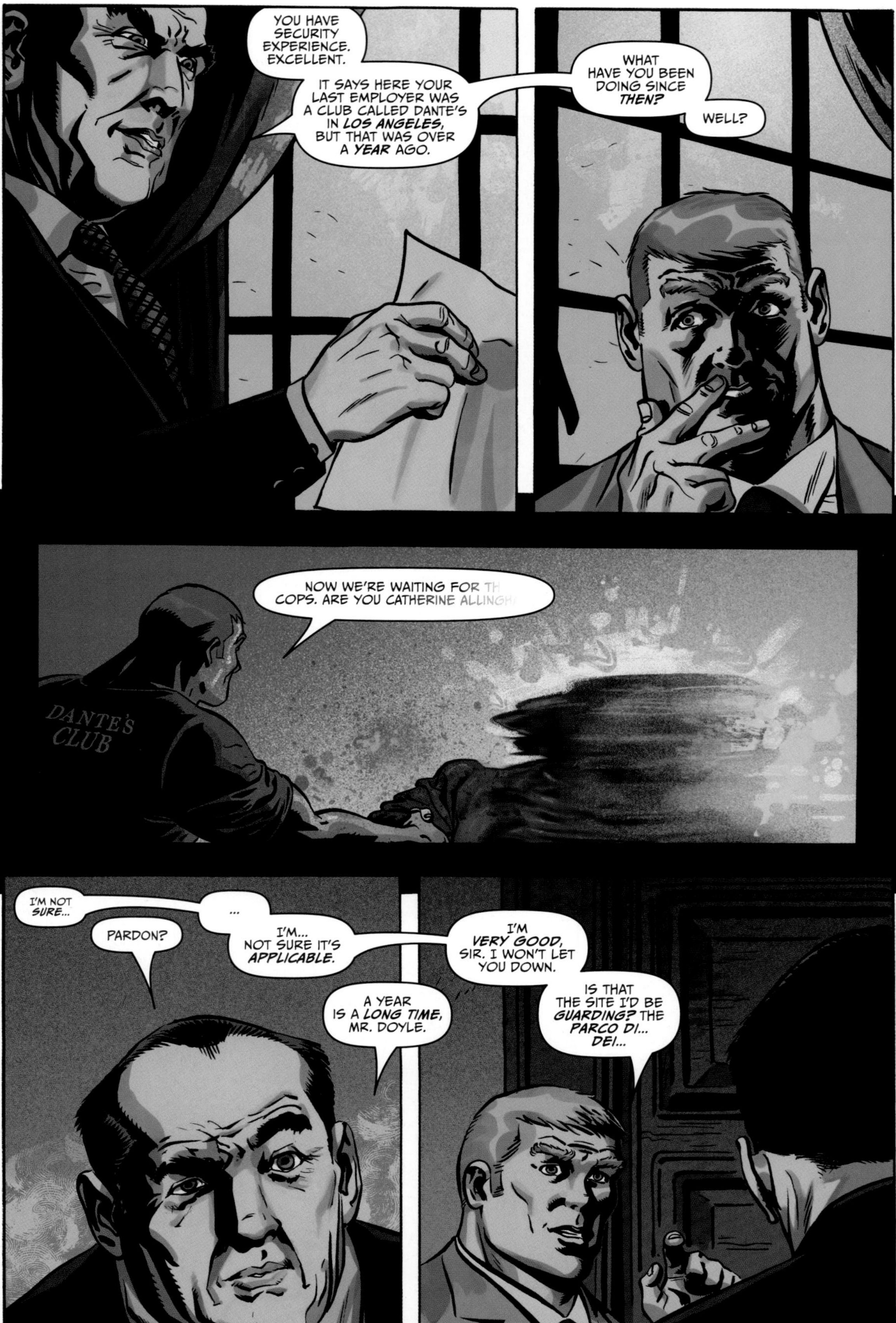
YOU HAVE SECURITY EXPERIENCE. EXCELLENT.
IT SAYS HERE YOUR LAST EMPLOYER WAS A CLUB CALLED DANTE'S IN LOS ANGELES, BUT THAT WAS OVER A YEAR AGO.
WHAT HAVE YOU BEEN DOING SINCE THEN?
WELL?
NOW WE'RE WAITING FOR TH COPS. ARE YOU CATHERINE ALLINGH
DANTE'S CLUB
I'M NOT SURE...
PARDON?
...
I'M... NOT SURE IT'S APPLICABLE.
A YEAR IS A LONG TIME, MR. DOYLE.
I'M VERY GOOD, SIR. I WON'T LET YOU DOWN.
IS THAT THE SITE I'D BE GUARDING? THE PARCO DI... DEI...

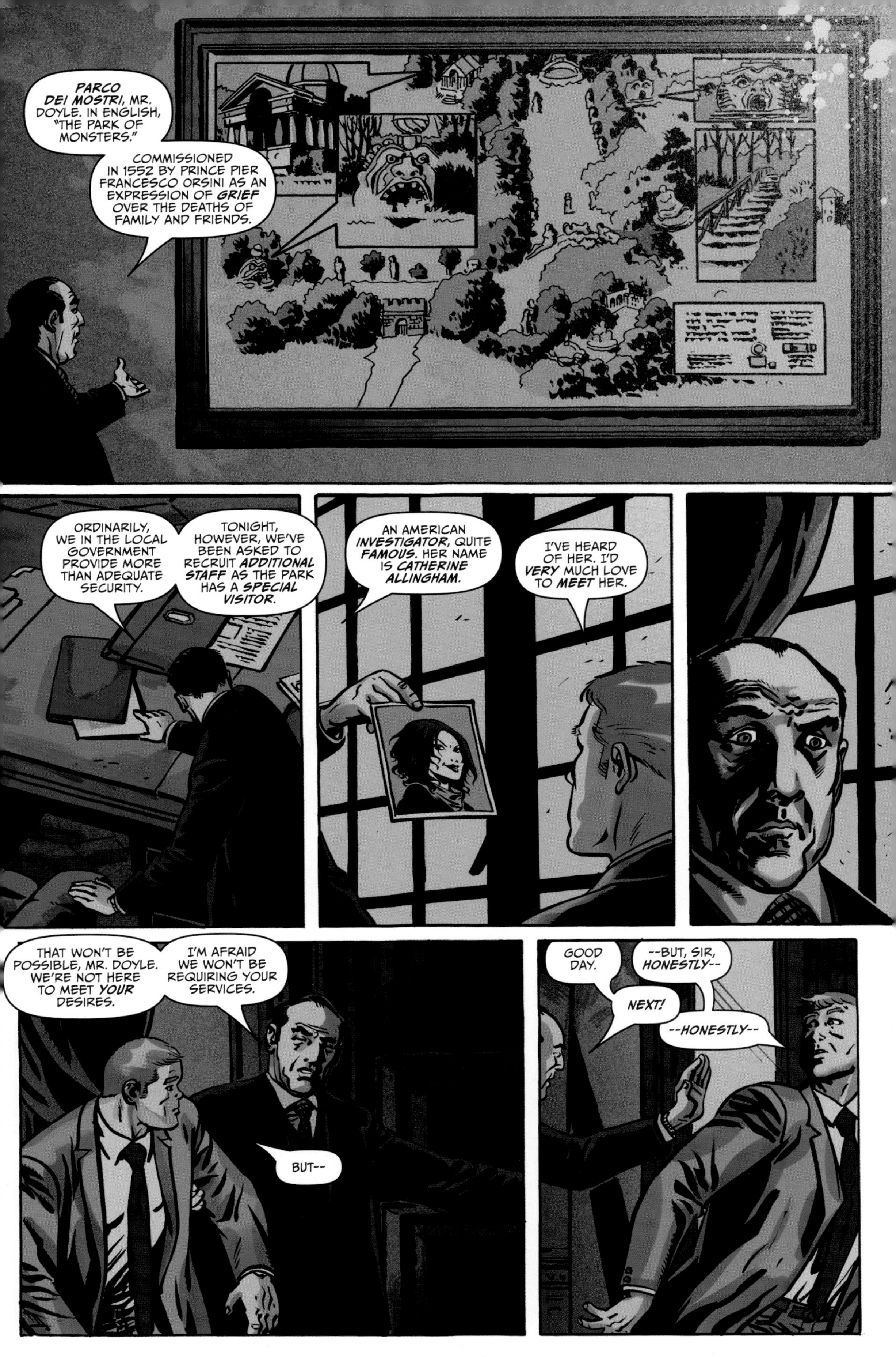
PARCO DEI MOSTRI, MR. DOYLE. IN ENGLISH, "THE PARK OF MONSTERS."
COMMISSIONED IN 1552 BY PRINCE PIER FRANCESCO ORSINI AS AN EXPRESSION OF GRIEF OVER THE DEATHS OF FAMILY AND FRIENDS.
ORDINARILY, WE IN THE LOCAL GOVERNMENT PROVIDE MORE THAN ADEQUATE SECURITY.
TONIGHT, HOWEVER, WE'VE BEEN ASKED TO RECRUIT ADDITIONAL STAFF AS THE PARK HAS A SPECIAL VISITOR.
AN AMERICAN INVESTIGATOR, QUITE FAMOUS. HER NAME IS CATHERINE ALLINGHAM.
I'VE HEARD OF HER. I'D VERY MUCH LOVE TO MEET HER.
THAT WON'T BE POSSIBLE, MR. DOYLE. WE'RE NOT HERE TO MEET YOUR DESIRES.
I'M AFRAID WE WON'T BE REQUIRING YOUR SERVICES.
BUT--
GOOD DAY.
--BUT, SIR, HONESTLY--
NEXT!
--HONESTLY--

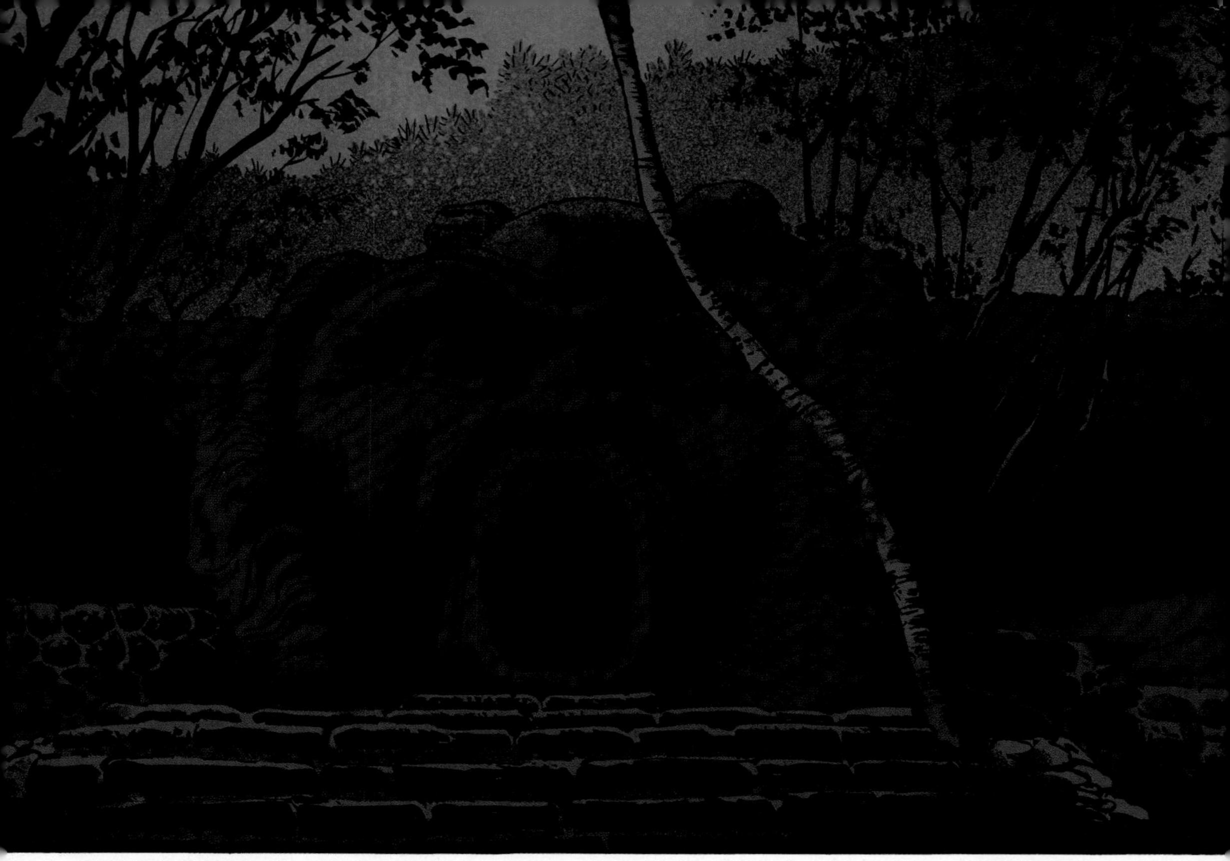

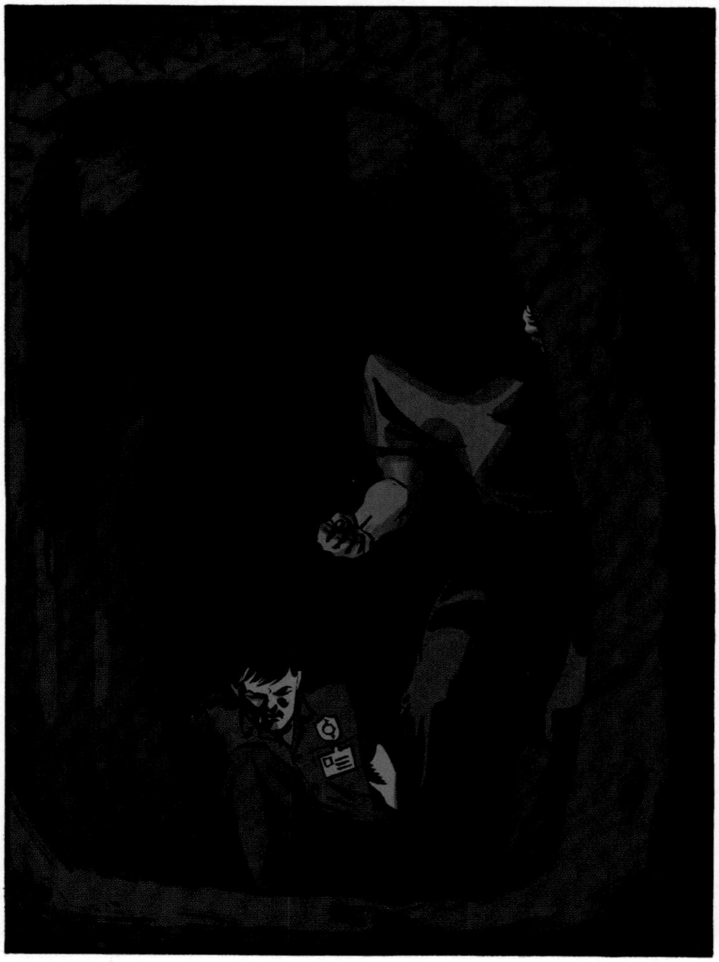

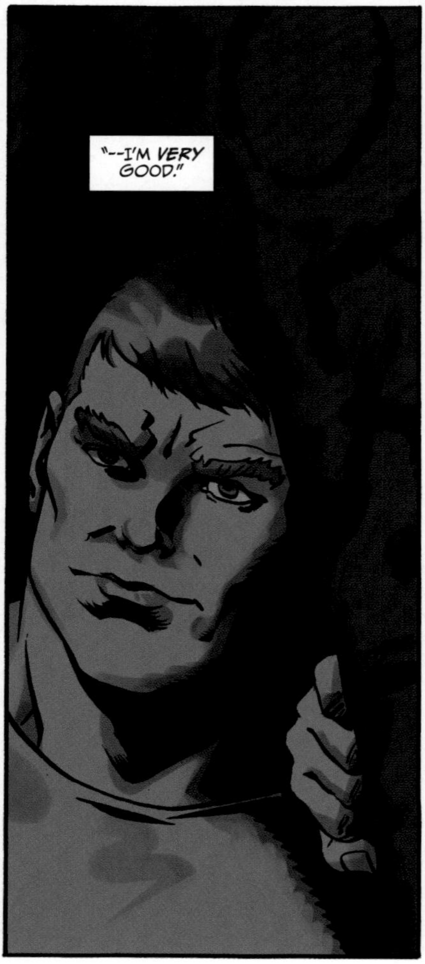
"--I'M VERY GOOD."

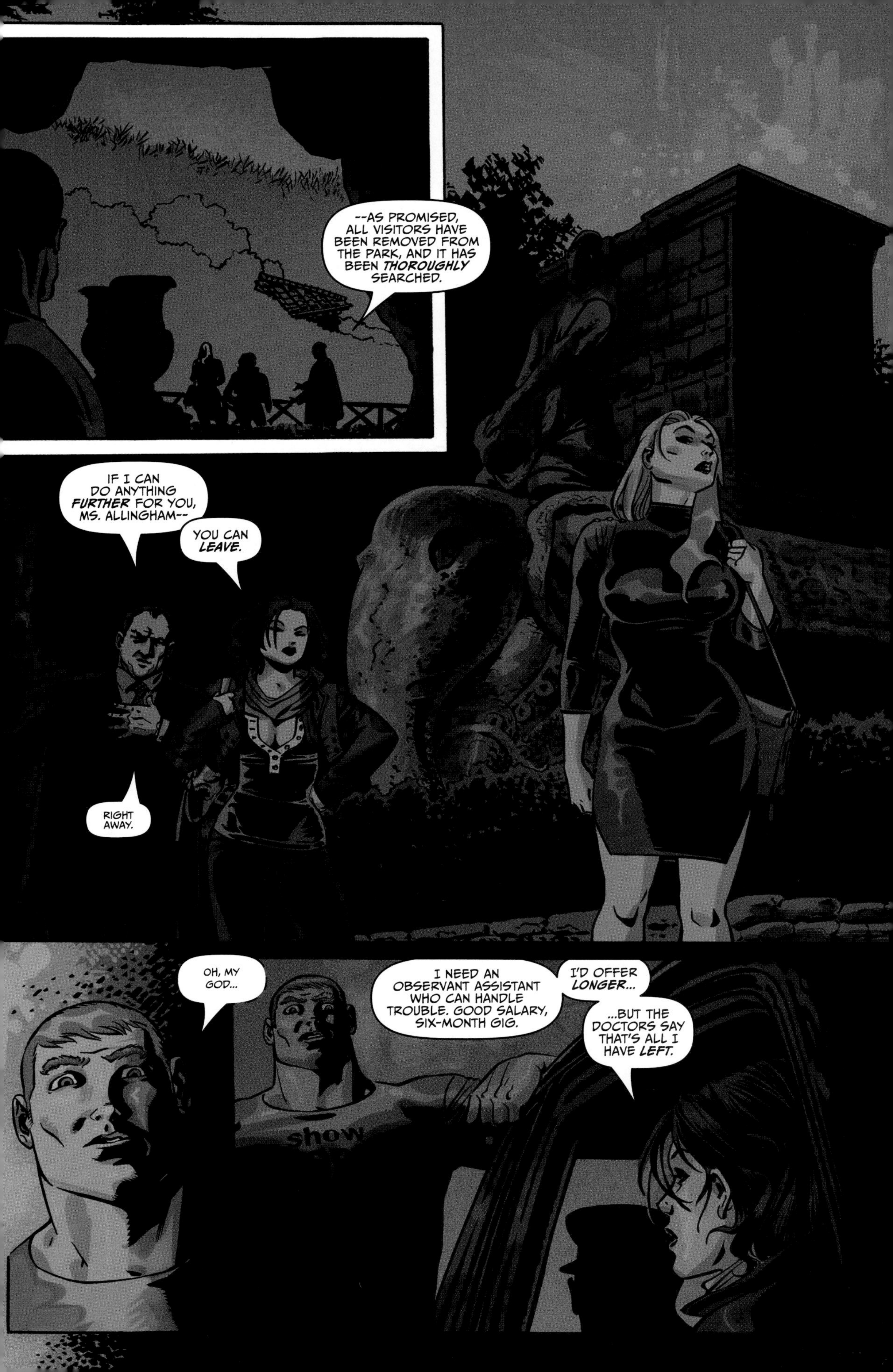
--AS PROMISED, ALL VISITORS HAVE BEEN REMOVED FROM THE PARK, AND IT HAS BEEN THOROUGHLY SEARCHED.
IF I CAN DO ANYTHING FURTHER FOR YOU, MS. ALLINGHAM--
YOU CAN LEAVE.
RIGHT AWAY.
OH, MY GOD...
I NEED AN OBSERVANT ASSISTANT WHO CAN HANDLE TROUBLE. GOOD SALARY, SIX-MONTH GIG.
I'D OFFER LONGER...
...BUT THE DOCTORS SAY THAT'S ALL I HAVE LEFT.
show

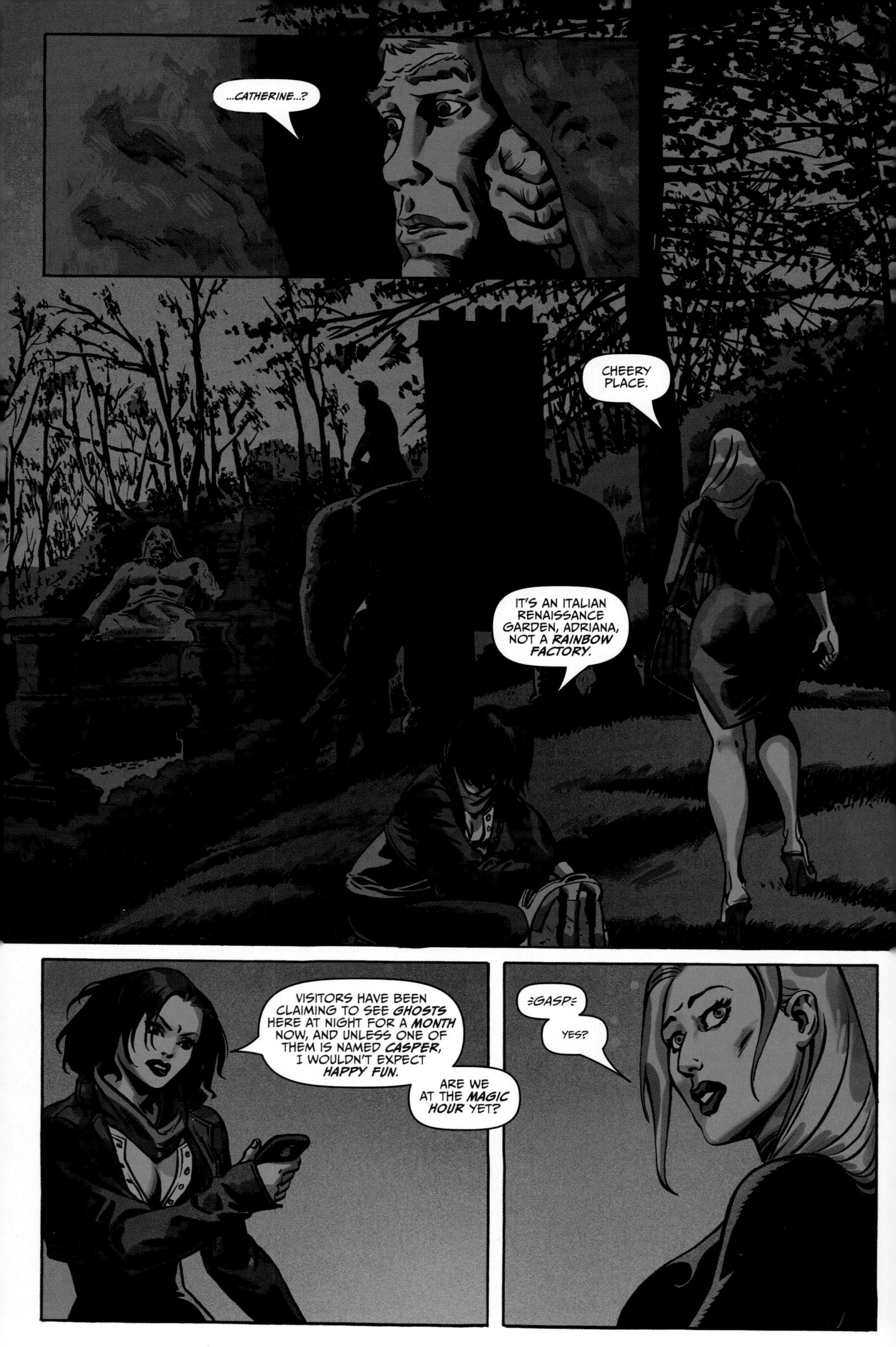
...CATHERINE...?
CHEERY PLACE.
IT'S AN ITALIAN RENAISSANCE GARDEN, ADRIANA, NOT A RAINBOW FACTORY.
VISITORS HAVE BEEN CLAIMING TO SEE GHOSTS HERE AT NIGHT FOR A MONTH NOW, AND UNLESS ONE OF THEM IS NAMED CASPER, I WOULDN'T EXPECT HAPPY FUN.
ARE WE AT THE MAGIC HOUR YET?
GASP
YES?

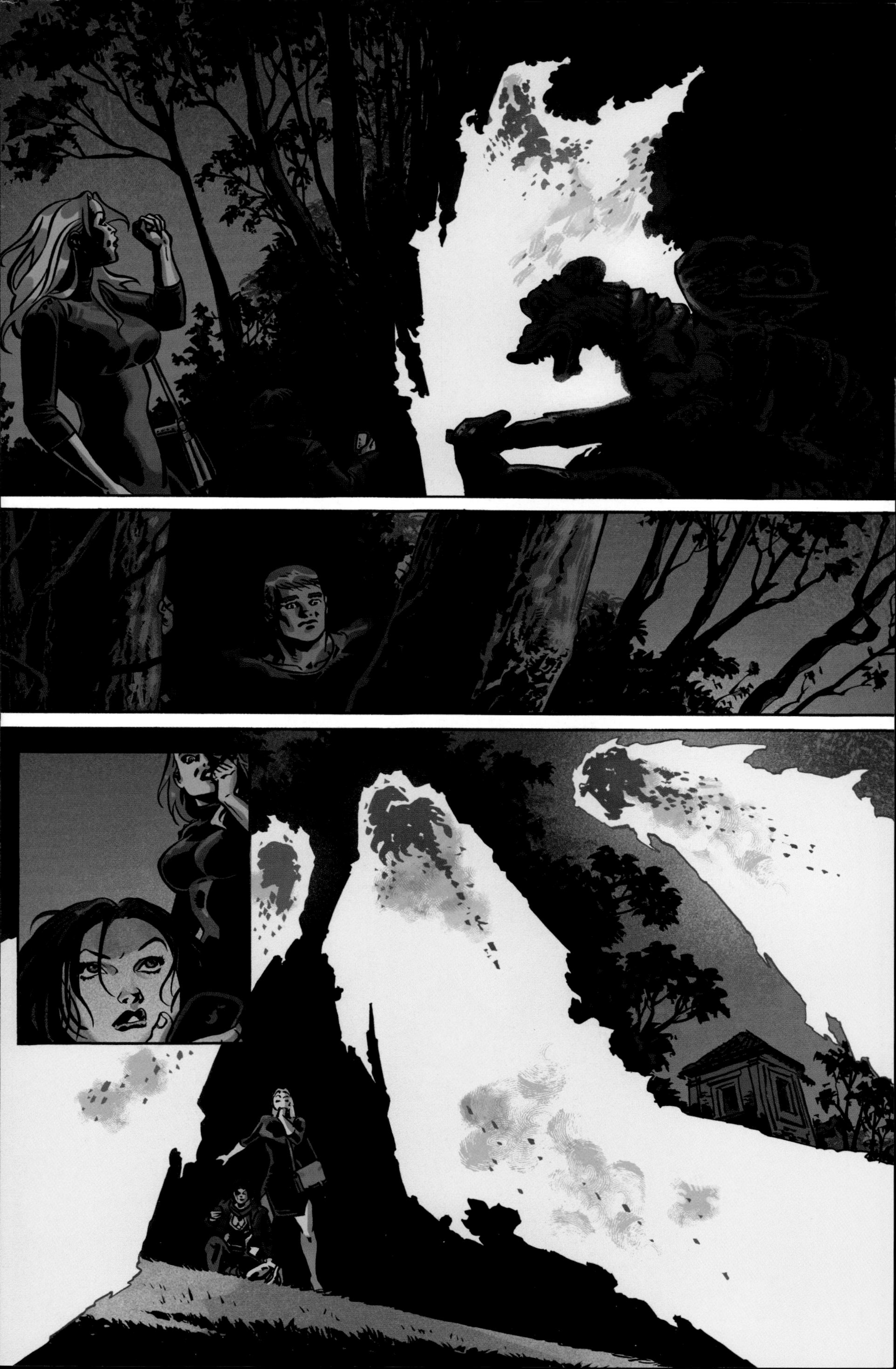

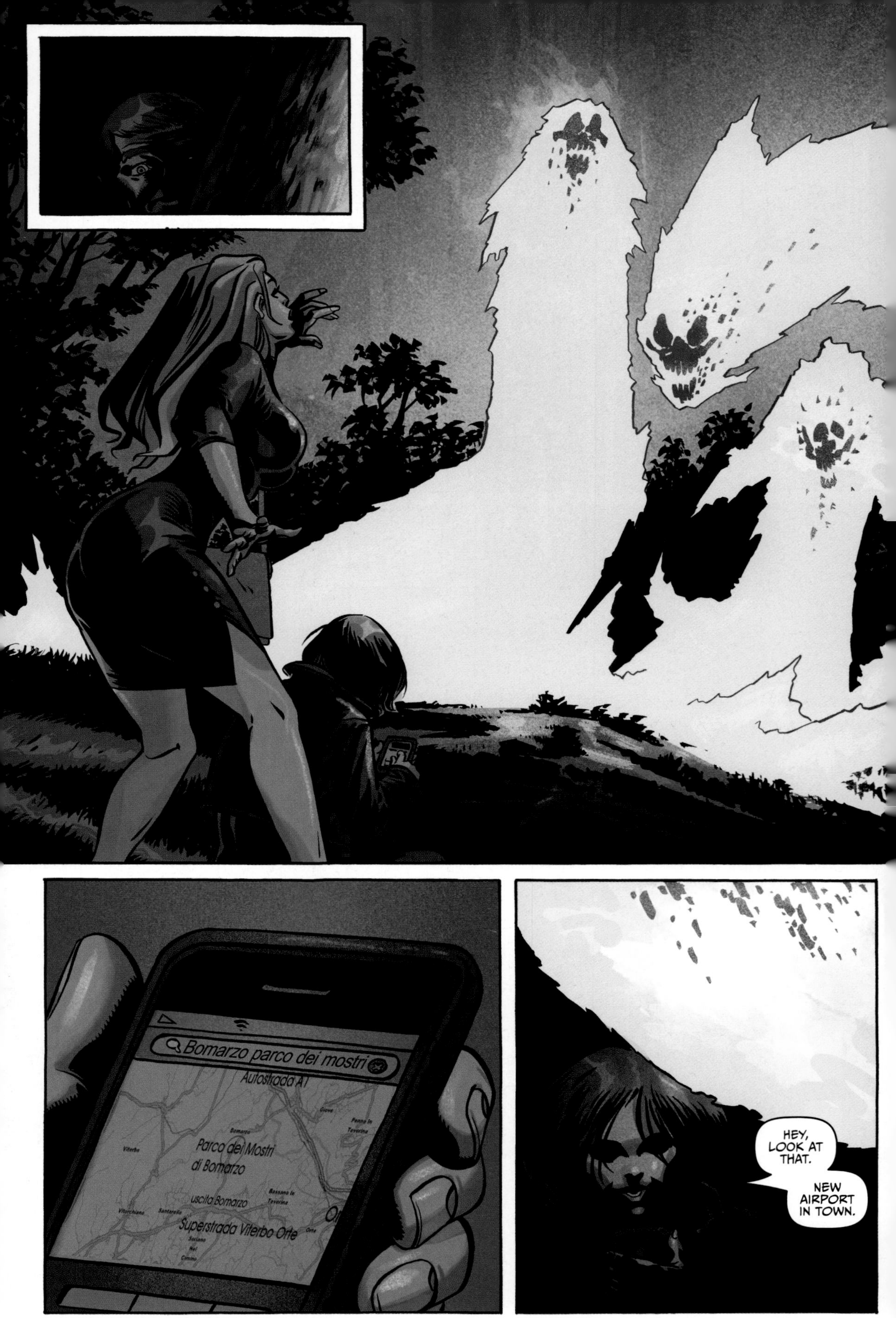
Bomarzo parco dei mostri
Autostrada A1
Parco dei Mostri di Bomarzo
uscita Bomarzo
Superstrada Viterbo Orte
HEY, LOOK AT THAT.
NEW AIRPORT IN TOWN.

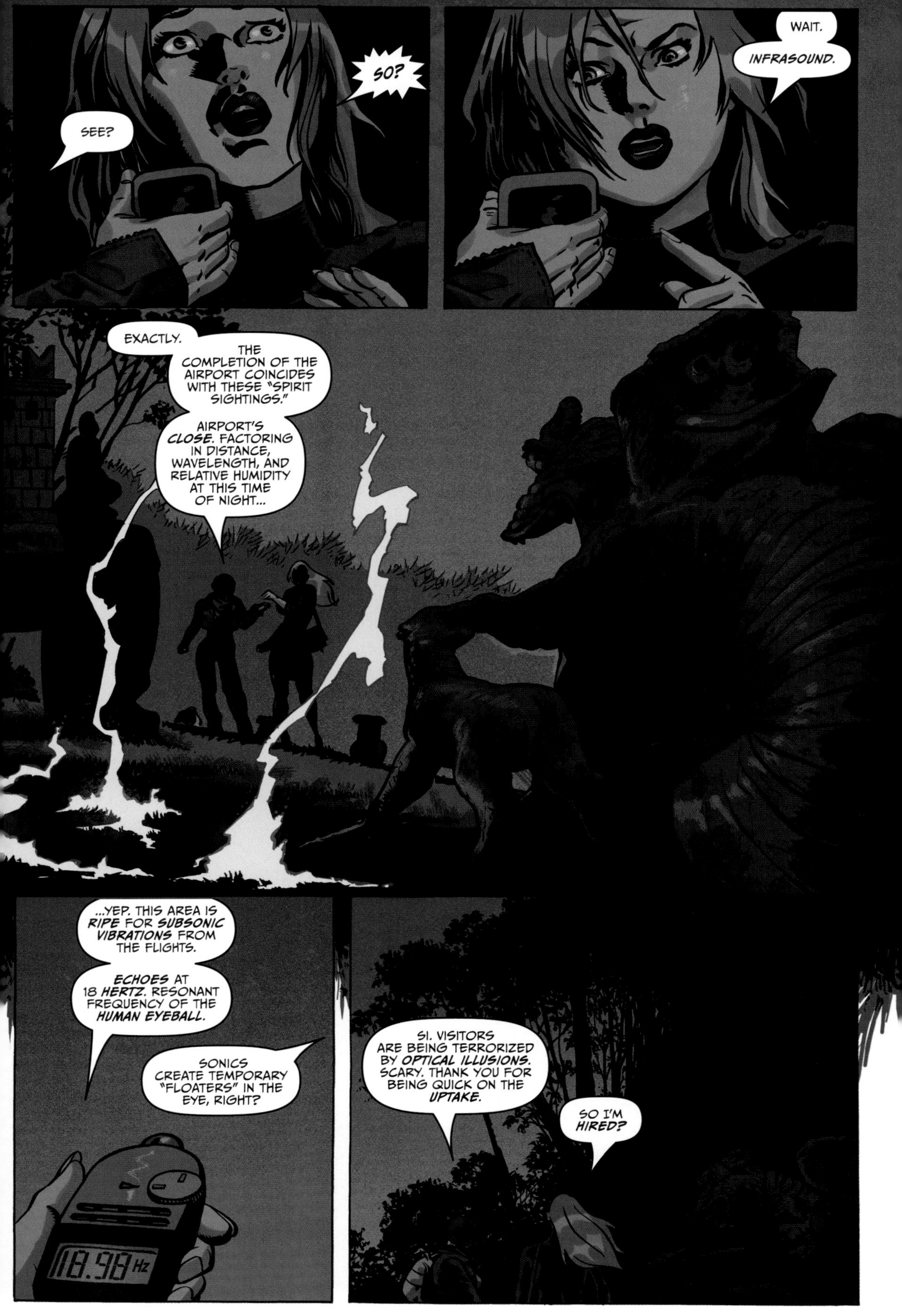
SEE?
SO?
WAIT.
INFRASOUND.
EXACTLY.
THE COMPLETION OF THE AIRPORT COINCIDES WITH THESE "SPIRIT SIGHTINGS."
AIRPORT'S CLOSE. FACTORING IN DISTANCE, WAVELENGTH, AND RELATIVE HUMIDITY AT THIS TIME OF NIGHT...
...YEP. THIS AREA IS RIPE FOR SUBSONIC VIBRATIONS FROM THE FLIGHTS.
ECHOES AT 18 HERTZ. RESONANT FREQUENCY OF THE HUMAN EYEBALL.
SONICS CREATE TEMPORARY "FLOATERS" IN THE EYE, RIGHT?
18.98 Hz
SI. VISITORS ARE BEING TERRORIZED BY OPTICAL ILLUSIONS. SCARY. THANK YOU FOR BEING QUICK ON THE UPTAKE.
SO I'M HIRED?

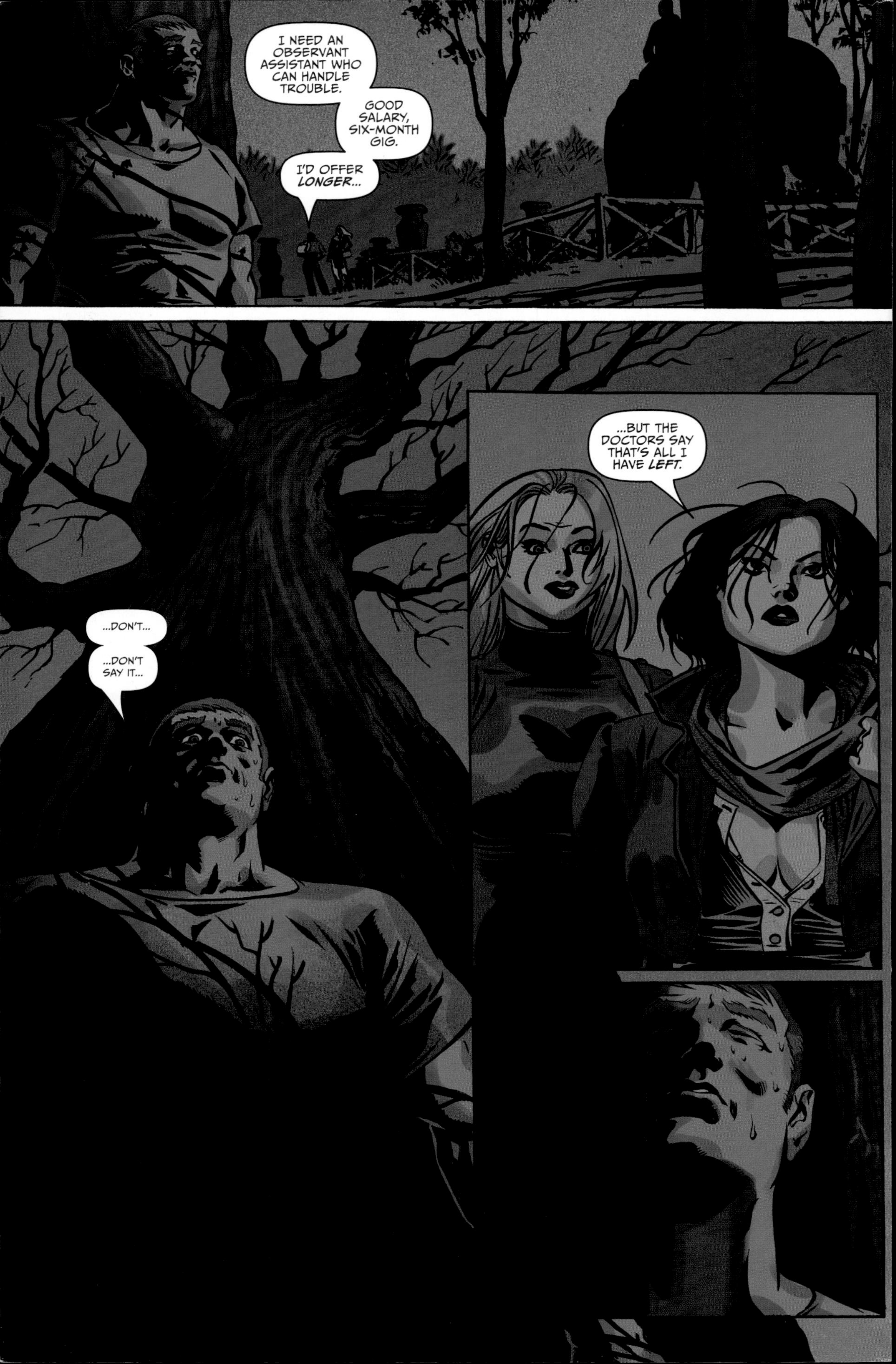
I NEED AN OBSERVANT ASSISTANT WHO CAN HANDLE TROUBLE.
GOOD SALARY, SIX-MONTH GIG.
I'D OFFER LONGER...
...BUT THE DOCTORS SAY THAT'S ALL I HAVE LEFT.
...DON'T...
...DON'T SAY IT...

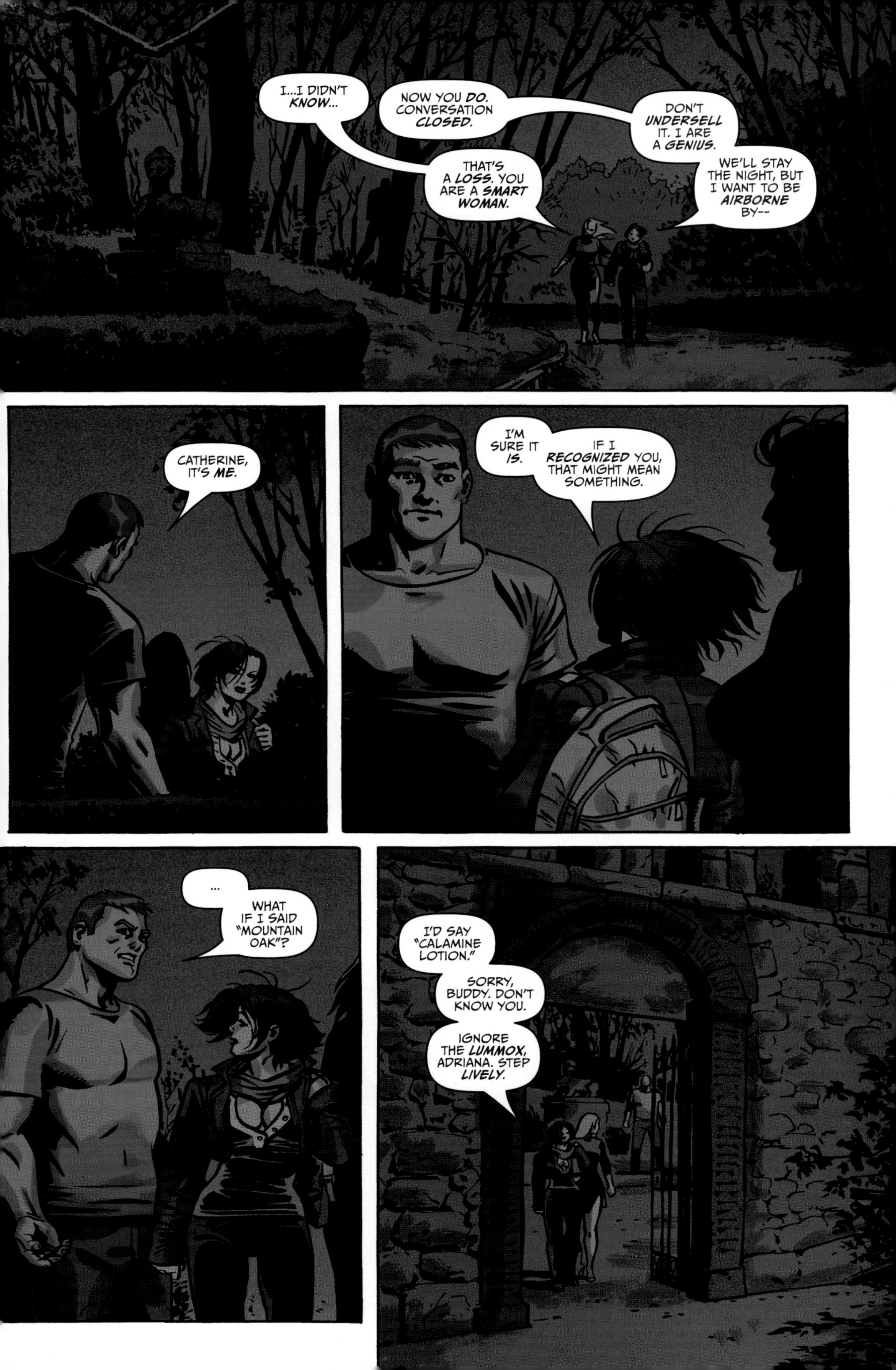
I...I DIDN'T KNOW...
NOW YOU DO. CONVERSATION CLOSED.
THAT'S A LOSS. YOU ARE A SMART WOMAN.
DON'T UNDERSELL IT. I ARE A GENIUS.
WE'LL STAY THE NIGHT, BUT I WANT TO BE AIRBORNE BY--
CATHERINE, IT'S ME.
I'M SURE IT IS.
IF I RECOGNIZED YOU, THAT MIGHT MEAN SOMETHING.
... WHAT IF I SAID "MOUNTAIN OAK"?
I'D SAY "CALAMINE LOTION."
SORRY, BUDDY. DON'T KNOW YOU.
IGNORE THE LUMMOX, ADRIANA. STEP LIVELY.

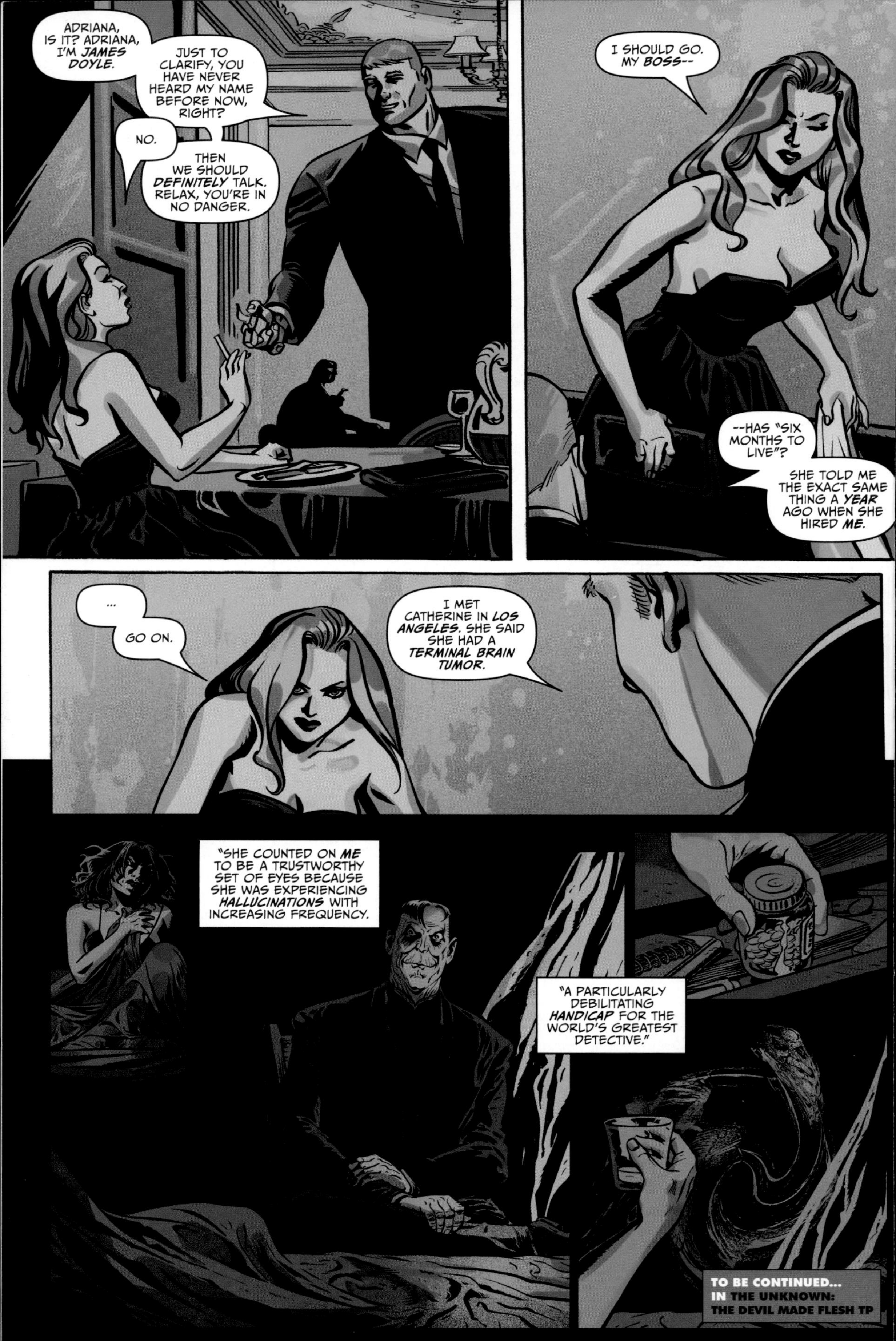
ADRIANA, IS IT? ADRIANA, I'M JAMES DOYLE.
JUST TO CLARIFY, YOU HAVE NEVER HEARD MY NAME BEFORE NOW, RIGHT?
NO.
THEN WE SHOULD DEFINITELY TALK. RELAX, YOU'RE IN NO DANGER.
I SHOULD GO. MY BOSS--
--HAS "SIX MONTHS TO LIVE"?
SHE TOLD ME THE EXACT SAME THING A YEAR AGO WHEN SHE HIRED ME.
... GO ON.
I MET CATHERINE IN LOS ANGELES. SHE SAID SHE HAD A TERMINAL BRAIN TUMOR.
"SHE COUNTED ON ME TO BE A TRUSTWORTHY SET OF EYES BECAUSE SHE WAS EXPERIENCING HALLUCINATIONS WITH INCREASING FREQUENCY.
"A PARTICULARLY DEBILITATING HANDICAP FOR THE WORLD'S GREATEST DETECTIVE."
TO BE CONTINUED... IN THE UNKNOWN: THE DEVIL MADE FLESH TP

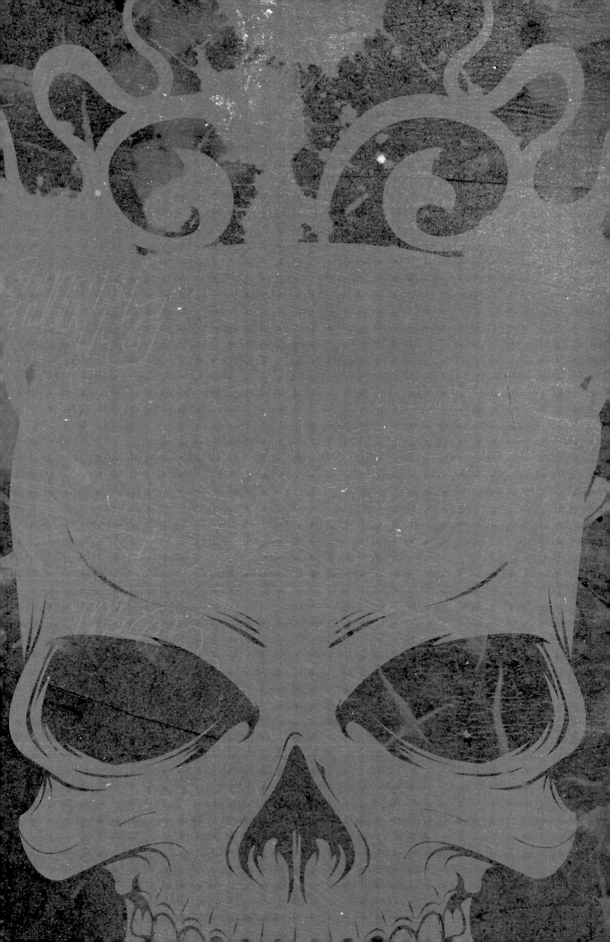

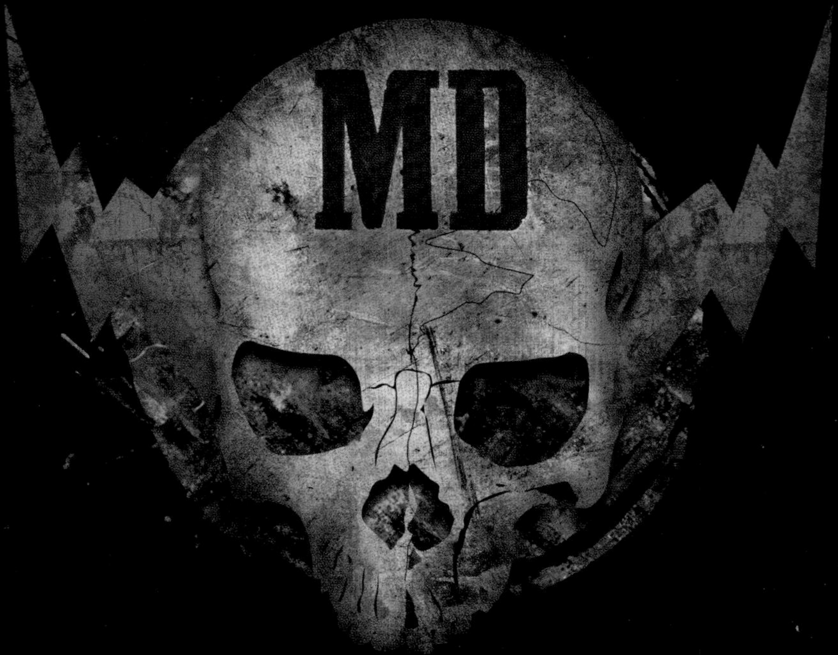
MD